366
LOW-FAT,
BRAND-NAME
RECIPES
in Minutes!

*More than
One Year of
Healthy Cooking
Using Your
Family's Favorite
Brand-Name
Foods*

By M.J. Smith,
M.A., R.D./L.D.

366 Low-Fat, Brand-Name Recipes in Minutes. ©1994
by M. J. Smith, M.A., R.D./L.D.

Library of Congress Cataloging-in-Publication Data

Smith, M. J. (Margaret Jane), 1955-
  366 low-fat, brand-name recipes in minutes: more than one
  year of healthy cooking using your family's favorite brand-
  name foods / by M.J. Smith.
      p.   cm.
  Includes index.
  ISBN 1-56561-049-0 ; $12.95

  1. Low-fat diet—Recipes. 2. Brand-name products.
  I. Title. II. Title: Three hundred sixty six low-fat, brand-
  name recipes in minutes. III. Title: Low-fat, brand-name
  recipes in minutes.
  Rm237.7. S583 1994
  641.5'635—dc20   94–15956
                                                         CIP

Edited by: Lisa Bartels-Rabb
Cover Design: Terry Dugan Design
Text Design: Nancy Nies
Editorial Production Manager: Donna Hoel
Art/Production Manager: Claire Lewis
Typesetting: Janet Hogge
Printed in the United States of America

Published by
CHRONIMED Publishing, Inc.
P.O. Box 47945
Minneapolis, MN 55447-9727

This book is dedicated to my children, Frederic and Elizabeth, who led me from spinach lasagna with fresh herbs to macaroni and cheese in the blue box.

Thank you:

- to my clients, family, and friends for continuing to be unselfish with their winning recipes.

- to Ms. Megan Bahlmann, who has provided invaluable assistance with computer nutrient analysis.

- to the folks at the Guttenberg Super Valu and Dick's Supermarket in Prairie du Chien for letting me stand and study new food products and labels in their busy aisles.

M.J. Smith, M.A., R.D./L.D., is a consulting dietitian and cookbook author. She lives in Guttenberg, Iowa, a small community along the Mississippi River, and has been in dietetic practice for 15 years. She has written many magazine articles and two best-selling books, *All-American Low-Fat Meals in Minutes* and *60 Days of Low-Cost, Low-Fat Meals in Minutes*. Despite a demanding writing schedule, she continues to counsel clients on dietary management of weight, cholesterol, and diabetes and takes pride in keeping up with American "tastes of the minute." With the introduction of the Food Pyramid, she has taken particular interest in developing recipes for complex carbohydrates—grain-based side dishes, whole-grain breads, low or no-meat entrees and vegetables. She has also endorsed the new food label and uses it as a teaching tool with clients and readers.

She is married to Andy Smith, M.D., a family physician. They have two children, Frederic, age 9, and Elizabeth, age 5, who are first lieutenants in her kitchen and at her tasting sessions. It was their entirely normal childhood food tastes that inspired this book on low-fat brand-name foods.

When Ms. Smith is not writing or cooking, she is committed to many professional and community volunteer activities. She serves as secretary of the Iowa Dietetic Association, is active in St. John Lutheran Church and Parents and Teachers Together and was appointed to the Mississippi River Parkway Commission. For fun, she takes walks, entertains in her home, follows political news, and opens up one of her husband's home-brewed beers.

CONTENTS

INTRODUCTION

THE TASTE OF TODAY

"What a lonnnng, strange trip it's been . . . " *

. . . my journey from a 1970s' foods lab, comparing soft and hard custards, to my role as a practicing dietitian and working mother.

You see, the difference between soft and hard custards has not really mattered in my work or in my life.

What has mattered to my clients, and ultimately to me personally, is the recipe for combining taste, convenience, and nutrition, in that order. Just a tip on the best brand of margarine or a head nod that it's OK to use a rice and vegetable mix on a low-fat diet is what people are looking for.

In nationwide surveys, Americans espouse nutrition as the factor most important in food selection. But health statistics and food consumption data belie that virtuous claim. Our public is literally gobbling up convenience foods, many reduced-fat varieties included. So this book is written for all of us who must have convenience and desire good nutrition—but not at the expense of taste.

* From "Truckin" by the Grateful Dead

1

How Were the Recipes Selected?

Do you ever tear out those slick food ads for the unbeatable (but alas high-fat) recipe? The recipes are usually both fast and tasty, and with just a little fixing, can be considered low-fat. Some recipes in brand-name ads are low-fat just as written, but the nutrient analysis is missing. So I have sorted those out for you. You will see a delectable "Dijonnaise Potato Salad" from Hellmann's with a few subtle changes and nutrient analysis that follows the new food-label format. Other recipes are simple variations of popular convenience foods, such as "Low-Fat Macaroni and Cheese." Take the "boring" out of the box, with seven easy ways to dress up an angel food cake. Or impress your weekend guests (and sleep in) with "Bakery-Style Blueberry Muffins" that start out with a Robin Hood mix and have fresh blueberries added.

And yes, the recipes are tested. Just as in my first two books, the recipes must be tasty to make it into the final manuscript. In fact, I'd like to share the checklist that I use to evaluate a recipe:

1. Does the recipe title describe the actual ingredients?

2. Does the recipe yield 4 servings? If it yields 8 servings, will the leftovers store well?

3. Is the "hands-on" preparation time less than 20 minutes?

4. Is the recipe based on a widely recognized brand-name food?

5. Can I improve the nutrition of the brand-name product by decreasing fat, cholesterol, calories, or sodium and by adding vitamins, minerals, fiber, or protein?

6. Can I vary the brand-name product to make it a more interesting dish?

7. Are the ingredients commonly found?

8. Does the recipe include a garnish or serving suggestion?

9. Is the recipe a particularly valuable source of calcium or fiber? If a single serving provides at least 20% of the Daily Value, this is highlighted.

10. Does it taste good?

If any one of these parameters are not met, the idea is thrown out.

The dietitian in me comes out in every recipe as I improve the nutrient density of brand-name products. For instance, Chi Chi's Salsa for dipping corn chips is enhanced with a mixture of fresh vegetables and beans ("Bean Salsa"). Reducing fat while adding fiber, vitamins, and minerals is the nutrition prescription found here. The Food Pyramid has and will continue to express the bottom line on a healthy diet: building a broad base from grains, adding ample fruits and vegetables, portion-controlled lean meats, low-fat dairy products, and scant amounts of fats and sugars. Following the recommendations of the Food Pyramid, there are whole chapters devoted to Low- or No-Meat Entrees and Grain-Based Side Dishes.

A caution about sodium . . . some recipes are based on brand-name foods that are high in sodium (such as canned soup). When the sodium count is high, directions in the nutrient analysis provide simple ingredient substitutions to reduce it.

Recipes in this book will fit with a food plan for weight control or diabetes. A "food exchange" value is found at the end of the nutrient listing. This value is based on the Exchange List for Meal Planning, a system developed and published by the American Dietetic Association and the American Diabetes Association. This system places foods into six groups, with the foods in each group having about the same nutritive value. They are: bread/starch, meat, vegetable, fruit, milk, and fat. This system, which simplifies menu planning, is widely used by people trying to control fat and calories or manage diabetes. Weight Watchers International uses a similar system for categorizing foods.

This book has added value for anyone with a bread machine. I have been using one for two years and am sharing recipes for the twenty different breads my family has chewed up in that time.

The book covers everything from beverages and appetizers to fifty desserts but will be most enjoyed by the busy cook who hates to serve the "same old thing" and takes pride in knowing there is good nutrition in every bite.

BEVERAGES

BEATS EGGNOG

1/2 c. Fleischmann's® Egg Beaters
1 pkg. Equal® sugar substitute
12 oz. evaporated skim milk
3/4 c. skim milk
1 tsp. vanilla
1 tsp. rum flavoring
Ground nutmeg

Whip Egg Beaters and Equal together and combine with two types of milk and flavoring. Mix well. Chill overnight if possible. Pour into tumblers and dust with nutmeg. *Preparation time = 10 minutes.*

Nutrition Facts (using egg substitute)
Serving size = 6 oz. • Servings per recipe = 4 • Calories = 118 • Calories from fat = 6

% Daily Value
Total fat 1 gm. = 2% • Saturated fat <1 gm. = 0 • Cholesterol 4 mg. = 1% • Sodium 190 mg. = 4% • Total carbohydrate 13 gm. = 4% • Dietary fiber = 0 • Protein 13 gm. = 22% • Calcium 349 mg. = 44% (High in calcium)

Exchange Values: 1 skim milk, 1/2 fat

BLOODY MARY MIX

1 qt. V-8® juice
2 Tbsp. Worcestershire sauce
1 Tbsp. lemon juice
1/4 tsp. sugar
1/4 tsp. pepper
1/4 tsp. hot pepper sauce
1/8 tsp. garlic powder

In a pitcher, thoroughly combine all ingredients. Chill. Serve over ice. Garnish with celery stalks and lemon wedges.
Preparation time = 10 minutes.

Nutrition Facts

Serving size = 8 oz. • Servings per recipe = 4 • Calories = 47 •
Calories from fat = 0

% Daily Value

Total fat = 0 • Saturated fat = 0 • Cholesterol = 0 • Sodium 756 mg. = 25%
(Choose Low Sodium V-8® to lower sodium.) • Total carbohydrate 11 gm. = 4% •
Dietary fiber = 0 • Protein 1 gm. = 2% • Calcium 27 mg. = 3%

Exchange Values: 2 vegetable

CONSTANT COMMENT®
HOLIDAY PUNCH

3 Constant Comment® tea bags
2 1/2 c. boiling water
1 qt. cranberry juice cocktail
12 oz. sugar-free lemon-lime soda

Place tea bags in a 2 qt. saucepan. Pour boiling water over tea bags
and let steep for five minutes. Remove tea bags and add cranberry
juice. Chill thoroughly. Just before serving, add soda. Pour into tall
glasses filled with ice. *Preparation time = 10 minutes.*

Nutrition Facts

Serving size = 8 oz. • Servings per recipe = 8 • Calories = 60 •
Calories from fat = 0

% Daily Value

Total fat = 0 • Saturated fat = 0 • Cholesterol = 0 • Sodium 3 mg. = 1% •
Total carbohydrate 15 gm. = 5% • Dietary fiber = 0 • Protein = 0 •
Calcium = 0

Exchange Values: 1 fruit

HOT SPICED CIDER

2 qt. Tree Top® cider
1 Tbsp. brown sugar
1 tsp. whole allspice
1 tsp. whole cloves
Dash of ground nutmeg
Cinnamon sticks (optional garnish)

Combine cider and spice ingredients in a large saucepan. Bring to a slow boil, cover, and simmer for 20 minutes. Remove from heat and pour through strainer.

An alternative method is to use an 8-cup electric percolator. Pour cider in pot, put spices in coffee basket, and percolate. Pour spiced cider into mugs or cups.

Add cinnamon stick to each mug for garnish.
Preparation time = 10 minutes.

Nutrition Facts
Serving size = 8 oz. • Servings per recipe = 8 • Calories = 123 •
Calories from fat = 0

% Daily Value
Total fat = 0 • Saturated fat = 0 • Cholesterol = 0 • Sodium 3 mg. = 1% •
Total carbohydrate 31 gm. = 10% • Dietary fiber = 0 • Protein = 0 •
Calcium 18 mg. = 0

Exchange Values: 2 fruit

Hot Spiced Tea

Nearly calorie-free warm-up for cold nights.

4 c. water
2 Tbsp. honey
4 whole cloves
4 cinnamon sticks
3 slices fresh lemon
3 slices fresh oranges
1 Tbsp. Lipton® instant tea

Boil water in saucepan. Meanwhile, place all other ingredients in a 1-quart teapot. Pour boiling water into pot. Steep for 5 minutes. Pour spiced tea through a strainer into mugs.
Preparation time = 10 minutes.

Nutrition Facts
Serving size = 8 oz. • Servings per recipe = 4 • Calories = 30 •
Calories from fat = 0

% Daily Value
Total fat = 0 • Saturated fat = 0 • Cholesterol = 0 • Sodium 4 mg. = 1% •
Total carbohydrate 7 gm. = 2% • Dietary fiber = 0 • Protein = 0 • Calcium = 0

Exchange Values: 1/2 fruit

Kahlua Warm-up

1/4 c. Nestles® semisweet chocolate chips
1/2 c. skim milk
1 tsp. butter flavoring
1/4 c. strong coffee or Kahlua
1 qt. skim milk

Place chocolate chips in a glass measuring cup; microwave at 60% power for 1 minute until softened. Stir in milk, butter flavor, and strong coffee. Meanwhile, heat skim milk in a saucepan just until bubbles begin to form around the side of the pan. Spoon 1/4 cup of chocolate mixture into each of the four mugs and add 1 cup skim milk to each. *Preparation time = 10 minutes.*

Nutrition Facts
Serving size = 8 oz. • Servings per recipe = 4 • Calories = 148 • Calories with
Kaluha = 196 • Calories from fat = 6

% Daily Value
Total fat 4 gm. = 6% • Saturated fat 2 gm. = 10% • Cholesterol 5 mg. = 2% •
Sodium 143 mg. = 5% • Total carbohydrate 20 gm. = 7% • Total carbohy-
drate with Kahlua 32 gm. = 11% • Dietary fiber = 0 • Protein 10 gm. = 17% •
Calcium 343 mg. = 43% (High in calcium)

Exchange Values: 1 skim milk, 1 fat

MEXICAN COFFEE

2 oranges
5 whole cloves
1 cinnamon stick, broken
1/2 c. Folger's® ground coffee
2 c. skim milk

Remove rind from one orange. Cut the rind into slivers and the
remaining orange into 8 slices (reserve for garnish). Combine slivered
rind, cloves, cinnamon sticks, and coffee in the basket of a cof-
feemaker. Add 8 cups of water and brew or percolate. Meanwhile,
heat milk to simmering in a small saucepan. Pour into a blender and
whirl 1 minute until frothy. Serve milk from a pitcher with hot coffee.
Garnish mugs with orange slices. *Preparation time = 10 minutes.*

Nutrition Facts
Serving size = 12 oz. • Servings per recipe = 8 • Calories = 23 •
Calories from fat = 0

% Daily Value
Total fat = 0 • Saturated fat = 0 • Cholesterol = 0 • Sodium 630 mg. = 21% •
Total carbohydrate 3 gm. = 1% • Dietary fiber = 0 • Protein 2 gm. = 3% •
Calcium 75 mg. = 9%

Exchange Values: 1 serving is a free food

ORANGE FOOLIE

This is a great afternoon snack...very satisfying.

> 6 oz. Minute Maid® frozen orange juice
>   concentrate
> 1 c. skim milk
> 1 c. water
> 1 tsp. vanilla
> 10 ice cubes
> 1 Tbsp. sugar or 2 packets Equal® sugar substitute

Combine all ingredients in a blender. Process for 1/2 minute or until ice cubes are crushed. Serve. *Preparation time = 10 minutes.*

Nutrition Facts
Serving size = 8 oz. • Servings per recipe = 4 • Calories = 52 • Calories from fat = 6

% Daily Value
Total fat <1 gm. = 1% • Saturated fat = 0 • Cholesterol = 0 • Sodium 33 mg. = 1% • Total carbohydrate 11 gm. = 4% • Dietary fiber = 0 • Protein 2 gm. = 4% • Calcium = 0

Exchange Values: 1 fruit

PEACH SLUSH

> 16 oz. frozen unsweetened peaches,
>   thawed slightly
> 12 oz. apricot nectar
> 6 oz. Minute Maid® frozen orange juice
>   concentrate
> 12 oz. Diet 7-Up®

In a blender, combine undrained peaches, nectar, and concentrate. Blend until smooth. Pour into a freezer container and freeze for 3 hours. To serve, spoon out slush into short glasses. Add 3 ice cubes to each glass and top with Diet 7-Up®.
Preparation time = 10 minutes. Freezer time = 3 hours.

Nutrition Facts
Serving size = 8 oz. • Servings per recipe = 8 • Calories = 83 •
Calories from fat = 0

% Daily Value
Total fat = 0 • Saturated fat = 0 • Cholesterol = 0 • Sodium = 0 • Total carbohydrate 20 gm. = 7% • Dietary fiber < 1 gm. = 2% • Protein = 0 • Calcium 12
mg. = 1%

Exchange Values: 1 1/2 fruit

PUNCH FOR A BUNCH

6 oz. Minute Maid® frozen pineapple-orange juice
   concentrate
6 oz. frozen grapefruit juice concentrate
1 qt. water
1 qt. sugar-free lemon-lime soft drink

Combine juice concentrates and water in a gallon container. Stir
well to mix. Just before serving, add soft drink.
Preparation time = 10 minutes.

Nutrition Facts
Serving size = 6 oz. • Servings per recipe = 12 • Calories = 55 •
Calories from fat = 0

% Daily Value
Total fat = 0 • Saturated fat = 0 • Cholesterol = 0 • Sodium = 0 •
Total carbohydrate 13 gm. = 4% • Dietary fiber = 0 • Protein = 0 • Calcium = 0

Exchange Values: 1 fruit

Red Rooster

6 c. Ocean Spray® Cranapple drink
6 oz. can frozen lemonade concentrate
1 tsp. rum flavoring

In a freezer container, combine cranberry-apple drink, lemonade concentrate, and rum flavoring. Freeze to an ice slush, about 3 hours. Spoon into tumblers. Serve with short straws.
Preparation time = 10 minutes.

Nutrition Facts

Serving size = 6 oz. • Servings per recipe = 8 • Calories = 123 • Calories from fat = 0

% Daily Value

Total fat = 0 • Saturated fat = 0 • Cholesterol = 0 • Sodium = 0 • Total carbohydrate 32 gm. = 11% • Dietary fiber = 0 • Protein = 0 • Calcium 13 mg. = 2%

Exchange Values: 2 fruit

Sangria

Festive wine punch!

1/2 c. water
1/2 c. Minute Maid® orange juice
1/4 cup brandy, optional
1/2 lemon, sliced and seeded
1 small orange, sliced and seeded
1 1/2 qt. red or white wine, chilled
    (may use nonalcoholic wine or sparkling grape juice)
12 oz. club soda
Ice cubes

Combine all ingredients, except club soda and ice, in a pitcher. Stir and refrigerate 1 hour. Just before serving, add club soda and pour over ice. *Preparation time = 10 minutes.*

Nutrition Facts
Serving size = 8 oz. • Servings per recipe = 8 • Calories = 138 •
Calories from fat = O

% Daily Value
Total fat = O • Saturated fat = O • Cholesterol = O • Sodium 22 mg = 1% •
Total carbohydrate 32 gm. = 10% • Dietary fiber = O • Protein 1 gm. = 2% •
Calcium 7 mg. = 1%

Exchange Values: 2 fruit

STRAWBERRY LIMEADE

16 oz. frozen whole strawberries, thawed
1 1 /2 c. cold water
1/2 c. RealLime® reconstituted lime juice
2 Tbsp. sugar
12 ice cubes
Whole strawberries or mint leaves for garnish,
optional

In a blender, combine strawberries, water, ReaLime, and sugar,
blending until sugar dissolves. Serve over 3 ice cubes in a short
glass. Garnish. *Preparation time = 10 minutes.*

Nutrition Facts
Serving size = 8 oz. • Servings per recipe = 4 • Calories = 49 •
Calories from fat = 3

% Daily Value
Total fat = O • Saturated fat = O • Cholesterol = O • Sodium = O • Total carbohydrate 13 gm. = 4% • Dietary fiber = O • Protein 1 gm. = 1% • Calcium 12
mg. = 1 %

Exchange Values: 1 fruit

Strawberry Sparkler

16 oz. frozen whole strawberries, thawed
1/2 c. ReaLime® reconstituted lime juice
1 bottle sparkling pink grape juice, chilled
1 qt. sugar-free lemon-lime soft drink, chilled
Lime slices for garnish

Press berries through a sieve into a bowl. Stir lime juice into strawberry pulp. Cover and chill. Put strawberry pulp into a large punch bowl. Carefully pour grape juice and soda into chilled pulp, stirring with an up-and-down motion. Garnish punch cups with lime slices. *Preparation time = 10 minutes.*

Nutrition Facts
Serving size = 6 oz. • Servings per recipe = 8 • Calories = 57 •
Calories from fat = 0

% Daily Value
Total fat = 0 • Saturated fat = 0 • Cholesterol = 0 • Sodium = 0 • Total carbohydrate 15 gm. = 5% • Dietary fiber = 0 • Protein = 0 • Calcium 6 mg. = 1%

Exchange Values: 1 fruit

BARBECUED
CHICKEN APPETIZERS

1 large skinless, boneless chicken breast
1 green pepper, cut into strips
1 medium onion, cut into thick strips
1/2 c. Heinz® catsup
1 Tbsp. mustard
1 Tbsp. brown sugar
1 Tbsp. vinegar
1/4 tsp. garlic powder
2 drops hot pepper sauce

Cut chicken breast into 16 chunks and place in a microwave-safe dish. Scatter pepper and onion strips on top of chicken. Combine remaining ingredients in a small bowl and pour over the chicken and vegetables. Cover and microwave on 70% power for 7 minutes or until chicken is white and tender. Serve with toothpicks. *Preparation time = 10 minutes.*

Nutrition Facts
Serving size = 4 chunks • Servings per recipe = 4 • Calories = 130 • Calories from fat = 18

% Daily Value
Total fat 2 gm.= 3% • Saturated fat < 1gm. = 2% • Cholesterol 37 mg. = 12% • Sodium 393 mg. = 13% • Total carbohydrate 14 gm. = 8% • Dietary fiber 1gm. = 4% • Protein 14 gm. = 25% • Calcium 29 mg. = 4%

Exchange Values: 2 lean meat, 1 vegetable

BLACK-BEAN DIP

15-oz. can black beans, rinsed and drained
1/2 c. Miracle Whip Free® dressing
1/2 c. nonfat sour cream
4 oz. chopped green chilies, drained
2 Tbsp. chopped fresh cilantro or
   1 Tbsp. dried cilantro
1 tsp. chili powder
1/2 tsp. garlic powder
Few drops of hot pepper sauce

Mash beans with a fork. Stir in remaining ingredients until well blended. Refrigerate and serve with tortilla chips. Look for chips that have 6 grams of fat, or less, per ounce. *Preparation time = 10 minutes.*

Nutrition Facts
Serving size = 1/4 cup • Servings per recipe = 8 • Calories = 85 • Calories from fat = 9

% Daily Value
Total fat 1gm. = 3% • Saturated fat 1 gm. = 5% • Cholesterol 5 gm. = 5% • Sodium 220 mg. = 2% • Total carbohydrate 15 mg. = 8% • Dietary fiber 3.5 gm. = 14% • Protein 4 gm. = 6% • Calcium 31 mg. = 4%

Exchange Values: 1 bread/starch

CELERY STUFFED WITH HAM AND CHEESE

3/4 c. Scott's of Wisconsin® smoky-flavored
   cheddar-cheese product
1/4 c. finely shredded lean ham
1/4 c. chopped dill pickle
1 tsp. Grey Poupon® Dijon mustard
32 3-inch celery sticks, chilled

Combine all ingredients, except celery, in a small bowl. Blend thoroughly. Stuff into celery, then chill until serving time. *Preparation time = 15 minutes.*

Nutrition Facts
Serving size = 4 stuffed sticks • Servings per recipe = 8 • Calories = 81 •
Calories from fat = 45

% Daily Value
Total fat 5 gm. = 7% • Saturated fat 2 gm. = 11% • Cholesterol 16 mg. = 6% •
Sodium 488 mg. = 16% • Total carbohydrate 5 gm. = 2% • Dietary fiber 1 gm.
= 4% • Protein 4 gm. = 7% • Calcium 108 mg. = 13%

Exchange Values: 1 lean meat, 1/2 fat

CRISPED CHIPS FOR MEXICAN DIPS

4 corn tortillas
Pam® vegetable oil spray

Lightly spray each side of tortillas with Pam®. Cut each tortilla into
eight wedges. Arrange on a baking sheet. Bake at 400° F. for 3 minutes on each side. Use with Mexican-style dips.
Preparation time = 15 minutes.

Nutrition Facts
Serving size = 4 crisps • Servings per recipe = 8 • Calories = 38 •
Calories from fat = 9

% Daily Value
Total fat 1 gm. = 2% • Saturated fat = 0 • Cholesterol = 0 • Sodium = 0 •
Total carbohydrate 7 gm. = 2% • Dietary fiber 1 gm. = 4% • Protein 1 gm. =
2% • Calcium = 0

Exchange Values: 1/2 bread/starch

CUCUMBER DILL DIP

8 oz. Kraft® Philadelphia Free cream cheese
1 c. Hellmann's® reduced-fat,
    cholesterol-free mayonnaise
2 medium cucumbers, peeled, seeded, and chopped
2 Tbsp. scallions, sliced
1 Tbsp. lemon juice
1/2 tsp. dried dill weed
1/2 tsp. hot pepper sauce

Beat cream cheese in medium bowl until smooth. Stir in mayonnaise, cucumbers, scallions, lemon juice, dill, and hot pepper sauce; cover and chill. Serve with fresh vegetables or melba rounds.
Preparation time = 15 minutes. Chilling time = 15 minutes.

Nutrition Facts
Serving size = 4 Tbsp. • Servings per recipe = 8 • Calories = 63 •
Calories from fat = 18

% Daily Value
Total fat 3 gm. = 5% • Saturated fat < 1 gm. = 5% • Cholesterol = 0 • Sodium
249 mg. = 8% • Total carbohydrate 5 gm. = 2% • Dietary fiber 1 gm. = 4% •
Protein 4 gm. = 7% • Calcium 31 mg. = 4%
Exchange Values: 1 vegetable, 1 fat

CUCUMBER SANDWICHES

These are always a hit

3 oz. Kraft® Philadelphia Free cream cheese
1 tsp. Lawry's® seasoned salt
24 slices cocktail rye bread
24 slices fresh cucumber (2 large cucumbers)
1 Tbsp. dried dill weed

Soften cream cheese in a small bowl. Stir in seasoned salt. Spread on rye. Top with a cucumber slice and dill weed. Leave peeling on the cucumber to add color and dietary fiber.
Preparation time = 20 minutes.

Nutrition Facts

Serving size = 3 • Servings per recipe = 8 • Calories = 95 •
Calories from fat = 9

% Daily Value

Total fat 1 gm. = 2% • Saturated fat = 0 • Cholesterol = 0 • Sodium 358 mg.
= 12% • Total carbohydrate 17 gm. = 6% • Dietary fiber 0.5 gm. = 2% •
Protein 3 gm. = 5% • Calcium 62 mg. = 7%

Exchange Values: 1 vegetable, 1 bread/starch

FIERY BEAN DIP

16 oz. Old El Paso® refried beans
4 oz. Velveeta Light® cheese, cubed
1 c. chunky salsa

Combine all ingredients in a 2-quart microwave-safe bowl.
Microwave at 50% power for 10 minutes, stirring several times.
Garnish with green onions. Serve with tortilla chips.
Preparation time = 5 minutes. Cooking time = 10 minutes.

Nutrition Facts

Serving size = 6 Tbsp. • Servings per recipe = 8 • Calories = 98 •
Calories from fat = 36

% Daily Value

Total fat 4 gm. = 6% • Saturated fat 2 gm. = 9% • Cholesterol 8 mg. = 3% •
Sodium 600 mg. = 20% (To reduce sodium, substitute no-added-salt tomatoes
for salsa.) • Total carbohydrate 11 gm. = 4% • Dietary fiber 4.1 gm. = 16% •
Protein 8 gm. = 14% • Calcium 156 mg. = 20% (High in calcium)

Exchange Values: 1 bread/starch, 1/2 lean meat

FRUITY CHEESE BALL

3 oz. Kraft® Philadelphia Free cream cheese, softened
1 Tbsp. sherry
2 oz. Kraft® Healthy Favorites cheddar cheese,
  shredded
2 Tbsp. dried apricots, chopped
2 Tbsp. green pepper, chopped
1/2 tsp. finely grated orange rind
1/4 c. parsley, chopped

Combine softened cream cheese and sherry in a small bowl, mixing until well blended. Add cheddar cheese, apricots, green pepper, and orange rind. Mix well. Chill for at least 1 hour. Then form into a ball and roll in parsley. Serve with Keebler® Harvest Crisp Sesame Crackers. *Preparation time = 15 minutes. Chilling time = 1 hour.*

Nutrition Facts
Serving size = 2 Tbsp • Servings per recipe = 8 • Calories = 70 •
Calories from fat = 27

% Daily Value
Total fat 3 gm. = 5% • Saturated fat 1 gm. = 15% • Cholesterol 7 mg. = 6% •
Sodium 68 mg. = 2% • Total carbohydrate 7 gm. = 2% • Dietary fiber 1 gm. =
4% • Protein 6 gm. = 10% • Calcium 178 mg. = 22% (High in calcium)
Exchange Values: 1 fruit, 1/2 fat

GUACAMOLE

1 large ripe avocado, seeded and peeled
1 Tbsp. ReaLime® lime juice from concentrate
1/2 tsp. garlic salt
1/2 tsp. sugar
1/4 tsp. pepper

Mash avocados in blender or food processor. Add remaining ingredients and mix well. Chill to blend flavors. Garnish with fresh tomato. Serve with tortilla chips or fresh vegetables.
Preparation time = 15 minutes. Chilling time = 15 minutes.

Nutrition Facts
Serving size = 2 Tbsp. • Servings per recipe = 8 • Calories = 35 •
Calories from fat = 27

% Daily Value
Total fat 3 gm. = 6% • Saturated fat < 1 gm. = 2% • Cholesterol = 0 • Sodium
135 mg. = 5% • Total carbohydrate = 0 • Dietary fiber = 0 • Protein = 0 •
Calcium 3 mg. = 1%

Exchange Values: 1 fat

HOT AND SPICY CRANBERRY DIP

16-oz. can Ocean Spray® jellied cranberry sauce
3 Tbsp. prepared horseradish
2 Tbsp. honey
1 Tbsp. Worcestershire sauce
1 Tbsp. lemon juice
1 garlic clove, minced
1/4 tsp. ground cayenne pepper
Pineapple chunks
Orange sections
Lean ham chunks

In a medium saucepan, combine the first seven ingredients and heat
to a boil. Reduce heat, cover, and simmer for 5 minutes. Serve warm
with pineapple, oranges, and ham chunks as dippers.
Preparation time = 15 minutes.

Nutrition Facts
Serving size = 1/4 cup • Servings per recipe = 8 • Calories = 121 •
Calories from fat = 0

% Daily Value
Total fat = 0 • Saturated fat = 0 • Cholesterol = 0 • Sodium 60 mg. = 2% •
Total carbohydrate 31 gm. = 10% • Dietary fiber = 0 • Protein = 0 •
Calcium = 0

Exchange Values: 2 fruit

HOT CHEESE DIP FOR PRETZELS

1 c. Velveeta® Light cheese, cubed
1 Tbsp. mustard
2 tsp. Worcestershire sauce

Combine all ingredients in a small microwave-safe bowl. Microwave on full power for 3 minutes, stopping twice to stir. Serve with sourdough pretzels. *Preparation time = 10 minutes.*

Nutrition Facts
Serving size = 2 Tbsp. • Servings per recipe = 8 • Calories = 81 •
Calories from fat = 45

% Daily Value
Total fat 5 gm.= 7% • Saturated fat 3 gm. = 14% • Cholesterol 20 mg. = 6% • Sodium 255 mg. = 8% • Total carbohydrate = 0 • Dietary fiber = 0 • Protein 9 gm. = 15% • Calcium 251 mg. = 31% (High in calcium)

Exchange Values: 1 lean meat, 1 fat

LINDA'S JAGIC

A Syrian appetizer that I was treated to by former college roomie, Linda Craig Nitch

16 oz. low-fat cottage cheese
8 oz. Kraft® Philadelphia Free cream cheese
1/3 c. I Can't Believe It's Not Butter® spread
5 green onions, chopped fine
1/4-1/2 c. finely chopped cilantro -
  (add according to your love of cilantro)
1 Hungarian hot wax pepper, finely chopped (or substitute 1 banana pepper or 2 jalapeno peppers)

Soften cream cheese to room temperature. Place in a blender, then add cottage cheese and spread. Process until smooth. Pour into a 2-quart bowl and stir in remaining ingredients. Chill. Use as a dip with pita chips or melba rounds.
Preparation time = 10 minutes. Chilling time = 15 minutes.

Nutrition Facts
Serving size = 1/4 cup • Servings per recipe = 16 • Calories = 53 •
Calories from fat = 18

% Daily Value
Total fat 2 gm. = 4% • Saturated fat < 1 gm. = 3% • Cholesterol 3 mg. = 1% •
Sodium 173 mg. = 6% • Total carbohydrate 3 gm. = 1% • Dietary fiber = 0 •
Protein 5 gm. = 9% • Calcium 65 mg. = 8%

Exchange Values: 1/2 skim milk, 1/2 fat

NO-BEAN CHILI DIP
FOR A GANG

15-oz. can Hormel® Chili, No Beans
10-oz. can tomatoes and green chilies, diced
1 c. Velveeta® Light, cubed
1/2 c. green onions, sliced
1/2 tsp. cayenne pepper

Combine all ingredients in a saucepan. Heat just until cheese melts, stirring frequently. Garnish dip with slices of green onion. Serve warm with assorted raw vegetable dippers or toasted French bread slices. *Preparation time = 10 minutes.*

Nutrition Facts
Serving size = 1/4 cup • Servings per recipe = 16 • Calories = 80 •
Calories from fat = 36

% Daily Value
Total fat 4 gm. = 7% • Saturated fat 2 gm. = 10% • Cholesterol 15 mg. = 5% •
Sodium 351 mg. = 12% • Total carbohydrate 5 gm.= 1% • Dietary fiber = 0 •
Protein 7 gm. = 9% • Calcium 144 mg. = 18%

Exchange Values: 2 vegetable, 1 fat

NUTTY SPINACH DIP

1 c. Hidden Valley Ranch® Low-Fat Original
   ranch dressing
10 oz. frozen chopped spinach, thawed and
   well drained
2 Tbsp. dry vegetable soup mix
2 Tbsp. chopped walnuts

Combine all ingredients in a medium bowl. Cover and refrigerate
at least 1 hour. Garnish with a few chopped nuts. Serve with fresh
vegetables or stuff into cherry tomatoes or mushroom caps.
Preparation time = 10 minutes. Chilling time = 1 hour.

Nutrition Facts
Serving size = 1/4 cup • Servings per recipe = 8 • Calories = 77 •
Calories from fat = 54

% Daily Value
Total fat 6 gm. = 9% • Saturated fat = 0 • Cholesterol 10 mg. = 3% • Sodium
560 mg. = 17% • Total carbohydrate 5 gm. = 2% • Dietary fiber 1 gm. = 4% •
Protein 1 gm. = 2% • Calcium 35 mg. = 5%

Exchange Values: 1 vegetable, 1 fat

ONION BAGEL CHIPS

1 envelope Lipton® onion soup mix
2 Tbsp. melted margarine
1 tsp. dried basil
1/2 tsp. dried oregano
1/4 tsp. garlic powder
4 plain bagels, cut into 1/8-inch slices

Preheat oven to 250° F. In a small bowl, thoroughly blend the first
five ingredients; then generously brush on both sides of bagel
slices. Arrange bagel slices on two ungreased baking sheets and
bake 50 minutes or until crisp and golden. Store in an airtight container up to 1 week. Serve with dips and spreads.
Preparation time = 10 minutes. Baking time = 50 minutes.

Nutrition Facts
Serving size = 4 chips • Servings per recipe = 8 • Calories = 135 •
Calories from fat = 24

% Daily Value
Total fat 4 gm. = 6% • Saturated fat 1 gm. = 3% • Cholesterol 1 mg. = 0 •
Sodium 691 mg. = 23 mg. (To reduce sodium, use just half of soup mix.) •
Total carbohydrate 22 gm. = 7% • Dietary fiber = 0 • Protein 5 gm. = 8% •
Calcium 7 mg. = 1%

Exchange Values: 1 1/2 bread/starch

PESTO AND CHEESE

1/2 c. chopped parsley
1/3 c. Grey Poupon® Dijon mustard
1/2 c. walnuts, chopped
1/4 c. grated Parmesan cheese
2 tsp. dried basil leaves
2 cloves garlic, crushed
6 oz. Kraft® Philadelphia Free cream cheese

Using a blender, combine the parsley, mustard, walnuts, Parmesan cheese, basil, and garlic to make a pesto. Set aside. Spread cream cheese on a 10-inch platter. Top with pesto. Serve with reduced-fat crackers such as Keebler® Harvest Crisps. *Preparation time = 15 minutes.*

Nutrition Facts
Serving size = 1/4 cup • Servings per recipe = 8 • Calories = 96 •
Calories from fat = 63

% Daily Value
Total fat 7 gm. = 11% • Saturated fat 1 gm. = 8% • Cholesterol 8 mg. = 3% •
Sodium 135 mg. = 4% • Total carbohydrate 4 gm. = 1% • Dietary fiber = 0 •
Protein 6 gm. = 10% • Calcium 175 mg. = 6%

Exchange Values: 1/2 skim milk, 1 fat

QUICK SALSA

14 1/2-oz. can Del Monte® Mexican Style
  stewed tomatoes
1/4 c. finely chopped onion
1 Tbsp. chopped fresh cilantro or
  1 Tbsp. dried cilantro
2 tsp. lemon juice
1 clove garlic, minced
1/4 tsp. hot pepper sauce

Place tomatoes in blender. Cover and process on low for 2 seconds to chop tomatoes. Pour into a 1-quart. bowl, add remaining ingredients, and serve with reduced-fat tortilla chips (such as Guiltless Gourmet®). *Preparation time = 10 minutes.*

Nutrition Facts
Serving size = 4 Tbsp. • Servings per recipe = 8 • Calories = 16 •
Calories from fat = 0

% Daily Value
Total fat = 0 • Saturated fat = 0 • Cholesterol = 0 • Sodium 130 mg. = 5% •
Total carbohydrate 4 gm. = 1% • Dietary fiber = 0 • Protein 1 gm. = 2% •
Calcium 18 mg. = 2%

Exchange Values: 1 vegetable

RED AND GREEN DIP

10 1/2 oz. Marie's® Lite blue cheese dressing
1/4 c. finely chopped celery
1/4 c. chopped green pepper
1/4 c. chopped red pepper
1 tsp. dried dill weed

Combine all ingredients in medium bowl. Cover and chill for at least 1 hour. Garnish with additional red and green peppers. Serve with red or green apples.
Preparation time = 10 minutes. Chilling time = 1 hour.

Nutrition Facts
Serving size = 1/4 cup • Servings per recipe = 8 • Calories = 51 •
Calories from fat = 27

% Daily Value
Total fat 3 gm. = 5% • Saturated fat 2 gm. = 12% • Cholesterol 13 mg. = 4% •
Sodium 699 mg. = 25% (To reduce sodium use half Marie's® dressing and half
nonfat yogurt.) • Total carbohydrate 5 gm. = 2% • Dietary fiber = 0 • Protein
3 gm. = 5% • Calcium 57 mg. = 7%

Exchange Values: 1 fat

SEAFOOD COCKTAIL SAUCE

1 c. catsup
3 drops Durkee® red hot sauce
3 Tbsp. horseradish
2 Tbsp. lemon juice

Combine all ingredients in a 2-cup bowl. Stir to mix and chill for 1
hour. Serve with crab sticks or shrimp.
Preparation time = 5 minutes. Chilling time = 1 hour.

Nutrition Facts
Serving size = 2 Tbsp. • Servings per recipe = 8 • Calories = 34 •
Calories from fat = 2

% Daily Value
Total fat = 0 • Saturated fat = 0 • Cholesterol = 0 • Sodium 388 mg. = 13% •
Total carbohydrate 8 gm. = 3% • Dietary fiber 0.5 gm. = 2% • Protein = 0 •
Calcium 6 mg. = 1%

Exchange Values: 1/2 fruit

SEAFOOD SPREAD

1 c. chopped mock crab
2 scallions, chopped fine
1/4 c. celery, chopped fine
1/2 c. Hellmann's® reduced-fat
   cholesterol-free mayonnaise dressing
1/4 c. Kraft® Free 1000 Island dressing
1/8 tsp. white pepper

Mix ingredients in a 2-cup bowl and chill. Serve as a spread for onion bagel chips.

Preparation time = 10 minutes. Chilling time = 30 minutes.

Nutrition Facts
Serving size = 1/4 cup • Servings per recipe = 8 • Calories = 84 • Calories from fat = 45

% Daily Value
Total fat 5 gm. = 8% • Saturated fat 1 gm. = 5% • Cholesterol 7 mg. = 2% • Sodium 432 mg. = 15% • Total carbohydrate 6 gm. = 2% • Dietary fiber = 0 • Protein 4 gm. = 6% • Calcium 7 mg. = 1%

Exchange Values: 1 lean meat, 1/2 fat

SMOKY CHEESE AND HERB DIP FOR PRETZELS

6 oz. Scott's® smoky cheddar cheese product,
   softened
1 tsp. basil
1 tsp. dried parsley
1 tsp. oregano
1 /2 tsp. dill seed
1/4 c. fresh chopped parsley for garnish

In a small bowl, stir herbs into softened cheese product. Form into a ball and roll in fresh parsley. Chill for 15 minutes. Serve cold with long pretzels or breadsticks.

Preparation time = 10 minutes. Chilling time = 15 minutes.

Nutrition Facts
Serving size = 2 Tbsp. • Servings per recipe = 8 • Calories = 60 •
Calories from fat = 36

% Daily Value
Total fat 4 gm. = 7% • Saturated fat 2 gm. = 11% • Cholesterol 15 mg. = 5% •
Sodium 352 mg. = 13% • Total carbohydrate 2 gm. = 1% • Dietary fiber = 0 •
Protein 3 gm. = 5% • Calcium 75 mg. = 9%

Exchange Values: 1/2 vegetable, 1 fat

SPINACH DIP

10 oz. frozen chopped spinach,
  thawed and drained
1 1/2 c. Land'O Lakes® No-Fat sour cream
1 c. Hellmann's® reduced-fat,
  cholesterol-free mayonnaise dressing
1 envelope Knorr® Vegetable soup mix
8 oz. water chestnuts, drained and chopped
3 scallions, finely chopped

In a medium bowl, combine spinach, sour cream, mayonnaise, soup mix, water chestnuts, and scallions. Cover and chill. Serve with fresh vegetables or breadsticks. Garnish with strips of red pepper or radish slices.
Preparation time = 15 minutes. Chilling time = 30 minutes.

Nutrition Facts
Serving size = 3 Tbsp. • Servings per recipe = 16 • Calories = 80 •
Calories from fat = 4

% Daily Value
Total fat 5 gm. = 8% • Saturated fat 1 gm. = 5% • Cholesterol = 0 • Sodium
163 mg. = 5% • Total carbohydrate 6 gm. = 2% • Dietary fiber 0.7 gm. = 3% •
Protein 2 gm. = 4% • Calcium 64 mg. = 8%

Exchange Values: 1 vegetable, 1 fat

SWEET-AND-SOUR COCKTAIL MEATBALLS

1 lb. lean ground beef
1 Tbsp. minced onion
1/4 c. bread crumbs
1/4 c. grape jelly
1/4 c. Heinz® catsup
1 Tbsp. horseradish

Combine lean ground beef, onion, and bread crumbs in a small bowl. Form meatballs, 2 tablespoons of meat each. Place in a shallow microwave-safe baking dish. Cook on 70% power for 7 minutes, stopping twice to stir the meatballs. Drain well. Use a paper towel to absorb remaining drippings. Transfer meatballs to a serving dish. In a small bowl, combine grape jelly, catsup, and horseradish. Heat sauce in the microwave for 1 minute on high power, pour over meatballs, and keep warm for serving. *Preparation time = 20 minutes.*

Nutrition Facts
Serving size = 4 meatballs • Servings per recipe = 8 • Calories = 103 • Calories from fat = 18

% Daily Value
Total fat 2 gm. = 3% • Saturated fat < 1 gm. = 1% • Cholesterol 30 mg. = 10% • Sodium 164 mg. = 6% • Total carbohydrate 8 gm. = 3% • Dietary fiber = 0 • Protein 14 gm. = 25% • Calcium 15 mg.= 2%

Exchange Values: 2 lean meat

TACO DIP ON A PLATTER

6 oz. Kraft® Philadelphia Free cream cheese
1/2 c. Land'O Lakes® No-Fat sour cream
2 tsp. chili powder
1 tsp. ground cumin
1/2 tsp. cayenne pepper
1/2 c. chunky salsa
2 c. shredded lettuce
2 oz. Kraft® Healthy Favorites
   cheddar cheese, shredded
1/2 c. diced tomatoes
1/2 c. sliced scallions

Combine cream cheese, sour cream, chili powder, cumin, and cayenne pepper in a large bowl; mix until well blended. Spread on a 10-inch serving platter. Top with salsa, lettuce, shredded cheese, tomatoes, and scallions. Serve with reduced-fat tortilla chips. Serve with Crisped Chips on page 17.
Preparation time = 20 minutes.

Nutrition Facts
Serving size = 1/2 cup • Servings per recipe = 8 • Calories = 61 • Calories from fat = 9

% Daily Value
Total fat 1 gm.= 2% • Saturated fat < 1 gm. = 1% • Cholesterol 5 mg. = 2% • Sodium 232 mg. = 8% • Total carbohydrate 4 gm. = 1% • Dietary fiber 0.5 gm. = 2% • Protein 5 gm. = 10% • Calcium 191 mg. = 24% (High in calcium)

Exchange Values: 1 vegetable, 1/2 skim milk

THREE BEAN AND SALSA PARTY DIP

15-oz. can kidney beans, drained
15-oz. can black-eyed peas, drained
15-oz. can garbanzo beans, drained
1/2 c. chopped onion
1/2 c. chopped celery
1/2 c. chopped pepper
14-oz. can chunky tomatoes, drained
1 c. Chi Chi's® hot salsa

Combine all ingredients in a large bowl. Chill or serve immediately with tortilla chips. Spoon leftover dip in flour tortillas, roll up, sprinkle with cheese, and heat through.
Preparation time = 10 minutes.

Nutrition Facts
Serving size = 1/2 cup • Servings per recipe = 12 • Calories = 130 • Calories from fat = 6

% Daily Value
Total fat < 1 gm. = 1% • Saturated fat = O • Cholesterol = O • Sodium 277 mg. = 9% • Total carbohydrate 24 gm. = 8% • Dietary fiber 6.5 gm. = 26% (High in fiber) • Protein 8 gm. = 14% • Calcium 30 mg. = 4%

Exchange Values: 1 1/2 bread/starch

ZESTY VEGETABLE DIP

16 oz. nonfat sour cream
1 pkg. dry vegetable soup mix
4 Tbsp. Durkee® red hot sauce

Combine all ingredients in a 1-quart mixing bowl. Cover and chill at least 1 hour. Serve with assorted fresh vegetables.
Preparation time = 5 minutes. Chilling time = 1 hour.

Nutrition Facts
Serving size = 1/4 cup • Servings per recipe = 8 • Calories = 65 •
Calories from fat = 4

% Daily Value
Total fat < 1 gm. = 1% • Saturated fat = 0 • Cholesterol 20 mg. = 7% •
Sodium 275 mg. = 9% • Total carbohydrate 8 gm. = 2% • Dietary fiber = 0 •
Protein 2 gm. = 4% • Calcium 81 mg. = 10%

Exchange Values: 1 vegetable, 1/2 skim milk

BREADS

ALL-PURPOSE LOW-FAT BRAN MUFFINS FROM A MIX

1 pkg. Kursteaz® oat bran muffin mix
1 c. water

Preheat oven to 425° F. Prepare muffin pans by spraying with Pam® or lining with cupcake papers. Mix muffin mix and water in a medium bowl, stirring just until moistened.

Optional additions to dress up your muffins:

Glorious Morning: Add 1 tsp. cinnamon, 1 c. diced fresh apples, 1/2 cup raisins.

Fruit and Fiber: Reduce water to 3/4 c. and add 1/2 c. unsweetened applesauce and 1 c. finely diced dried apricot.

Nutty Muffins: Add 1/4 c. sunflower seeds.

Bake for 18 minutes or until muffins test done.
Preparation time = 10 minutes. Baking time = 18 minutes.

Nutrition Facts
Serving size = 1 muffin • Servings per recipe = 12 • Calories = 142 • Calories from fat = 36

% Daily Value
Total fat 4 gm. = 6% • Saturated fat 2 gm. = 10% • Cholesterol = 0 • Sodium 232 mg. = 8% • Total carbohydrate 22 gm. = 7% • Dietary fiber 3 gm. = 12% • Protein 2 gm. = 3% • Calcium 48 mg = 6%

Exchange Values: 1 bread/starch, 1/2 fat, 1/2 fruit

Bakery-Style Blueberry Muffins

1/2 c. oatmeal
2 7-oz. pkg. Robin Hood® blueberry muffin mix
2 eggs or 1/2 c. liquid egg substitute
1/2 c. skim milk
1 c. fresh blueberries
2 Tbsp. sugar
1/4 tsp. nutmeg

Preheat oven to 400° F. Prepare 16 muffin cups with liners or spray with Pam®. In a medium mixing bowl, combine muffin mixes with oatmeal. Add skim milk and egg; mix until moist. Fold in fresh blueberries. Spoon batter into prepared muffin cups. Mix sugar and nutmeg in a small bowl. Sprinkle over muffin batter. Bake for 15 to 19 minutes or until golden brown and tops spring back when touched lightly. *Preparation time = 15 minutes. Baking time = 19 minutes.*

Nutrition Facts

Serving size = 1 muffin • Servings per recipe = 16 • Calories = 133 • Calories from fat = 16

% Daily Value

Total fat 4 gm. = 6% • Saturated fat < 1 gm. = 1% • Cholesterol 22 mg. = 7% • Sodium 183 mg. = 6% • Total carbohydrate 22 gm. = 7% • Dietary fiber 0.6 gm. = 2% • Protein 3 gm. = 5% • Calcium 32 mg. = 4%

Exchange Values: 1 bread/starch, 1 fat

BLUEBERRY PANCAKES IN THE OVEN

1 c. Aunt Jemima® Original pancake and
   waffle mix
1 Tbsp. margarine
16-oz. can blueberries, well drained

Preheat oven to 350° F. Prepare pancake mix according to package directions; set aside. Melt butter in a 10-inch pie plate in the oven. Remove from heat. Spoon berries into bottom of pie plate. Carefully pour batter on top. Bake for 18 minutes in 350° oven or until the top of the pancake springs back. Loosen edges and invert on a serving plate. Cut into 4 wedges and serve with your favorite topping.

You can substitute your favorite fruit. These also freeze well. *Preparation time = 10 minutes. Baking time = 18 minutes.*

Nutrition Facts
Serving size = 1 wedge • Servings per recipe = 4 • Calories = 174 •
Calories from fat = 45

% Daily Value
Total fat 5 gm. = 7% • Saturated fat 1 gm. = 3% • Cholesterol 0 • Sodium 384 mg. = 13% • Total carbohydrate 30 gm. = 10% • Dietary fiber 0.6 gm. = 2% • Protein 4 gm. = 7% • Calcium 79 mg. = 10%

Exchange Values: 1 bread/starch, 1 fruit, 1 fat

BUTTERMILK ZUCCHINI
BREAD

2/3 c. brown sugar
2/3 c. white sugar
3 eggs or 3/4 c. liquid egg substitute
1/2 c. buttermilk
1/2 c. vegetable oil
3 c. flour
1 tsp. soda
1/4 tsp. baking powder
2 tsp. Tone's® ground cinnamon
2 c. shredded zucchini
1/4 c. chopped walnuts or pecans

Preheat oven to 375° F. Prepare two loaf pans by spraying them with Pam®. Combine brown and white sugars with eggs in a large mixing bowl, beating well. Stir in buttermilk and oil. Add all remaining ingredients, except nuts, and mix well. Pour batter into two prepared loaf pans. Sprinkle the top of the batter with chopped nuts. Bake for 40 to 45 minutes or until lightly browned. Check for doneness by inserting a wooden pick into the center of the bread. It should return clean with no sign of batter. This bread freezes very well. *Preparation time = 20 minutes. Baking time = 45 minutes.*

Nutrition Facts
Serving size = 1 slice/16 slices per loaf • Servings per recipe = 32 slices from 2 loaves • Calories = 153 • Calories from fat = 45

% Daily Value
Total fat 5 gm. = 8% • Saturated fat < 1 gm. = 2% • Cholesterol = 0 with egg substitute • Cholesterol = 40 mg. with real eggs = 13% • Sodium 18 mg. = 1% • Total carbohydrate 4 gm. = 6% • Dietary fiber 0.2 gm. = 1% • Protein 4 gm. = 6% • Calcium 17 mg. = 2%

Exchange Values: 1 fat, 1 bread/starch, 1 vegetable

COCOA BANANA MUFFINS

Finally, high-fiber chocolate!

1 c. all-purpose flour
2 tsp. baking powder
1/2 tsp. salt
2 Tbsp. cocoa powder
1/3 c. sugar
1 1/2 c. Kelloggs® All-Bran cereal
3/4 c. milk
1 egg or 1/4 c. liquid egg substitute
2 Tbsp. vegetable oil
1 c. mashed banana (about 1 large ripe banana)

Preheat oven to 400° F. Line 12 muffin cups with paper liners or spray with Pam®. In a medium bowl, stir together flour, baking powder, salt, cocoa powder, and sugar. Combine cereal and milk in a large mixing bowl and let stand for 2 minutes or until cereal softens. Add egg and oil to cereal. Beat well and stir in banana. Add flour mixture, stirring only until combined and evenly moist. Spoon batter into prepared muffin cups. Bake for 25 minutes or until muffins are lightly browned.
Preparation time = 15 minutes. Baking time 25 = minutes.

Nutrition Facts
Serving size = 1 muffin • Servings per recipe = 12 • Calories = 133 • Calories from fat = 27

% Daily Value
Total fat 3 gm. = 5% • Saturated fat 1 gm. = 2% • Cholesterol = 0 with egg substitute • Cholesterol 18 mg. = 6% with real egg • Sodium 129 mg. = 4% • Total carbohydrate 28 gm. = 9% • Dietary fiber 1.2 gm. = 5% • Protein 4 gm. = 7% • Calcium 61 mg. = 7%

Exchange Values: 1 bread/starch, 1 fat

CRANBERRY POPPY SEED LOAF

2 1/2 c. flour
1/2 c. sugar
2 Tbsp. poppy seed
1 Tbsp. baking powder
1 1/8 c. skim milk
1/4 c. melted margarine
1 egg or 1/4 c. liquid egg substitute
1 tsp. vanilla
2 tsp. grated lemon or orange peel
1 c. Ocean Spray® cranberries, chopped

Optional topping:

1 Tbsp. sifted powdered sugar

Preheat oven to 350° F. Spray a loaf pan with Pam® and set aside. In a large bowl, mix flour, sugar, poppy seed, and baking powder; set aside. Blend milk, margarine, eggs, vanilla, and lemon or orange peel. Stir into flour mixture just until moist. Stir in chopped cranberries and spread batter in the prepared loaf pan. Bake for 50 to 60 minutes or until done. When bread is completely cool, dust with sifted powdered sugar.

Preparation time = 20 minutes. Baking time = 60 minutes.

Nutrition Facts

Serving size = 1 slice • Servings per recipe = 16 • Calories = 183 • Calories from fat = 9

% Daily Value

Total fat 4 gm. = 5% • Saturated fat < 1 gm. = 3% • Cholesterol = 0 with egg substitute • Cholesterol 13 mg. = 4% with real egg • Sodium 42 mg. = 2% • Total carbohydrate 41 gm. = 14% • Dietary fiber = 0 • Protein 6 gm. = 10% • Calcium 65 mg. = 8%

Exchange Values: 1 bread/starch, 1 fruit, 1 fat

ORANGE-TOPPED CRANBERRY PUMPKIN BREAD

3 1/2 c. flour
1 c. sugar
2 tsp. baking soda
2 tsp. pumpkin pie spice
3/4 tsp. salt
1 tsp. baking powder
16-oz. can whole-berry cranberry sauce
16-oz. Libby's® solid pack pumpkin
1/2 c. vegetable oil
4 eggs or 1 c. liquid egg substitute
1/4 c. chopped walnuts or pecans
1 Tbsp. finely grated orange peel

Preheat oven to 350° F. Spray two loaf pans with Pam®. In a large mixing bowl, combine flour, sugar, baking soda, pumpkin pie spice, salt, and baking powder. In a second bowl, combine remaining ingredients, except nuts and orange peel, stirring until well mixed. Add pumpkin mixture to flour mixture and stir until well moistened. Pour batter into loaf pans. Sprinkle batter with nuts and orange peel. Bake for 60 minutes or until bread is done. Cool in pans 10 minutes, then remove. *Preparation time = 25 minutes. Baking time = 60 minutes.*

Nutrition Facts
Serving size = 1 slice/16 slices per loaf • Servings per recipe = 32 slices for 2 loaves • Calories = 161 • Calories from fat = 45

% Daily Value
Total fat 5 gm. = 8% • Saturated fat < 1 gm. = 2% • Cholesterol = 0 with egg substitute • Cholesterol 26 mg. = 9% with real egg • Sodium 144 mg. = 5% • Total carbohydrate 30 gm. = 10% • Dietary fiber = 0 • Protein 4 gm. = 8% • Calcium 17 mg. = 2%

Exchange Values: 1 fat, 1 bread/starch, 1/2 fruit

GRATED CARROT AND PINEAPPLE MUFFINS

2 1/3 c. flour
2 tsp. baking powder
1 1/2 tsp. soda
2 tsp. ground cinnamon
1 tsp. salt
1/8 tsp. nutmeg
1/8 tsp. cloves
1/8 tsp. allspice
1 c. sugar
1/4 c. vegetable oil
1/2 c. Land 'O Lakes® nonfat sour cream
3 eggs, well-beaten, or 3/4 c. liquid egg substitute
2 c. grated carrots
8 oz. crushed pineapple in juice, well drained

Preheat oven to 425° F. Prepare 24 muffin cups with paper liners or spray with Pam®. Sift together flour, baking powder, baking soda, cinnamon, salt, nutmeg, cloves, and allspice into a large bowl; set aside. In a mixing bowl, combine sugar, oil, sour cream, and eggs; beat until smooth. Add carrots and drained pineapple. Fold in dry ingredients, mixing just until moistened. Spoon batter into muffin cups and bake for 15 to 20 minutes or until muffins test done. *Preparation time = 20 minutes. Baking time = 25 minutes.*

Nutrition Facts
Serving size = 1 muffin • Servings per recipe = 24 • Calories = 153 • Calories from fat = 7

% Daily Value
Total fat 3 gm. = 5% • Saturated fat < 1 gm. = 2% • Cholesterol 2 mg. = 1% with egg substitute • Cholesterol 26 mg. = 9% with real egg • Sodium 113 mg. = 4% • Total carbohydrate 32 gm. = 10% • Dietary fiber 0.6 gm. = 2% • Protein 4 gm. = 7% • Calcium 36 mg. = 5 %

Exchange Values: 1 fruit, 1 bread/starch

GREEN CHILI SPOON BREAD

1 c. water
1 Tbsp. margarine
1 1/2 tsp. sugar
1/2 tsp. salt
2/3 c. yellow cornmeal
1/2 c. skim milk
2 eggs, well beaten, or 1/2 c. liquid egg substitute
4 oz. Old El Paso® chopped green chilies,
    well drained

Preheat oven to 375° F. Bring water, margarine, sugar, and salt to a boil in a saucepan. Slowly add cornmeal, whisking constantly. Bring to simmering. Remove from heat. Quickly whisk in milk, eggs, and green chilies. Pour into a 5-cup soufflé dish that has been sprayed with Pam®. Bake for 30 minutes until golden brown. *Preparation time = 15 minutes. Baking time = 30 minutes.*

Nutrition Facts
Serving size = 1 slice • Servings per recipe = 8 • Calories = 109 •
Calories from fat = 27

% Daily Value
Total fat 3 gm. = 4% • Saturated fat < 1 gm. = 2% • Cholesterol = 0 with egg substitute • Cholesterol 93 mg. = 18% with real egg • Sodium 184 mg. = 6% • Total carbohydrate 18 gm. = 6% • Dietary fiber 1 gm. = 4% • Protein 5 gm. = 8% • Calcium 32 mg. = 4%

Exchange Values: 1 1/2 bread/starch

JEWELED PINEAPPLE RINGS

1 pkg. Pillsbury® hot roll mix
2 Tbsp. sugar
1/2 c. water
1/2 c. pineapple juice
1 Tbsp. margarine, softened
1 egg or 1/4 c. liquid egg substitute
1/2 c. candied pineapple
1/4 c. powdered sugar
1 1/2 tsp. pineapple juice

Spray a large baking sheet with Pam®. In a large bowl, combine roll mix, contents of yeast packet, and sugar, stirring until well blended. In a small saucepan, heat water and 1/2 c. pineapple juice until very warm but not boiling. Stir warm liquid, margarine, and egg into flour mixture until dough pulls away from the side of the bowl. Turn dough out onto a floured surface. Knead for 5 minutes. Place dough back in the bowl, cover, and let rise for 5 minutes. With a rolling pin, roll the dough into a rectangle on a floured surface. Spread with candied pineapple. Roll up cinnamon-roll fashion and cut into 16 rolls. Place rolls on a cookie sheet. Bake for 20 minutes at 375° F. until golden brown. Cool rolls on a rack. Combine powdered sugar and pineapple juice and drizzle over cool rolls. For a breakfast treat, prepare rolls the night before, refrigerate, and bake in the morning. *Preparation time = 25 minutes. Baking time = 20 minutes.*

Nutrition Facts
Serving size = 1 roll • Servings per recipe = 16 • Calories = 84 • Calories from fat = 18

% Daily Value
Total fat 2 gm. = 3% • Saturated fat < 1 gm. = 2% • Cholesterol = 0 with egg substitute • Cholesterol 13 mg. = 4% with real egg • Sodium 85 mg. = 3% • Total carbohydrate 14 gm. = 5% • Dietary fiber = 0 • Protein 1 gm. = 2% • Calcium 40 mg. = 5%

Exchange Values: 1 bread/starch

ORANGE BLOSSOM SPECIAL

1 pkg. Pillsbury® hot roll mix
2 Tbsp. sugar
2 Tbsp. grated orange peel
1/2 c. water
1/2 c. orange juice
1 Tbsp. margarine, softened
1 egg or 1/4 c. liquid egg substitute
1/4 c. Simply Fruit® raspberry preserves
1/4 c. powdered sugar
1 1/2 tsp. orange juice

Spray a large baking sheet with Pam®. In a large bowl, combine yeast from roll mix, sugar, and orange peel with flour mixture. Blend well. In a small saucepan, heat water and 1/2 c. orange juice until very warm but not boiling. Stir warm liquid, margarine, and egg into flour mixture until dough pulls away from the side of the bowl. Turn dough out onto a floured surface. Knead for 5 minutes. Place dough back in the bowl, cover, and let rise for 5 minutes. With a rolling pin, roll the dough into a rectangle on a floured surface. Spread with raspberry preserves. Roll up cinnamon-roll fashion and cut into 16 rolls. Place rolls on a cookie sheet. Bake for 20 minutes at 375° F. until golden brown. Cool rolls on a rack. Combine powdered sugar and orange juice and drizzle over cool rolls. For a breakfast treat, prepare rolls the night before, refrigerate, and bake in the morning. *Preparation time = 25 minutes. Baking time = 20 minutes.*

Nutrition Facts
Serving size = 1 roll • Servings per recipe = 16 • Calories = 87 • Calories from fat = 18

% Daily Value
Total fat 2 gm. = 3% • Saturated fat < 1 gm. = 0 • Cholesterol = 0 with egg substitute • Cholesterol 13 mg. = 4% with real egg • Sodium 89 mg. = 3% • Total carbohydrate 16 gm. = 5% • Dietary fiber = 0 • Protein 1 gm. = 2% • Calcium 40 mg. = 5%

Exchange Values: 1 bread/starch

Strawberry Spread for Breads and Bagels

3 oz. Kraft® Philadelphia Free cream cheese
1/4 c. coarsely chopped strawberries
2 packets Equal® sugar substitute

Combine ingredients and use as a spread for quick breads and bagels. Refrigerate. This keeps for 3 days. *Preparation time = 10 minutes.*

Nutrition Facts

Serving size = 1 Tbsp. • Servings per recipe = 8 • Calories = 21 • Calories from fat = 2

% Daily Value

Total fat < 1 gm. = 1% • Saturated fat = 0 • Cholesterol = 0 • Sodium 16 mg. = 1% • Total carbohydrate 3 gm. = 1% • Dietary fiber = 0 • Protein 1 gm. = 2% • Calcium 9 mg. = 1%

Exchange Values: Free Food

Surprise Me Muffins

2 c. Aunt Jemima® Original pancake and waffle mix
1/4 c. sugar
1 1/4 c. skim milk
1 egg, beaten, or 1/4 c. liquid egg substitute
2 Tbsp. vegetable oil

Preheat oven to 425° F. Line 12 muffin cups with papers or spray with Pam®. In a medium mixing bowl, combine pancake mix and sugar. Add milk, egg, and oil, mixing just until dry ingredients are moist. Then choose one of the flavor options. Fill prepared muffin cups and bake for 17 minutes until golden brown.
Preparation time = 15 minutes. Baking time = 17 minutes.

Flavor options:

Blueberry—Add 3/4 c. fresh or frozen blueberries to batter.
Raspberry, Strawberry, Orange, or Apricot—Fill muffin cups 1/2 full with batter, spoon 1 tsp. of fruit preserves into the center of each muffin. Top with remaining batter.

Nutrition Facts

Serving size = 1 muffin • Servings per recipe = 12 • Calories = 121 • Calories from fat = 18

% Daily Value

Total fat 3 gm. = 5% • Saturated fat < 1 gm. = 2% • Cholesterol = 0 with egg substitute • Cholesterol 18 mg. = 6% with real egg • Sodium 260 mg. = 8% • Total carbohydrate 19 gm. = 6% • Dietary fiber 0.3 gm. = 1% • Protein 3 gm. = 6% • Calcium 82 mg. = 10%

Exchange Values: 1 1/2 bread/starch

TWO BRAN MUFFINS

1 1 /2 c. flour
1 c. Kelloggs® Bran Flakes
1 c. oat bran
1/2 c. brown sugar
1/4 tsp. salt
1/4 c. crushed pineapple in juice, drained
1 1/2 tsp. baking soda
1 1/4 c. buttermilk
1 egg, slightly beaten, or 1/4 c. liquid egg substitute
1/4 c. vegetable oil

Preheat oven to 400° F. Prepare 12 muffin cups with paper liners or by spraying with Pam®. Combine first seven ingredients in a large mixing bowl. In a small bowl, mix together buttermilk, egg, and oil; add to flour mixture stirring only until blended. Spoon into prepared muffin cups and bake for 25 minutes.

Preparation time = 15 minutes. Baking time = 25 minutes.

Nutrition Facts

Serving size = 1 muffin • Servings per recipe = 12 small muffins • Calories = 137 • Calories from fat = 27

% Daily Value

Total fat 3 gm. = 5% • Saturated fat = 0 • Cholesterol = 0 with egg substitute • Cholesterol 18 mg. = 6% with real egg • Sodium 57 mg. = 2% • Total carbohydrate 25 gm. = 8% • Dietary fiber 2 gm. = 8% • Protein 4 gm. = 8% • Calcium 23 mg. = 3%

Exchange Values: 1 1/2 bread/starch

Zucchini-Cheddar Bread

1 c. chopped onion
2 Tbsp. vegetable oil
2 Tbsp. skim milk
2 1/2 c. Bisquick Light® baking mix
1 Tbsp. snipped parsley
1/2 tsp. dried basil
1/2 tsp. dried thyme
1/4 c. skim milk
3 eggs or 3/4 c. liquid egg substitute
1 1/2 c. shredded fresh zucchini
2 oz. Kraft® Healthy Favorites
    cheddar cheese, shredded

Preheat oven to 400° F. Spray a loaf pan with Pam®. In a mixing bowl, combine onions, oil, milk, baking mix, parsley, basil, thyme, and eggs. Beat for 1 minute. Stir in remaining ingredients. Spread in the loaf pan and bake for 40 to 45 minutes or until wooden pick inserted in the center comes out clean. Cool slightly and remove from pan.
Preparation time = 15 minutes. Baking time = 40 minutes.

Nutrition Facts

Serving size = 1 slice • Servings per recipe = 16 • Calories = 88 • Calories from fat = 27

% Daily Value

Total fat 3 gm. = 4% • Saturated fat < 1 gm. = 2% • Cholesterol 2 mg. = 1% with egg substitute • Cholesterol 40 mg. = 13% with real egg • Sodium 182 mg. = 6% • Total carbohydrate 10 gm. = 3% • Dietary fiber 0.6 gm. = 2% • Protein 4 gm. = 7% • Calcium 77 mg. = 10%

Exchange Values: 1 bread/starch

Bread-Machine Breads

Applesauce Bread

1/2 c. apple juice
2/3 c. applesauce
1/2 c. grated apple
Pinch nutmeg
1/2 tsp. cinnamon
4 Tbsp. sugar
1/2 tsp. salt
1 1/2 Tbsp. nonfat dry milk
3/4 c. whole-wheat flour
2 1/4 c. Gold Medal® Better for Bread flour
1 1/2 tsp. dry yeast
1 Tbsp. margarine

Add ingredients to pan in order listed (recipe tested with Hitachi® Automatic Home Bakery). If your machine calls for dry ingredients first, then invert the order of ingredients. Program for "bread" or regular setting. Push "start." Remove bread from machine approximately 4 hours later. Recipe makes one large (3 cup flour) loaf. *Preparation time = 10 minutes. Baking time = 4 hours.*

Nutrition Facts
Serving size = 1/2 slice • Servings per recipe = 24 half slices •
Calories = 110 • Calories from fat = 9

% Daily Value
Total fat 1 gm. = 2% • Saturated fat = 0 • Cholesterol = 0 • Sodium 152 mg.
= 5% • Total carbohydrate 22 gm. = 9% • Dietary fiber 0.3 gm. = 1% •
Protein 3 gm. = 5% • Calcium 8 mg. = 1%

Exchange Values: 1 bread/starch, 1/2 fruit

BEER CHEESE BREAD

10 oz. beer, flat
3 c. Gold Medal® Better for Bread flour
1 Tbsp. sugar
1 1/2 tsp. salt
1 1/2 Tbsp. nonfat dry milk
1 1/2 tsp. dry yeast
1 Tbsp. margarine
2 oz. shredded Kraft® Healthy Favorites
Jack cheese

Add ingredients to pan in order listed (recipe tested with Hitachi® Automatic Home Bakery). If your machine calls for dry ingredients first, then invert the order of ingredients. Program for "bread" or regular setting. Push "start." Remove bread from machine approximately 4 hours later. Recipe makes one large (3 cup flour) loaf. *Preparation time = 10 minutes. Baking time = 4 hours.*

Nutrition Facts

Serving size = 1/2 slice • Servings per recipe = 24 half slices • Calories = 120 • Calories from fat = 9

% Daily Value

Total fat 2 gm. = 4% • Saturated fat = 0 • Cholesterol = 0 • Sodium 152 mg. = 5% • Total carbohydrate 22 gm. = 9% • Dietary fiber 0.3 gm. = 1% • Protein 4 gm. = 7% • Calcium 8 mg. = 1%

Exchange Values: 1 1/2 bread/starch

BLUEBERRY BREAD

1/4 c. water
1/4 c. drained blueberry juice
3 c. Gold Medal® Better for Bread flour
1/2 tsp. salt
1 1/2 Tbsp. nonfat dry milk
2 Tbsp. sugar
1 1/2 tsp. yeast
1 Tbsp. margarine
16 1/2 oz. blueberries, drained with juice reserved.

Drain blueberries, reserving the juice. Add first seven ingredients to pan in order listed (recipe tested with Hitachi® Automatic Home Bakery). If your machine calls for dry ingredients first, then invert the order of ingredients. Program for "mix bread" or the setting that allows ingredients such as seeds or fruit to be folded into the dough. Push "start" and wait for the signal to add drained blueberries. Remove the bread from the pan when done, approximately 3 1/2 hours later. Recipe makes one large (3 cup flour) loaf. *Preparation time = 10 minutes. Baking time = 4 hours.*

Nutrition Facts
Serving size = 1/2 slice • Servings per recipe = 24 half slices •
Calories = 125 • Calories from fat = 9

% Daily Value
Total fat 1 gm. = 2% • Saturated fat = 0 • Cholesterol = 0 • Sodium 152 mg.
= 5% • Total carbohydrate 32 gm. = 11% • Dietary fiber 0.3 gm. = 1% •
Protein 3 gm. = 5% • Calcium 8 mg. = 1%

Exchange Values: 1 1/2 bread/starch

Buttermilk Cheese Bread

1/4 c. water
1 c. buttermilk
3 c. bread flour
1 tsp. baking powder
1 tsp. salt
1 Tbsp. sugar
1 1/2 tsp. yeast
1 c. shredded Kraft® Healthy Favorites
cheddar cheese

Add ingredients to pan in order listed (recipe tested with Hitachi® Automatic Home Bakery). If your machine calls for dry ingredients first, then invert the order of ingredients. Program for "bread" or regular setting. Push "start." Remove bread from machine approximately 4 hours later. Recipe makes one large (3 cup flour) loaf. *Preparation time = 10 minutes. Baking time = 4 hours.*

Nutrition Facts

Serving size = 1/2 slice • Servings per recipe = 24 half slices • Calories = 125 • Calories from fat = 9

% Daily Value

Total fat 1 gm. = 2% • Saturated fat = 0 • Cholesterol = 0 • Sodium 152 mg. = 5% • Total carbohydrate 32 gm. = 11% • Dietary fiber 0.3 gm. = 1% • Protein 3 gm. = 5% • Calcium 105 mg. = 13%

Exchange Values: 1 1/2 bread/starch

CALIFORNIA DIP BREAD

1/2 c. water
3/4 c. low-fat cottage cheese
3/4 c. nonfat sour cream
1 egg or 1/4 c. liquid egg substitute
3 1/3 c. bread flour
1/4 tsp. baking soda
3 Tbsp. sugar
1 envelope Lipton's® onion soup mix
1 1/2 tsp. dry yeast
1 Tbsp. margarine

Add ingredients to pan in order listed (recipe tested with Hitachi® Automatic Home Bakery). If your machine calls for dry ingredients first, then invert the order of ingredients. Program for "bread" or regular setting. Push "start." Remove bread from machine approximately 4 hours later. Recipe makes one large (3 cup flour) loaf. *Preparation time = 10 minutes. Baking time = 4 hours.*

Nutrition Facts
Serving size = 1/2 slice • Servings per recipe = 24 half slices • Calories = 135 • Calories from fat = 9

% Daily Value
Total fat 1 gm. = 2% • Saturated fat = 0 • Cholesterol = 0 with egg substitute • Cholesterol 8 mg. = 3% with real egg • Sodium 201 mg. = 7% • Total carbohydrate 32 gm. = 11% • Dietary fiber 0.3 gm. = 1% • Protein 5 gm. = 9% • Calcium 8 mg. = 1%

Exchange Values: 1 1/2 bread/starch

CHOCOLATE CHIP BREAD

1/4 c. water
1 c. milk
1 egg or 1/4 c. liquid egg substitute
3 c. Gold Medal® Better for Bread flour
2 Tbsp. brown sugar
2 Tbsp. white sugar
1 tsp. salt
1 tsp. cinnamon
1 1/2 tsp. dry yeast
2 Tbsp. margarine
1/2 c. semisweet chocolate chips

Add first 10 ingredients to pan in order listed (recipe tested with Hitachi® Automatic Home Bakery). If your machine calls for dry ingredients first, then invert the order of ingredients. Program for "mix bread" or the setting that allows ingredients such as seeds or fruit to be folded into the dough. Push "start." Wait for the signal and add the chocolate chips. Remove from the pan when done, approximately 3 1/2 hours. Recipe makes one large (3 cup flour) loaf. *Preparation time = 10 minutes. Baking time = 4 hours.*

Nutrition Facts

Serving size = 1/2 slice • Servings per recipe = 24 half slices •
Calories = 140 • Calories from fat = 18

% Daily Value

Total fat 2 gm. = 4% • Saturated fat 1 gm. = 4% • Cholesterol = 0 with egg substitute • Cholesterol 8 mg. = 3% with real egg • Sodium 109 mg. = 3% • Total carbohydrate 32 gm. = 11% • Dietary fiber 0.3 gm. = 1% • Protein 3 gm. = 5% • Calcium 8 mg. = 1%

Exchange Values: 1 bread/starch, 1 fruit

CORN, CHILIES, AND CHEESE BREAD

1 1/4 c. water
1 egg or 1/4 c. egg substitute
3 c. Gold Medal® Better for Bread flour
3/4 c. yellow cornmeal
1/2 tsp. salt
2 tsp. sugar
1 1/2 Tbsp. nonfat dry milk
1 1/2 tsp. dry yeast
1 Tbsp. margarine
1/2 c. whole-kernel canned corn, drained well
1 Tbsp. chopped green chilies
1/2 c. shredded Kraft® Healthy Favorites
    cheddar cheese

Add first eight ingredients to pan in order listed (recipe tested with Hitachi® Automatic Home Bakery). If your machine calls for dry ingredients first, then invert the order of ingredients. Program for "mix bread" or the setting that allows ingredients such as seeds or fruit to be folded into the dough. Push "start." Wait for the signal and add the corn, chilies, and cheese. Remove the bread from the pan when done, approximately 3 1/2 hours later. Recipe makes one large (3 cup flour) loaf. *Preparation time = 10 minutes. Baking time = 4 hours.*

Nutrition Facts
Serving size = 1/2 slice • Servings per recipe = 24 half slices • Calories = 150 • Calories from fat = 9

% Daily Value
Total fat 1 gm. = 2% • Saturated fat = 0 • Cholesterol = 0 with egg substitute • Cholesterol 8 mg. = 3% with real egg • Sodium 70 mg. = 2% • Total carbohydrate 32 gm. = 11% • Dietary fiber 1 gm. = 3% • Protein 6 gm. = 10% • Calcium 8 mg. = 1%

Exchange Values: 2 bread/starch

CRAISIN BREAD

1 1/8 c. water
2 3/4 c. Gold Medal® Better for Bread flour
1 1/2 Tbsp. nonfat dry milk
3 Tbsp. sugar
1 tsp. cinnamon
1 1/2 tsp. salt
1 1/2 tsp. dry yeast
1 Tbsp. margarine
3/4 c. craisins
(dried cranberries, found with dried fruits)

Add first eight ingredients to pan in order listed (recipe tested with Hitachi® Automatic Home Bakery). If your machine calls for dry ingredients first, then invert the order of ingredients. Program for "mix bread" or the setting that allows ingredients such as seeds or fruit to be folded into the dough. Push "start." When the signal sounds add the craisens. Remove the bread from the pan when done, approximately 3 1/2 hours later. Recipe makes one large (3 cup flour) loaf. *Preparation time = 10 minutes. Baking time = 4 hours.*

Nutrition Facts
Serving size = 1/2 slice • Servings per recipe = 24 half slices •
Calories = 125 • Calories from fat = 9

% Daily Value
Total fat 1 gm. = 2% • Saturated fat = 0 • Cholesterol 0 mg. = 0 • Sodium 152 mg. = 5% • Total carbohydrate 30 gm. = 11% • Dietary fiber 0.6 gm. = 2% • Protein 3 gm. = 5% • Calcium 8 mg. = 1%

Exchange Values: 1 1/2 bread/starch

DRIED FRUIT BREAD

1 1/8 c. water
2 3/4 c. Gold Medal® Better for Bread flour
1 1/2 Tbsp. nonfat dry milk
3 Tbsp. sugar
1 tsp. cinnamon
1 1/2 tsp. salt
1 1/2 tsp. dry yeast
1 Tbsp. margarine
3/4 c. mixed dried fruit bits (pineapple, apple)

Add first eight ingredients to pan in order listed (recipe tested with Hitachi® Automatic Home Bakery). If your machine calls for dry ingredients first, then invert the order of ingredients. Program for "mix bread" or the setting that allows ingredients such as seeds or fruit to be folded into the dough. Push "start." When the signal sounds, add the dried fruit. Remove the bread from the pan when done, approximately 3 1/2 hours later. Recipe makes one large (3 cup flour) loaf. *Preparation time = 10 minutes. Baking time = 4 hours.*

Nutrition Facts
Serving size = 1/2 slice • Servings per recipe = 24 half slices •
Calories = 125 • Calories from fat = 9

% Daily Value
Total fat 1 gm. = 2% • Saturated fat = 0 • Cholesterol = 0 • Sodium 152 mg.
= 5% • Total carbohydrate 30 gm. = 11% • Dietary fiber 0.6 gm. = 2% •
Protein 3 gm. = 5% • Calcium 8 mg. = 1%

Exchange Values: 1 1/2 bread/starch

FRENCH BREAD

2 stiffly beaten egg whites
1 c., less 1 Tbsp. water
3 c. Gold Medal® Better for Bread flour
2 Tbsp. sugar
1 tsp. salt
1 1/2 tsp. dry yeast
2 Tbsp. margarine

Add ingredients to pan in order listed (recipe tested with Hitachi® Automatic Home Bakery). If your machine calls for dry ingredients first, then invert the order of ingredients. Program for "bread" or regular setting. Push "start." Remove bread from the pan when done, approximately 4 hours later. Recipe makes one large (3 cup flour) loaf. *Preparation time = 10 minutes. Baking time = 4 hours.*

Nutrition Facts

Serving size = 1/2 slice • Servings per recipe = 24 half slices •
Calories = 120 • Calories from fat = 9

% Daily Value

Total fat 1 gm. = 2% • Saturated fat = 0 • Cholesterol = 0 • Sodium 62 mg. = 2% • Total carbohydrate 27 gm. = 9% • Dietary fiber = 0 • Protein 4 gm. = 7% • Calcium 25 mg. = 3%

Exchange Values: 1 1/2 bread/starch

GRANOLA BREAD

3/4 c. water
1/2 c. buttermilk
1 egg or 1/4 c. egg substitute
2 Tbsp. honey
2 c. bread flour
3/4 c. whole-wheat flour
3/4 tsp. salt
2 tsp. sugar
1 c. Kelloggs® Low-Fat Granola
1 1/2 tsp. dry yeast
1 Tbsp. margarine

Add ingredients to pan in order listed (recipe tested with Hitachi® Automatic Home Bakery). If your machine calls for dry ingredients first, then invert the order of ingredients. Program for "bread" or regular setting. Push "start." Remove bread from the pan when done, approximately 4 hours later. Recipe makes one large (3 cup flour) loaf. *Preparation time = 10 minutes. Baking time = 4 hours.*

Nutrition Facts

Serving size = 1/2 slice • Servings per recipe = 24 half slices • Calories = 108 • Calories from fat = 9

% Daily Value

Total fat 1 gm. = 2% • Saturated fat = 0 • Cholesterol = 0 with egg substitute • Cholesterol 8 mg. = 3% with real egg • Sodium 81 mg. = 3% • Total carbohydrate 24 gm. = 8% • Dietary fiber 0.6 gm. = 2% • Protein 3 gm. = 5% • Calcium 8 mg. = 1%

Exchange Values: 1 1/2 bread/starch

Hawaiian Coconut Bread

1/2 c. water
1/2 c. pineapple juice
1 egg or 1/4 c. egg substitute
3 c. Gold Medal® Better for Bread flour
2 tsp. salt
1 Tbsp. sugar
1/4 c. nonfat dry milk
2 Tbsp. margarine
1 1/2 tsp. dry yeast
3/4 c. shredded coconut
1/4 c. macadamia nuts
1/2 c. crushed pineapple, well drained

Add first nine ingredients to pan in order listed (recipe tested with Hitachi® Automatic Home Bakery). If your machine calls for dry ingredients first, then invert the order of ingredients. Program for "mix bread" or the setting that allows ingredients such as seeds or fruit to be folded into the dough. Push "start." When the signal sounds, add the coconut, nuts, and pineapple. Remove the bread from the pan when done, approximately 3 1/2 hours later. Recipe makes one large (3 cup flour) loaf. *Preparation time = 10 minutes. Baking time = 4 hours.*

Nutrition Facts

Serving size = 1/2 slice • Servings per recipe = 24 half slices •
Calories = 185 • Calories from fat = 63

% Daily Value

Total fat 7 gm. = 10% • Saturated fat 3 gm. = 15% • Cholesterol = 0 with egg
substitute • Cholesterol 8 mg. = 3% with real egg • Sodium 210 mg. = 7% •
Total carbohydrate 30 gm. = 11% • Dietary fiber 0.6 gm. = 2% • Protein 5 gm. =
5% • Calcium 8 mg. = 1%

Exchange Values: 1 bread/starch, 1 fruit, 1 fat

ITALIAN BREAD

1 1/8 c. water
3 c. Gold Medal® Better for Bread flour
1 1/2 Tbsp. nonfat dry milk
1 1/2 tsp. salt
3 Tbsp. sugar
1 tsp. dried oregano
1 tsp. dried basil
2 Tbsp. Parmesan cheese
1/4 tsp. garlic powder
1 Tbsp. dried onion
1 1/2 tsp. dry yeast
2 Tbsp. margarine

Add ingredients to pan in order listed (recipe tested with Hitachi® Automatic Home Bakery). If your machine calls for dry ingredients first, then invert the order of ingredients. Program for "bread" or regular setting. Push "start." Remove bread from pan when done, approximately 4 hours later. Recipe makes one large (3 cup flour) loaf. *Preparation time = 10 minutes. Baking time = 4 hours.*

Nutrition Facts
Serving size = 1/2 slice • Servings per recipe = 24 half slices • Calories = 120 • Calories from fat = 9

% Daily Value
Total fat 1 gm. = 2% • Saturated fat = 0 • Cholesterol = 0 • Sodium 164 mg. = 5% • Total carbohydrate 27 gm. = 9% • Dietary fiber = 0 • Protein 4 gm. = 7% • Calcium 25 mg. = 3%

Exchange Values: 1 1/2 bread/starch

LEMON BREAD

3/4 c. milk
2 eggs or 1/2 c. liquid egg substitute
3 c. Gold Medal® Better for Bread flour
1/2 tsp. salt
1/4 c. sugar
1/4 tsp. lemon extract
2 tsp. freshly grated lemon peel
1 1/2 tsp. yeast
2 Tbsp. margarine

Add ingredients to pan in order listed (recipe tested with Hitachi® Automatic Home Bakery). If your machine calls for dry ingredients first, then invert the order of ingredients. Program for "bread" or regular setting. Push "start." Remove bread from pan when done, approximately 4 hours later. Recipe makes one large (3 cup flour) loaf. *Preparation time = 10 minutes. Baking time = 4 hours.*

Nutrition Facts
Serving size = 1/2 slice • Servings per recipe = 24 half slices •
Calories = 124 • Calories from fat = 9

% Daily Value
Total fat 1 gm. = 2% • Saturated fat = 0 • Cholesterol = 0 with egg substitute • Cholesterol 18 mg. = 6% with real egg • Sodium 67 mg. = 2% • Total carbohydrate 26 gm. = 11% • Dietary fiber 0.3 gm. = 1% • Protein 3 gm. = 5% • Calcium 8 mg. = 1%

Exchange Values: 1 1/2 bread/starch

OAT BRAN BANANA BREAD

3/4 c. water
1/2 c. mashed banana
1 egg or 1/4 c. liquid egg substitute
1/2 c. oat bran
2 3/4 c. Gold Medal® Better for Bread flour
3 Tbsp. sugar
1 1/2 tsp. salt
1 1/2 Tbsp. nonfat dry milk
1 1/2 tsp. dry yeast

Add ingredients to pan in order listed (recipe tested with Hitachi®
Automatic Home Bakery). If your machine calls for dry ingredients
first, then invert the order of ingredients. Program for "bread" or
regular setting. Push "start." Remove bread from pan when done,
approximately 4 hours later. Recipe makes one large (3 cup flour)
loaf. *Preparation time = 10 minutes. Baking time = 4 hours.*

Nutrition Facts
Serving size = 1/2 slice • Servings per recipe = 24 half slices •
Calories = 124 • Calories from fat = 9

% Daily Value
Total fat 1 gm. = 2% • Saturated fat = 0 • Cholesterol = 0 with egg substitute •
Cholesterol 8 mg. = 3% with real egg • Sodium 67 mg. = 2% • Total carbohy-
drate 26 gm. = 11% • Dietary fiber 1 gm. = 4% • Protein 3 gm. = 5% •
Calcium 8 mg. = 1%

Exchange Values: 1 1/2 bread/starch

Oat Bran Carrot Bread

1 c. water
1 egg or 1/4 c. liquid egg substitute
1/2 c. oat bran
2 3/4 c. Gold Medal® Better for Bread flour
3 Tbsp. sugar
1 1/2 tsp. salt
1 1/2 Tbsp. nonfat dry milk
1 1/2 tsp. dry yeast
1/2 c. grated carrots

Add first eight ingredients to pan in order listed (recipe tested with Hitachi® Automatic Home Bakery). If your machine calls for dry ingredients first, then invert the order of ingredients. Program for "mix bread" or the setting that allows ingredients such as seeds or fruit to be folded into the dough. Push "start." When the signal sounds, add the carrots. Remove from the pan when done, approximately 3 1/2 hours later. Recipe makes one large (3 cup flour) loaf. *Preparation time = 10 minutes. Baking time = 4 hours.*

Nutrition Facts
Serving size = 1/2 slice • Servings per recipe = 24 half slices •
Calories = 124 • Calories from fat = 9

% Daily Value
Total fat 1 gm. = 2% • Saturated fat = 0 • Cholesterol = 0 with egg substitute •
Cholesterol 8 mg. = 3% with real egg • Sodium 67 mg. = 2% • Total carbohy-
drate 26 gm. = 11% • Dietary fiber 1 gm. = 4% • Protein 3 gm. = 5% •
Calcium 8 mg. = 1%

Exchange Values: 1 1/2 bread/starch

OAT BRAN RAISIN BREAD

1 c. water
1 egg or 1/4 c. egg substitute
1/2 c. oat bran
2 3/4 c. Gold Medal® Better for Bread flour
3 Tbsp. sugar
1 1/2 tsp. salt
1 1/2 Tbsp. nonfat dry milk
1 1/2 tsp. dry yeast
1/2 c. raisins

Add first eight ingredients to pan in order listed (recipe tested with Hitachi® Automatic Home Bakery). If your machine calls for dry ingredients first, then invert the order of ingredients. Program for "mix bread" or the setting that allows ingredients such as seeds or fruit to be folded into the dough. Push "start." When the signal sounds, add the raisins. Remove the bread when done, approximately 3 1/2 hours later. Recipe makes one large (3 cup flour) loaf. *Preparation time = 10 minutes. Baking time = 4 hours.*

Nutrition Facts
Serving size = 1/2 slice • Servings per recipe = 24 half slices •
Calories = 124 • Calories from fat = 9

% Daily Value
Total fat 1 gm. = 2% • Saturated fat = 0 • Cholesterol = 0 with egg substitute •
Cholesterol 8 mg. = 3% with real egg • Sodium 67 mg. = 2% • Total carbohy-
drate 26 gm. = 11% • Dietary fiber 1 gm. = 4% • Protein 3 gm. = 5% •
Calcium 8 mg. = 1%

Exchange Values: 1 1/2 bread/starch

ONION DILL BREAD

1/4 c. water
3/4 c. low-fat cottage cheese
3/4 c. nonfat sour cream
1 egg or 1/4 c. liquid egg substitute
3 1/3 c. Gold Medal® Better for Bread flour
1/4 tsp. baking soda
1 1/2 tsp. dry yeast
1/4 tsp. salt
3 Tbsp. sugar
1 Tbsp. margarine
3 Tbsp. minced dried onion
2 Tbsp. whole dill seed

Add first eight ingredients to pan in order listed (recipe tested with Hitachi® Automatic Home Bakery). If your machine calls for dry ingredients first, then invert the order of ingredients. Program for "mix bread" or the setting that allows ingredients such as seeds or fruit to be folded into the dough. Push "start." When the signal sounds, add the dried onion and dill seed. Remove the bread from the pan when done, approximately 3 1/2 hours later. Recipe makes one large (3 cup flour) loaf. *Preparation time = 10 minutes. Baking time = 4 hours.*

Nutrition Facts

Serving size = 1/2 slice • Servings per recipe = 24 half slices •
Calories = 132 • Calories from fat = 9

% Daily Value

Total fat 1 gm. = 2% • Saturated fat = 0 • Cholesterol = 0 with egg substitute •
Cholesterol 8 mg. = 3% with real egg • Sodium 67 mg. = 2% • Total
carbohydrate 31 gm. = 11% • Dietary fiber = 0 • Protein 3 gm. = 5% •
Calcium 15 mg. = 2%

Exchange Values: 1 1/2 bread/starch

ORANGE BREAD

1/4 c. water
1 c. orange juice
1 egg or 1/4 c. egg substitute
2 Tbsp. grated orange rind
3 c. Gold Medal® Better for Bread flour
1 1/2 Tbsp. nonfat dry milk
1/4 c. sugar
1 tsp. salt
1 1/2 tsp. dry yeast
1 Tbsp. margarine

Add ingredients to pan in order listed (recipe tested with Hitachi® Automatic Home Bakery). If your machine calls for dry ingredients first, then invert the order of ingredients. Program for "bread" or regular setting. Push "start." Remove bread when done, approximately 4 hours later. Recipe makes one large (3 cup flour) loaf. *Preparation time = 10 minutes. Baking time = 4 hours.*

Nutrition Facts
Serving size = 1/2 slice • Servings per recipe = 24 half slices •
Calories = 124 • Calories from fat = 9

% Daily Value
Total fat 1 gm. = 2% • Saturated fat = 0 • Cholesterol = 0 with egg substitute • Cholesterol 8 mg. = 3% with real egg • Sodium 67 mg. = 2% •
Total carbohydrate 26 gm. = 11% • Dietary fiber = 0 • Protein 3 gm. = 5% •
Calcium 15 mg. = 2%
Exchange Values: 1 1/2 bread/starch

Overnight Pecan Rolls

1 c. water
1 egg or 1/4 c. liquid egg substitute
3 c. Gold Medal® Better for Bread flour
1/4 c. sugar
2 Tbsp. nonfat dry milk
1 1/2 tsp. salt
1 1/2 tsp. dry yeast
1 Tbsp. margarine

Filling:

1 Tbsp. margarine
1/4 c. brown sugar
1 tsp. cinnamon
2 Tbsp. chopped pecans

Add first eight ingredients to pan in order listed (recipe tested with Hitachi® Automatic Home Bakery). If your machine calls for dry ingredients first, then invert the order of ingredients. Program for "dough" setting and push "start." When dough preparation is complete (approximately 1 hour and 40 minutes) remove the soft dough from the pan and roll out on a floured surface. Spread with margarine and sprinkle with brown sugar, cinnamon, and pecans. Roll up the dough and slice into 24 rolls. Place on a greased baking sheet and cover loosely with plastic wrap. Refrigerate overnight. In the morning, place the rolls in a cold oven and preheat the oven to 375° F. When the oven reaches 375° F., set the timer for 15 minutes. If your oven does not have an indicator for when the temperature is attained, allow 12 minutes, making total oven time 27 minutes. Rolls are done when they are golden brown.

Preparation time = 30 minutes. Bread Machine time = 1 hour 40 minutes. Baking time (including preheating) = 27 minutes.

Nutrition Facts

Serving size = 1 roll • Servings per recipe = 24 rolls • Calories = 136 • Calories from fat = 18

% Daily Value

Total fat 2 gm. = 4% • Saturated fat = 0 • Cholesterol = 0 with egg substitute • Cholesterol 8 mg. = 3% with real egg • Sodium 67 mg. = 2% • Total carbohydrate 31 gm. = 11% • Dietary fiber 1 gm. = 4% • Protein 3 gm. = 5% • Calcium 13 mg. = 2%

Exchange Values: 1 1/2 bread/starch

PEANUT BUTTER BREAD

1 1/4 c. water
1/2 c. peanut butter
3 c. Gold Medal® Better for Bread flour
1 1/2 Tbsp. nonfat dry milk
1/4 c. brown sugar
1 1/2 tsp. dry yeast

Add ingredients to pan in order listed (recipe tested with Hitachi®
Automatic Home Bakery). If your machine calls for dry ingredients
first, then invert the order of ingredients. Program for "bread" or
regular setting and push "start." Remove bread when done, approximately 4 hours later. Recipe makes one large (3 cup flour) loaf.
Preparation time = 10 minutes. Baking time = 4 hours.

Nutrition Facts
Serving size = 1/2 slice • Servings per recipe = 24 half slices •
Calories = 146 • Calories from fat = 27

% Daily Value
Total fat 3 gm. = 5% • Saturated fat = 0 • Cholesterol = 0 • Sodium 67 mg. =
2% • Total carbohydrate 30 gm. = 10% • Dietary fiber 1 gm. = 4% • Protein
5 gm. = 8% • Calcium 8 mg. = 1%

Exchange Values: 1 bread/starch, 1 fruit

Pecan and Red Onion Bread

1 c. plus 1 Tbsp. milk
3 c. Gold Medal® Better for Bread flour
1 1/2 tsp. salt
3 Tbsp. sugar
1 1/2 tsp. yeast
1 Tbsp. margarine
1/2 c. fresh red onion, chopped
1/4 c. pecans or walnuts, chopped

Add first six ingredients to pan in order listed (recipe tested with Hitachi® Automatic Home Bakery). If your machine calls for dry ingredients first, then invert the order of ingredients. Program for "mix bread" or the setting that allows ingredients such as seeds or fruit to be folded into the dough. Push "start." When the signal sounds, add the onion and nuts. Remove the bread from the pan when done, approximately 3 1/2 hours later. Recipe makes one large (3 cup flour) loaf. *Preparation time = 10 minutes. Baking time = 4 hours.*

Nutrition Facts
Serving size = 1/2 slice • Servings per recipe = 24 half slices •
Calories = 130 • Calories from fat = 45

% Daily Value
Total fat 5 gm. = 8% • Saturated fat = 0 • Cholesterol = 0 • Sodium 67 mg.
= 2% • Total carbohydrate 30 gm. = 11% • Dietary fiber 1 gm. = 4% •
Protein 3 gm. = 5% • Calcium 15 mg. = 2%

Exchange Values: 1 1/2 bread/starch

POTATO BREAD

1 c. water
1 egg or 1/4 c. liquid egg substitute
3 c. Gold Medal® Better for Bread flour
1/4 c. instant mashed-potato flakes
1 1/2 tsp. nonfat dried milk
3 Tbsp. sugar
1 1/2 tsp. salt
1 1/2 tsp. dry yeast
1 Tbsp. margarine

Add ingredients to pan in order listed (recipe tested with Hitachi® Automatic Home Bakery). If your machine calls for dry ingredients first, then invert the order of ingredients. Program for "bread" or regular setting and push "start." Remove bread when done, approximately 4 hours later. Recipe makes one large (3 cup flour) loaf. *Preparation time = 10 minutes. Baking time = 4 hours.*

Nutrition Facts
Serving size = 1/2 slice • Servings per recipe = 24 half slices •
Calories = 120 • Calories from fat = 9

% Daily Value
Total fat 1 gm. = 2% • Saturated fat = 0 • Cholesterol = 0 with egg substitute •
Cholesterol 8 mg. = 3% with real egg • Sodium 150 mg. = 2% •
Total carbohydrate 27 gm. = 9% • Dietary fiber = 0 • Protein 4 gm. = 7% •
Calcium 25 mg. = 3%

Exchange Values: 1 1/2 bread/starch

PUMPKIN BREAD

1 1/3 c. water
1/4 c. orange juice
1/2 c. canned pumpkin
1 egg or 1/4 c. liquid egg substitute
3 c. Gold Medal® Better for Bread flour
1/2 c. whole-wheat flour
1 tsp. salt
1 tsp. ground pumpkin pie spice (or substitute 3/4
    tsp. cinnamon, 1/8 tsp. allspice, and a pinch each
    of ginger, nutmeg, and cloves)
3 Tbsp. brown sugar
1 1/2 tsp. dry yeast
2 Tbsp. margarine

Add ingredients to pan in order listed (recipe tested with Hitachi®
Automatic Home Bakery). If your machine calls for dry ingredients
first, then invert the order of ingredients. Program for "bread" or
regular setting, and push "start." Remove bread when done, approximately 4 hours later. Recipe makes one large (3 cup flour) loaf.
Preparation time = 10 minutes. Baking time = 4 hours.

Nutrition Facts
Serving size = 1/2 slice • Servings per recipe = 24 half slices •
Calories = 130 • Calories from fat = 9

% Daily Value
Total fat 1 gm. = 2% • Saturated fat = 0 • Cholesterol = 0 with egg substitute •
Cholesterol 8 mg. = 3% with real egg • Sodium 100 mg. = 2% • Total carbohy-
drate 26 gm. = 11% • Dietary fiber 0.3 gm. = 1% • Protein 3 gm. = 5% •
Calcium 8 mg. = 1%

Exchange Values: 1 1/2 bread/starch

REUBEN BREAD

1 c. plus 1 Tbsp. water
1 Tbsp. molasses
1 c. rye flour
2 c. Gold Medal® Better for Bread flour
1 1/2 tsp. salt
1 1/2 Tbsp. nonfat dry milk
3 Tbsp. sugar
1 1/2 tsp. dry yeast
1 Tbsp. margarine
2 tsp. caraway seed
2 tsp. dried minced onion

Add first eight ingredients to pan in order listed (recipe tested with Hitachi® Automatic Home Bakery). If your machine calls for dry ingredients first, then invert the order of ingredients. Program for "mix bread" or the setting that allows ingredients such as seeds or fruit to be folded into the dough. Push "start." When the signal sounds, add the dried onion and caraway seed. Remove the bread from the pan when done, approximately 3 1/2 hours later. Recipe makes one large (3 cup flour) loaf. *Preparation time = 10 minutes. Baking time = 4 hours.*

Nutrition Facts
Serving size = 1/2 slice • Servings per recipe = 24 half slices •
Calories = 110 • Calories from fat = 9

% Daily Value
Total fat 1 gm. = 2% • Saturated fat = 0 • Cholesterol = 0 • Sodium 140 mg.
= 3% • Total carbohydrate 28 gm. = 9% • Dietary fiber 0.5 gm. = 2% •
Protein 4 gm. = 7% • Calcium 25 mg. = 3%

Exchange Values: 1 1/2 bread/starch

RUSSIAN BLACK BREAD

1 c. plus 2 Tbsp. water
2 Tbsp. molasses
2 Tbsp. cider vinegar
1/2 oz. unsweetened chocolate, melted
1 1/2 c. Gold Medal® Better for Bread flour
1 1/2 c. medium rye flour
1/4 c. whole-wheat flour
1/2 c. bran flakes
1 tsp. salt
1 tsp. instant coffee
1 Tbsp. sugar
1 1/2 Tbsp. nonfat dry milk
1 1/2 tsp. yeast
2 Tbsp. margarine
1 Tbsp. caraway seeds
1/4 tsp. fennel seeds

Add all ingredients, except caraway and fennel seeds, to pan in order listed (recipe tested with Hitachi® Automatic Home Bakery). If your machine calls for dry ingredients first, then invert the order of ingredients. Program for "mix bread" or the setting that allows ingredients such as seeds or fruit to be folded into the dough. Push "start." When the signal sounds, add the caraway and fennel seed. Remove the bread from the pan when done, approximately 3 1/2 hours later. Recipe makes one large (3 cup flour) loaf. *Preparation time = 10 minutes. Baking time = 4 hours.*

Nutrition Facts
Serving size = 1/2 slice • Servings per recipe = 24 half slices • Calories = 120 • Calories from fat = 9

% Daily Value
Total fat 1 gm. = 2% • Saturated fat = 0 • Cholesterol = 0 • Sodium 109 mg. = 3% • Total carbohydrate 27 gm. = 9% • Dietary fiber 1 gm. = 4% • Protein 4 gm. = 7% • Calcium 25 mg. = 3%

Exchange Values: 1 1/2 bread/starch

Salads

August Salad

2 c. peeled, sliced cucumbers
   (2 medium cucumbers)
1 c. peeled, chunked tomatoes
2 Tbsp. chopped fresh green pepper
1 Tbsp. chopped fresh onion
1/3 c. Marie's® lite blue cheese dressing
1/4 c. croutons

Layer ingredients in a clear salad bowl. Chill or serve immediately.
Preparation time = 10 minutes.

Nutrition Facts
Serving size = 1 cup • Servings per recipe = 4 • Calories = 95 •
Calories from fat = 54

% Daily Value
Total fat 6 gm. = 9% • Saturated fat 2 gm. = 9% • Cholesterol 5 mg. = 2% •
Sodium 20 mg. = 1% • Total carbohydrate 9 gm. = 3% • Dietary fiber 2 gm. =
8% • Protein 2 gm. = 4% • Calcium 45 mg. = 6%

Exchange Values: 2 vegetable, 1 fat

BARTLES AND JAYMES® TROPICAL FRUIT SALAD

1 c. fresh orange sections
1 c. strawberries
1 c. kiwi slices (2 kiwi)
1 c. Bartles and Jaymes® Premium
   Tropical wine cooler

Combine fruits in a clear bowl. Pour wine cooler over fruits. Allow to marinate 10 minutes or up to overnight. Use a ladle and serve in large fruit or cereal bowls. *Preparation time = 10 minutes.*

Nutrition Facts
Serving size = 1 cup • Servings per recipe = 4 • Calories = 71 • Calories from fat = 4

% Daily Value
Total fat < 1 gm. = 1% • Saturated fat = 0 • Cholesterol = 0 • Sodium = 0 • Total carbohydrate 18 gm. = 6% • Dietary fiber 3 gm. = 12% • Protein 1 gm. = 2% • Calcium 45 mg. = 6%

Exchange Values: 1 fruit

BLUE CHEESE LOVER'S POTATO SALAD

8 medium red-skinned potatoes
1/2 c. green onions, thinly sliced
1/4 tsp. garlic salt, divided
1/4 tsp. black pepper
1 c. plain nonfat Dannon® yogurt
2 Tbsp. buttermilk
1/4 c. blue cheese, crumbled

Cut potatoes into 3/4-inch pieces, leaving skins on. Cook in boiling water for 15 to 20 minutes or until tender; drain. Combine potatoes, onions, 1/8 tsp. garlic salt, and pepper, tossing gently. Stir together yogurt, buttermilk, 1/8 tsp. garlic salt. Add to potatoes and toss gently to coat. Cover and chill at least 30 minutes. *Preparation time = 30 minutes. Chilling time = 30 minutes.*

Nutrition Facts
Serving size = 3/4 cup • Servings per recipe = 8 • Calories = 164 •
Calories from fat = 27

% Daily Value
Total fat 3 gm. = 4% • Saturated fat 2 gm. = 8% • Cholesterol 8 mg. = 3% •
Sodium 132 mg. = 5% • Total carbohydrate 30 gm. = 10% • Dietary fiber 2
gm. = 8% • Protein 6 gm. = 10% • Calcium 104 mg. = 13%

Exchange Values: 2 bread/starch

BROCCOLI FOR
A BUNCH

Flowerettes from 1 large bunch of broccoli
1/2 red onion, thinly sliced
4 strips bacon, cut into small pieces and fried crisp
1/2 c. raisins

Dressing:
1/2 c. Hellman's® reduced-fat mayonnaise
2 Tbsp. brown sugar
1/2 c. nonfat sour cream
1 Tbsp. vinegar

Combine flowerettes, onion, bacon, and raisins in a large salad
bowl. Combine dressing ingredients in a 1-cup bowl. Pour dressing
over salad, toss to coat, and serve. *Preparation time = 15 minutes.*

Nutrition Facts
Serving size = 1 cup • Servings per recipe = 8 • Calories = 120 •
Calories from fat = 18

% Daily Value
Total fat 2 gm. = 3% • Saturated fat 0.5 gm. = 3% • Cholesterol 3 mg. =
1% • Sodium 279 mg. = 10% • Total carbohydrate 23 gm. = 8% • Dietary
fiber 4 gm. = 16% • Protein 6 gm. = 10% • Calcium 106 mg. = 13%

Exchange Values: 1 bread/starch, 1/2 fruit

CARROT AND LENTIL SALAD

1 c. dry lentils
1 c. diced carrots
1/2 tsp. garlic powder
1 bay leaf

Dressing:

1/2 c. celery, finely chopped
1/4 c. fresh parsley, finely chopped
2 Tbsp. vegetable oil
1/4 c. ReaLemon® lemon juice
1/4 tsp. salt
1/2 tsp. dried thyme
1/4 tsp. pepper

In a Dutch oven, combine lentils, carrots, garlic, and bay leaf. Cover with 1 inch of water. Bring to a boil and simmer for 15 minutes or until lentils are tender. Remove bay leaf, drain, and cool. Meanwhile, combine all ingredients for dressing. Pour over lentil mixture. Cover and refrigerate at least 30 minutes. *Preparation time = 30 minutes. Chilling time = 30 minutes.*

Nutrition Facts
Serving size = 3/4 cup • Servings per recipe = 8 • Calories = 130 • Calories from fat = 36

% Daily Value
Total fat 4 gm. = 6% • Saturated fat 0.3 gm. = 2% • Cholesterol = 0 • Sodium 96 mg. = 3% • Total carbohydrate 18 gm. = 6% • Dietary fiber 2 gm. = 8% • Protein 8 gm. = 13% • Calcium 36 gm. = 5%

Exchange Values: 1 vegetable, 1 bread/starch, 1/2 fat

CHILLED TOMATO SALAD

1 envelope Good Seasons® Italian dressing mix
2 Tbsp. oil
1/4 c. red wine vinegar
1/2 c. water
16-oz. can chopped tomatoes, drained
1/4 c. chopped red onion
1/2 c. thinly sliced celery
1 medium carrot, grated
1 Tbsp. crumbled blue cheese

Combine dressing mix, oil, red wine vinegar, and water in a cruet. Set aside. Combine remaining ingredients. Add half of the dressing. Cover and refrigerate until ready to serve. Save the remaining dressing for later use on green salads. *Preparation time = 10 minutes.*

Nutrition Facts
Serving size = 3/4 cup • Servings per recipe = 4 • Calories = 90 • Calories from fat = 45

% Daily Value
Total fat 5 gm. = 8% • Saturated fat 2 gm. = 8% • Cholesterol 5 gm. = 2% • Sodium 490 mg. = 16% • Total carbohydrate 10 gm. = 3% • Dietary fiber 1 gm. = 4% • Protein 2 gm. = 4% • Calcium 68 mg. = 9%

Exchange Values: 2 vegetable, 1 fat

COPPER CARROTS

2 lb. carrots, thinly sliced
1/4 c. water
1 green pepper, thinly sliced into rings
1 med. onion, thinly sliced
1 tsp. Worcestershire sauce
1/4 c. sugar
3/4 c. white vinegar
1 tsp. prepared mustard
1 can Campbell's® Healthy Request tomato soup
2 Tbsp. vegetable oil
1/4 tsp. pepper

Place carrots in a microwave-safe dish. Sprinkle with 1/4 cup water, cover, and microwave on high power for 5 minutes, stopping to stir at least twice during the cooking. When carrots are cool, alternate layers of carrots with pepper and onion slices. Combine Worcestershire sauce and remaining ingredients in a bowl. Pour sauce mixture over vegetables. Cover and refrigerate at least 1 hour. *Preparation time = 20 minutes. Chilling time = 1 hour.*

Nutrition Facts
Serving size = 1 cup • Servings per recipe = 8 • Calories = 143 • Calories from fat = 45

% Daily Value
Total fat 5 gm. = 7% • Saturated fat < 1 gm. = 2% • Cholesterol = 0 • Sodium 342 mg. = 12% • Total carbohydrate 26 gm. = 9% • Dietary fiber 5 gm. = 20% • Protein 3 gm. = 4% • Calcium 41 mg. = 5%

Exchange Values: 1 bread/starch, 1 vegetable, 1 fat

Cottage Cheese and Vegetable Salad

1 3-oz. box Jello® sugar-free orange gelatin
1 c. hot water
1/4 c. reduced-fat mayonnaise
1/2 c. nonfat cottage cheese
1/2 c. grated carrots
1/2 c. finely diced celery
1 Tbsp. finely chopped onion
1/2 c. chopped green pepper

Dissolve gelatin in hot water. While hot, add mayonnaise. Allow to cool, then add remaining ingredients. Refrigerate until set. *Preparation time = 20 minutes. Chilling time = 2 hours.*

Nutrition Facts
Serving size = 3/4 cup • Servings per recipe = 4 • Calories = 92 • Calories from fat = 4

% Daily Value
Total fat 5 gm. = 8% • Saturated fat 1 gm. = 5% • Cholesterol 6 mg. = 2% • Sodium 244 mg. = 8% • Total carbohydrate 8 gm. = 3% • Dietary fiber 2 gm. = 8% • Protein 4 gm. = 7% • Calcium 39 mg. = 5%

Exchange Values: 2 vegetable, 1 fat

CRANBERRY DELIGHT

3 oz. sugar-free lemon gelatin
1 c. boiling water
16-oz. can Ocean Spray® whole-berry cranberry sauce
8-oz. can crushed pineapple in juice
1/4 c. chopped pecans
1 c. diced yellow apples

Dissolve gelatin in boiling water. Mix the cranberry sauce with a fork to break it up, then add to the gelatin. Add the pineapple and juice, and chill until thickened. Fold in pecans and apples. Pour into a clear bowl and chill. *Preparation time = 10 minutes. Chilling time = 2 hours.*

Nutrition Facts
Serving size = 1/2 cup • Servings per recipe = 8 • Calories = 186 • Calories from fat = 45

% Daily Value
Total fat 5 gm. = 8% • Saturated fat < 1 gm. = 2% • Cholesterol = 0 • Sodium 21 mg. = 1% • Total carbohydrate 38 gm. = 13% • Dietary fiber 0.5 gm. = 2% • Protein 1 gm. = 2% • Calcium 11 mg. = 2%

Exchange Values: 2 1/2 fruit, 1 fat

CREAMY APPLE SLAW

1 Tbsp. vinegar
2 tsp. lemon juice
1 tsp. sugar
1/4 tsp. prepared mustard
3/4 c. Land 'O Lakes® nonfat sour cream
2 c. shredded cabbage
2 c. cubed apples, dipped in lemon juice
1/4 c. grated carrot
3 Tbsp. finely chopped celery

Blend vinegar, lemon juice, sugar, mustard, and salt. Fold in sour cream. Cover and chill. When ready to serve, toss cabbage, apples, carrot, and celery together in a bowl. Add dressing and toss again. *Preparation time = 15 minutes.*

Nutrition Facts
Serving size = 1 cup • Servings per recipe = 4 • Calories = 138 •
Calories from fat = 9

% Daily Value
Total fat < 1 gm. = 1% • Saturated fat = 0 • Cholesterol = 0 • Sodium 83 mg.
= 3% • Total carbohydrate 31 gm. = 10% • Dietary fiber 6 gm. = 24% (High in
fiber) • Protein 5 gm. = 9% • Calcium 190 mg. = 24%

Exchange Values: 1 fruit, 3 vegetable

CREAMY ITALIAN DRESSING FOR GREEN SALADS

1 c. Land 'O Lakes® nonfat sour cream
1/2 c. Hellmann's® reduced-fat mayonnaise
1 envelope Italian salad dressing mix
1/2 c. buttermilk

Mix the sour cream, mayonnaise, and salad dressing mix. Gradually add buttermilk, stirring until smooth. This makes 2 cups. *Preparation time = 10 minutes.*

Nutrition Facts

Serving size = 1/4 cup • Servings per recipe = 8 • Calories = 46 • Calories from fat = 3

% Daily Value

Total fat < 1 gm. = 1% • Saturated fat = 0 • Cholesterol = 0 • Sodium 427 mg. = 14% • Total carbohydrate 8 gm. = 3% • Dietary fiber = 0 • Protein 3 gm. = 5% • Calcium 100 mg. = 13%

Exchange Values: 1/2 skim milk

CREAMY RED-SKINNED POTATO SALAD WITH BACON AND MUSTARD DRESSING

4 large red-skinned potatoes, cut into 1-inch chunks
1/4 c. water
1 Tbsp. red-wine vinegar
1 tsp. vegetable oil
1 Tbsp. Dijon mustard
1/4 tsp. salt
1/2 tsp. dried basil
1/4 tsp. pepper
2 slices bacon, snipped into small pieces
    and fried crisp
1/2 c. finely chopped celery
2 Tbsp. finely chopped red onion
1/4 c. Dannon® nonfat plain yogurt
2 Tbsp. nonfat sour cream

Place potatoes in a microwave-safe dish. Sprinkle with 1/4 c. water and cover. Microwave on high power for 5 minutes; stop to stir the potatoes and turn the dish twice during cooking. Drain the potatoes and transfer to a salad bowl; chill for 20 minutes. Meanwhile, in a small serving bowl, whisk the vinegar, oil, mustard, salt, and basil. Add dressing to cooled potatoes, then stir in bacon, celery, and onion. Stir yogurt and sour cream together, then pour over potatoes, folding carefully just until evenly combined. Serve. *Preparation time = 15 minutes. Chilling time = 20 minutes.*

Nutrition Facts
Serving size = 1/2 cup • Servings per recipe = 8 • Calories = 99 • Calories from fat = 15

% Daily Value
Total fat 2 gm. = 4% • Saturated fat < 1 gm. = 1% • Cholesterol 1 mg. = 1% • Sodium 142 mg. = 5% • Total carbohydrate 18 gm. = 6% • Dietary fiber 1.5 gm. = 6% • Protein 3 gm. = 5% • Calcium 38 mg. = 5%

Exchange Values: 1 bread/starch

CUCUMBER, RADISH, AND TOMATO SALAD

1 large cucumber, peeled and sliced 1/4-inch thick
6 medium radishes, sliced 1/8 inch thick
1 medium tomato, thinly sliced
3 Tbsp. Kraft Free® Italian dressing
1 Tbsp. Parmesan cheese

Layer cucumbers, radishes, and tomato in a clear glass bowl. Add dressing and Parmesan. Marinate in the refrigerator for 20 minutes. Serve. *Preparation time = 10 minutes. Chilling time = 20 minutes.*

Nutrition Facts
Serving size = 1 cup • Servings per recipe = 4 • Calories = 48 • Calories from fat = 18

% Daily Value
Total fat 2 gm. = 4% • Saturated fat < 1 gm. = 4% • Cholesterol 3 mg. = 1% • Sodium 161 mg. = 5% • Total carbohydrate 5 gm. = 2% • Dietary fiber 0.8 gm. = 3% • Protein 2 gm. = 4% • Calcium 65 mg. = 8%

Exchange Values: 2 vegetable

CUCUMBER, RADISH, AND TOMATO SALAD NUMBER 2

1 large cucumber, peeled and sliced 1/4-inch thick
6 medium radishes, sliced 1/8 inch thick
1 medium tomato, thinly sliced
3 Tbsp. Kraft Free® Peppercorn Ranch
   nonfat dressing
1 Tbsp. fresh parsley

Layer cucumbers, radishes, and tomato in a clear glass bowl. Add dressing and parsley. Marinate in the refrigerator for 20 minutes. Serve. *Preparation time = 10 minutes. Chilling time = 20 minutes.*

Nutrition Facts
Serving size = 1 cup • Servings per recipe = 4 • Calories = 33 •
Calories from fat = 2

% Daily Value
Total fat < 1 gm. = 1% • Saturated fat = 0 • Cholesterol = 0 • Sodium 125 mg.
= 4% • Total carbohydrate 7 gm. = 2% • Dietary fiber 0.8 gm. = 3% • Protein
1 gm. = 2% • Calcium 20 mg. = 3%

Exchange Values: 1 vegetable

DIJONNAISE POTATO SALAD

1/3 c. Hellman's® reduced-fat mayonnaise
2 Tbsp. Hellman's® Dijonnaise creamy
  mustard blend
1 Tbsp. vinegar
1 Tbsp. chopped fresh dill or parsley
1/8 tsp. salt
1/4 tsp. pepper
4 medium potatoes, peeled, cubed, and cooked
1/2 c. finely sliced celery
1/4 c. thinly sliced green onions

Combine first six ingredients in a large salad bowl. Stir in potatoes, celery, and onions. Cover and chill for at least 30 minutes. *Preparation time (including micro-cooking of potatoes) = 20 minutes. Chilling time = 30 minutes.*

Nutrition Facts
Serving size = 3/4 cup • Servings per recipe = 8 • Calories = 108 •
Calories from fat = 30

% Daily Value
Total fat 5 gm. = 8% • Saturated fat 1 gm. = 5% • Cholesterol 4 mg. = 2% •
Sodium 145 mg. = 5% • Total carbohydrate 15 gm. = 5% • Dietary fiber 2 gm.
= 8% • Protein 2 gm. = 3% • Calcium 14 mg. = 2%

Exchange Values: 1 bread/starch, 1 fat

FANCY SPRING SALAD

2 3-oz. pkgs. sugar-free strawberry gelatin
1 c. boiling water
8 oz. Land 'O Lakes® nonfat sour cream
3-oz. can crushed pineapple, drained well
1 c. pineapple, lemon, or orange sherbet
4 oz. nonfat cottage cheese

In a 2-quart bowl, pour boiling water over gelatin. Stir until gelatin is completely dissolved. Add remaining ingredients and pour into a 6-cup mold. Chill until firm, about 4 hours. Remove from mold onto a serving plate lined with fresh greens. *Preparation time = 15 minutes. Chilling time = 4 hours.*

Nutrition Facts
Serving size = 1/2 cup • Servings per recipe = 8 • Calories = 82 • Calories from fat = 4

% Daily Value
Total fat < 1 gm. = 1% • Saturated fat = 0 • Cholesterol 3 mg. = 1% • Sodium 100 mg. = 4% • Total carbohydrate 15 gm. = 5% • Dietary fiber = 0 • Protein 5 gm. = 8% • Calcium 112 mg. = 14%

Exchange Values: 1 1/2 fruit

LENTIL SALAD

1 c. lentils, rinsed
3 c. water
1/2 tsp. garlic powder
3 Tbsp. ReaLemon® lemon juice
1 tsp. vegetable oil
1 tsp. ground coriander
1/2 tsp. pepper
1/2 tsp. salt
1 red pepper, cored, seeded, and diced
4 green onions, trimmed and finely sliced
1/4 c. chopped fresh cilantro (optional)

Cover lentils with boiling water in a large bowl and let stand for 30 minutes. Drain and place lentils and garlic powder in a saucepan with garlic. Cover with water and boil. Reduce heat to low and simmer, partially covered, for 10 minutes or until lentils are tender. Drain lentils and set aside. Meanwhile, whisk together lemon juice, oil, coriander, salt, and pepper in a large bowl. Add the lentils, red pepper, green onions, and optional cilantro and toss. Serve immediately. This salad is best when the dressing is added just before serving. *Lentil soaking time = 30 minutes. Preparation time = 20 minutes.*

Nutrition Facts
Serving size = 3/4 cup • Servings per recipe = 8 • Calories = 92 • Calories from fat = 9

% Daily Value
Total fat 1 gm. = 2% • Saturated fat = 0 • Cholesterol = 0 • Sodium 136 mg. = 5% • Total carbohydrate 15 gm. = 5% • Dietary fiber 0.3 gm. = 1% • Protein 7 gm. = 12% • Calcium 16 mg. = 2%

Exchange Values: 1 bread/starch

MAKE-YOUR-OWN
BLUE CHEESE DRESSING

1 c. Dannon® nonfat plain yogurt
1/4 c. reduced-fat mayonnaise
2 Tbsp. crumbled blue cheese
2 tsp. sugar
1/2 tsp. celery seed
2 drops hot pepper sauce

Combine all ingredients in a salad dressing container. Refrigerate.
Preparation time = 10 minutes. Chilling time = 15 minutes.

Nutrition Facts
Serving size = 1 Tbsp. • Servings per recipe = 8 • Calories = 39 •
Calories from fat = 9

% Daily Value
Total fat 1 gm. = 2% • Saturated fat < 1 gm. = 4% • Cholesterol 4 mg. = 1% •
Sodium 164 mg. = 6% • Total carbohydrate 5 gm. = 2% • Dietary fiber = 0 •
Protein 3 gm. = 4% • Calcium 76 mg. = 10%

Exchange Values: 1/2 skim milk

Marinated Tomato Medley

This is an excellent side dish with grilled meats.

> 2 large tomatoes, sliced
> 1 medium onion, sliced
> 1 small green pepper, sliced into rings
> 1/2 c. ReaLemon® lemon juice
> 1 Tbsp. vegetable oil
> 1 Tbsp. sugar
> 1/8 tsp. salt
> 1/8 tsp. garlic powder

Combine tomatoes, onion, and green pepper in a salad bowl. Combine remaining ingredients in a small bowl, whisking until well blended. Pour liquid over vegetables.
Preparation time = 10 minutes.

Nutrition Facts
Serving size = 1/2 cup • Servings per recipe = 4 • Calories = 68 • Calories from fat = 36

% Daily Value
Total fat 4 gm. = 6% • Saturated fat = 0 • Cholesterol = 0 • Sodium 73 mg. = 2% • Total carbohydrate 9 gm. = 3% • Dietary fiber 1 gm. = 4% • Protein 1 gm. = 2% • Calcium 9 mg. = 1%
Exchange Values: 1 fat, 1 vegetable

MARINATED VEGETABLE SALAD

> 1 small head cauliflower, cleaned and cut into bite-
> sized pieces
> 1 bunch broccoli, cleaned and cut into
> bite-sized pieces
> 4 carrots, cleaned, peeled, and sliced into thin coins
> 3 celery ribs, cleaned and cut into 1/4-inch slices
> 20 cherry tomatoes, halved
> 1/2 c. vinegar
> 1/2 c. Dole® pineapple juice
> 3 Tbsp. sugar
> 3 Tbsp. vegetable oil
> 1 Tbsp. minced onion
> 3/4 tsp. dill weed
> 1/4 tsp. black pepper
> 1/8 tsp. garlic powder

Combine cauliflower, broccoli, carrots, celery, and tomatoes in a large salad bowl. In a salad dressing shaker container, combine remaining ingredients. Pour dressing over vegetables and refrigerate until ready to serve. *Preparation time = 20 minutes.*

Nutrition Facts

Serving size = 1 cup • Servings per recipe = 12 • Calories = 102 • Calories from fat = 36

% Daily Value

Total fat 4 gm. = 6% • Saturated fat = 0 • Cholesterol = 0 • Sodium 58 mg. = 2% • Total carbohydrate 16 gm. = 6% • Dietary fiber 4 gm. = 16% • Protein 4 gm. = 7% • Calcium 5 mg. = 7%

Exchange Values: 2 vegetable, 1 fat

Old-Fashioned Potato Salad

The buttermilk makes it just like Grandma used to make!

> 6 c. cooked, diced potatoes (4 large potatoes)
> 1/4 c. sliced green onion
> 2 hard-cooked eggs, coarsely chopped
> 1/2 c. Hellman's® reduced-fat mayonnaise
> 1/4 tsp. celery seed
> 1 tsp. prepared mustard
> 1 Tbsp. vinegar
> 1 tsp. sugar
> 2 Tbsp. buttermilk
> 1/4 tsp. salt
> 1/2 tsp. white pepper

Combine potatoes, onion, and eggs in a salad bowl. Whisk remaining ingredients together in a small bowl. Pour dressing over potato mixture, carefully blending with a large spoon.
Preparation time = 30 minutes.

Nutrition Facts
Serving size = 1/2 cup • Servings per recipe = 8 • Calories = 177 • Calories from fat = 63

% Daily Value
Total fat 7 gm. = 11% • Saturated fat 2 gm. = 8% • Cholesterol 60 mg. = 20% • Sodium 165 mg. = 5% • Total carbohydrate 24 gm. = 8% • Dietary fiber 1.6 gm. = 7% • Protein 5 gm. = 9% • Calcium 70 gm. = 9%

Exchange Values: 1 1/2 bread/starch, 1 fat

PAT'S WONDER SALAD

Sent to me by a wonderful cook and former neighbor,
Pat Nederhizer

1 pkg. beef-flavored ramen noodles
1 large pkg. Dole® coleslaw mix
1/4 c. sunflower seeds
1 bunch green onion, thinly sliced
1/4 c. sliced almonds

Dressing:
2 Tbsp. oil
1/2 c. water
1/2 flavor packet from ramen noodles
2 Tbsp. cider vinegar
1/4 c. sugar

Break noodles into pieces and mix with coleslaw, sunflower seeds, onions, and almonds in a large salad bowl. Combine ingredients for dressing in a shaker container. Pour over vegetable mixture shortly before serving. *Preparation time = 15 minutes.*

Nutrition Facts
Serving size = 3/4 cup • Servings per recipe = 12 • Calories = 147 •
Calories from fat = 62

% Daily Value
Total fat 7 gm. = 12% • Saturated fat 1 gm. = 4% • Cholesterol 8 mg. = 3% •
Sodium 94 mg. = 3% • Total carbohydrate 18 gm. = 6% • Dietary fiber 2 gm. =
8% • Protein 5 gm. = 9% • Calcium 26 mg. = 3%

Exchange Values: 2 vegetable, 1/2 bread/starch, 1 fat

PEA-NUTTY SALAD

10-oz. pkg. frozen peas, thawed
2 slices crisply cooked bacon, crumbled
1/2 c. chopped celery
1/4 c. chopped onion
1/8 c. peanuts
1/2 c. Land 'O Lakes® nonfat sour cream
1/8 tsp. salt.

Drain peas and place on a paper towel if still wet. Mix all ingredients in a salad bowl and chill until serving time.
Preparation time = 15 minutes.

Nutrition Facts
Serving size = 1/2 cup • Servings per recipe = 8 • Calories = 73 •
Calories from fat = 27

% Daily Value
Total fat 3 gm. = 4% • Saturated fat 1 gm. = 3% • Cholesterol 2 mg. = 1% •
Sodium 118 mg. = 4% • Total carbohydrate 9 gm. = 3% • Dietary fiber 0.6
mg. = 2% • Protein 5 gm. = 8% • Calcium 59 mg. = 8%

Exchange Values: 2 vegetable, 1/2 fat

PIÑA COLADA FRUIT SALAD

1 c. sliced banana
1/2 c. pineapple tidbits
1/2 c. sliced kiwifruit
2 Tbsp. coconut
12 oz. Seagrams® piña colada cooler

Combine fruits in a salad bowl. Sprinkle with coconut. Pour cooler
over all. Use a ladle to serve fruit into bowls.
Preparation time = 10 minutes.

Nutrition Facts
Serving size = 1/2 cup • Servings per recipe = 4 • Calories = 158 •
Calories from fat = 36

% Daily Value
Total fat 4 gm. = 6% • Saturated fat 3 gm. = 15% • Cholesterol = 0 • Sodium
15 mg. = 0 • Total carbohydrate 32 gm. = 11% • Dietary fiber 2 gm. = 6% •
Protein 1 gm. = 2% • Calcium 20 mg. = 2%

Exchange Values: 2 fruit, 1 fat

RED, WHITE, AND BLUE SLAW SALAD

6 c. coarsely shredded green cabbage
2 strips bacon, cooked crisp and crumbled
1/4 c. crumbled blue cheese
1/2 c. Marzetti® Light Slaw dressing
5 cherry tomatoes, halved

Combine cabbage, bacon, and blue cheese in a salad bowl. Pour
dressing over all and toss to coat. Garnish the outside edge of the
salad with halved cherry tomatoes.
Preparation time = 15 minutes.

Nutrition Facts
Serving size = 1 cup • Servings per recipe = 8 • Calories = 133 •
Calories from fat = 54

% Daily Value
Total fat 6 gm. = 9% • Saturated fat 2 gm. = 10% • Cholesterol 11 mg. = 4% •
Sodium 249 mg. = 8% • Total carbohydrate 11 gm. = 4% • Dietary fiber 4 gm. =
16% • Protein 5 gm. = 8% • Calcium 120 mg. = 15%

Exchange Values: 1 fat, 3 vegetable

Snap-Bean Salad

1 Tbsp. vegetable oil
2 Tbsp. wine vinegar
1/4 c. chicken broth
(may prepare by mixing 1/4 tsp. chicken
bouillon with 1/4 c. hot water)
1/8 tsp. salt
1/2 tsp. onion powder
1/4 tsp. pepper
1 Tbsp. fresh parsley, finely chopped
16-oz. can Del Monte® whole green beans,
well drained

Mix first seven ingredients in a salad bowl. Add drained beans.
Allow to marinate at least 20 minutes. Serve chilled.
Preparation time = 10 minutes. Chilling time = 20 minutes.

Nutrition Facts
Serving size = 1/2 cup • Servings per recipe = 4 • Calories = 55 •
Calories from fat = 27

% Daily Value
Total fat 3 gm. = 4% • Saturated fat = 0 • Cholesterol = 0 • Sodium 432 mg.
= 14% • Total carbohydrate 5 gm. = 2% • Dietary fiber 1 gm. = 4% • Protein
1 gm. = 2% • Calcium 30 mg. = 4%

Exchange Values: 1 vegetable, 1/2 fat

SPICED CARROT SALAD

8 large carrots
1/4 tsp. cinnamon
1/2 tsp. cumin
1/2 tsp. paprika
1/4 tsp. black pepper
1/8 tsp. salt
1/4 c. ReaLemon® lemon juice
2 Tbsp. honey
1 Tbsp. vegetable oil

Clean, peel, and cut carrots into 3-inch sticks. Place in microwave-safe dish and sprinkle with 2 Tbsp. water. Cover and microwave on high power for 4 minutes. Drain. Combine spices with lemon juice, honey, and oil. Pour over carrots. Chill until serving. *Preparation time = 15 minutes.*

Nutrition Facts
Serving size = 3/4 cup • Servings per recipe = 8 • Calories = 63 •
Calories from fat = 18

% Daily Value
Total fat 2 gm. = 3% • Saturated fat = 0 • Cholesterol = 0 • Sodium 59 mg.
= 2% • Total carbohydrate 12 gm. = 4% • Dietary fiber 3 gm. = 12% •
Protein 1 gm. = 2% • Calcium 20 mg. = 3%

Exchange Values: 2 vegetable, 2 fat

Spicy Bean and Corn Salad

16-oz. can black beans, rinsed and drained
8-oz. can whole-kernel corn, drained
3/4 c. sliced green onions with tops
3/4 c. finely sliced celery
1 small red bell pepper, diced
3/4 c. Chi Chi's® salsa
1 Tbsp. oil
2 Tbsp. lemon juice
1/4 tsp. cumin

Combine beans, corn, onions, celery, and pepper in a salad bowl. Mix salsa with oil, lemon juice, and cumin in a shaker container. Pour over vegetables and serve. *Preparation time = 10 minutes.*

Nutrition Facts

Serving size = 3/4 cup • Servings per recipe = 8 • Calories = 147 • Calories from fat = 7

% Daily Value

Total fat 3 gm. = 4% • Saturated fat = 0 • Cholesterol = 0 • Sodium 818 mg. = 27% (To reduce sodium, substitute fresh tomatoes for salsa.) • Total carbohydrate 27 gm. = 9% • Dietary fiber 1 gm. = 4% • Protein 7 gm. = 12% • Calcium 109 mg. = 14%

Exchange Values: 1 bread/starch, 1 vegetable, 1 fat

THREE-BEAN SALAD

16-oz. can Del Monte® cut green beans
16-oz. can yellow wax beans
16-oz. can red kidney beans
1 small green pepper, finely chopped
1 small onion, finely chopped
1/4 c. sugar
1 tsp. salt
1/2 tsp. freshly ground pepper
1/2 c. vinegar
2 Tbsp. salad oil

Drain the liquid from the three cans of beans. Place beans in a glass bowl and mix in green pepper and onion. Combine sugar, salt, pepper, vinegar, and oil in a shaker container. Pour over beans and mix well. Refrigerate until ready to serve.
Preparation time = 10 minutes.

Nutrition Facts
Serving size = 1 cup • Servings per recipe = 12 • Calories = 136 • Calories from fat = 36

% Daily Value
Total fat 3 gm. = 4% • Saturated fat = 0 • Cholesterol = 0 • Sodium 271 mg. = 9% • Total carbohydrate 22 gm. = 7% • Dietary fiber 1 gm. = 4% • Protein 6 gm. = 11% • Calcium 43 mg. = 5%

Exchange Values: 1 1/2 bread/starch, 1 fat

WALDORF SLAW SALAD

6 c. shredded green cabbage
1 Delicious apple, cut into bite-size chunks
1/2 c. raisins
3/4 c. Marzetti's® Light Slaw dressing

Combine cabbage, apple, and raisins in a salad bowl. Pour dressing over the salad and toss gently to coat well. Garnish with a few chopped walnuts. *Preparation time = 10 minutes.*

Nutrition Facts

Serving size = 1 cup • Servings per recipe = 8 • Calories = 136 • Calories from fat = 45

% Daily Value

Total fat 5 gm. = 8% • Saturated fat 1 gm. = 5% • Cholesterol 7 mg. = 2% • Sodium 181 mg. = 6% • Total carbohydrate 22 gm. = 7% • Dietary fiber 5 gm. = 20% • Protein 3 gm. = 5% • Calcium 89 mg. = 11%

Exchange Values: 1 fat, 1 fruit, 1 vegetable

SOUPS & STEWS

AMERICAN INDIAN SLOW-COOK STEW

*From The Parson's Inn, a bed and breakfast
in Glen Haven, Wisconsin*

1/2 c. lentils, rinsed
1/2 c. navy beans, rinsed
2 c. chopped onion
2 c. sliced celery
5 carrots, scrubbed and sliced 1/2-inch thick
1/4 c. brown sugar
1 c. barley
1/2 tsp. thyme
1/4 tsp. garlic powder
2 bay leaves
1 tsp. black pepper
1/2 c. red cooking wine
1 qt. V-8® juice
2 c. water

Combine all ingredients in a slow cooker. Cook for 4 to 6 hours on
high heat or for 8 to 10 hours on low heat. Remove bay leaves before
serving. *Preparation time = 15 minutes. Slow cooker time = 4 to 6
hours on high or 8 to 10 hours on low.*

Nutrition Facts
Serving size = 1 1/2 cup • Servings per recipe = 8 • Calories = 246 •
Calories from fat = 8

% Daily Value
Total fat 1 gm. = 2% • Saturated fat = 0 • Cholesterol = 0 • Sodium 123 mg.
= 4% • Total carbohydrate 51 gm. = 17% • Dietary fiber 6 gm. = 24% (High
in fiber) • Protein 5 gm. = 9% • Calcium 34 mg. = 4%

Exchange Values: 2 starch, 2 vegetable

BEER AND CHEESE SOUP

This makes a meal with a green salad or coleslaw.

> 1/2 c. chopped onion
> 1 tsp. margarine
> 2 c. cubed raw potatoes
> 12 oz. beer
> 1 1/2 c. water
> 1 c. cubed Velveeta Light® processed cheese
> 1/2 tsp. hot pepper sauce

In a stockpot, sauté onions in margarine until tender. Add potatoes, beer, and water; bring mixture to a boil. Reduce heat to a simmer and cook for 20 minutes or until potatoes are tender. Add cheese and hot pepper sauce, stirring until cheese is melted. Serve. *Preparation time = 30 minutes.*

Nutrition Facts
Serving size = 3/4 cup • Servings per recipe = 8 • Calories = 149 • Calories from fat = 63

% Daily Value
Total fat 7 gm. = 10% • Saturated fat 4 gm. = 20% • Cholesterol 20 mg. = 7% • Sodium 439 mg. = 15% • Total carbohydrate 16 gm. = 5% • Dietary fiber 1 gm. = 4% • Protein 6 gm. = 11% • Calcium 158 mg. = 20% (High in calcium)

Exchange Values: 1 bread/starch, 1 1/2 fat

BLACK BEAN CHILI IN THE CROCKPOT

1 lb. boneless stew meat, trimmed and cut
    into 1-inch cubes
3 TB. chili powder
1 tsp. cumin
1/4 tsp. salt
1/2 tsp. oregano
1/2 tsp. pepper
2 Tbsp. Hunt's® tomato paste
14-oz. can Hunt's® whole tomatoes
1/2 tsp. garlic powder
2 large onions, finely chopped
2 15-oz. cans black beans, rinsed and drained
1 large jalapeno pepper, seeded and minced
    (optional)

Pat beef dry with paper towels and place in a slow cooker. In a cup, mix chili powder, cumin, salt, oregano, and black pepper. Sprinkle over beef, tossing to coat. Stir tomato paste into the whole tomatoes. Pour into pot. Add remaining ingredients and cook on low for 8 hours or on high for 4 to 6 hours. *Preparation time = 15 minutes. Slow cooker time = 4 to 6 hours on high heat or 8 to 10 hours on low heat.*

Nutrition Facts
Serving size = 1 1/2 cup • Servings per recipe = 8 • Calories = 157 •
Calories from fat = 8

% Daily Value
Total fat 1 gm. = 2% • Saturated fat < 1 gm. = 1% • Cholesterol 8 mg. = 3% •
Sodium 179 mg. = 6% • Total carbohydrate 27 gm. = 9% • Dietary fiber 4 gm.
= 16% • Protein 12 gm. = 20% • Calcium 48 mg. = 6%

Exchange Values: 1 bread/starch, 1 lean meat, 1 vegetable

BLACK-EYED PEA CHOWDER

4 strips bacon, diced fine
1 c. chopped celery
1 c. chopped onion
1 c. chopped green pepper
2 16-oz. cans black-eyed peas,
    rinsed and drained
10 1/2-oz. can beef consomme
2 14 1/2-oz. cans Del Monte® diced tomatoes

In a stockpot, cook diced bacon until crispy. Drain off grease. Add celery, onion, and green pepper to the pot. Cook over medium heat until vegetables are tender. Add remaining ingredients and heat through. Garnish with celery tops. *Preparation time = 20 minutes.*

Nutrition Facts
Serving size = 1 1/2 cup • Servings per recipe = 8 • Calories = 160 •
Calories from fat = 18

% Daily Value
Total fat 2 gm. = 4% • Saturated fat < 1 gm. = 3% • Cholesterol 3 mg. = 1% •
Sodium 444 mg. = 9% • Total carbohydrate 28 gm. = 9% • Dietary fiber 4 gm.
= 16% • Protein 10 gm. = 17% • Calcium 82 mg. = 10%

Exchange Values: 1 bread/starch, 1 vegetable, 1 lean meat

Border Barley and Lentil Soup

1 Tbsp. vegetable oil
2/3 c. chopped onion
2/3 c. chopped celery
1/2 tsp. garlic powder
14-oz. can beef consommé
1 c. water
2 c. Del Monte® diced tomatoes
2/3 c. lentils, rinsed
2/3 c. pearl barley
2 Tbsp. chopped green chilies
1 tsp. coriander
2 tsp. chili powder
2 tsp. cumin
Pinch of cayenne powder
Nonfat sour cream for garnish

In a stockpot, cook onion, celery, and garlic powder in oil until tender. Add consommé, water, tomatoes, lentils, barley, chilies, and seasonings. Bring mixture to a boil and then reduce heat. Cover and simmer for 30 minutes. Garnish each bowl of soup with a dollop of nonfat sour cream. *Preparation time = 10 minutes. Cooking time = 30 minutes.*

Nutrition Facts
Serving size = 1 cup • Servings per recipe = 8 • Calories = 123 • Calories from fat = 18

% Daily Value
Total fat 2 gm. = 3% • Saturated fat < 1 gm. = 1% • Cholesterol = 0 • Sodium 443 mg. = 15% • Total carbohydrate 20 gm. = 7% • Dietary fiber 0.5 gm. = 2% • Protein 8 gm. = 14% • Calcium 43 mg. = 6%

Exchange Values: 1 1/2 bread/starch

CABBAGE AND RAISIN STEW

Thanks Metcalf cooks!

7 c. finely sliced raw cabbage
2 1/2 c. sliced fresh mushrooms
1 c. chopped onions
1 c. julienned red pepper
2 c. water
1 c. Sunmaid® raisins
1/2 tsp. garlic powder
1 Tbsp. lemon juice
2 tsp. paprika
2 tsp. tarragon
1 tsp. margarine
1/4 tsp. salt
1 c. skim milk

Combine first ten ingredients in a stockpot. Cook over medium heat for 20 minutes. In a small saucepan, melt margarine, then blend in flour and salt until smooth. Gradually stir cold milk into the flour and cook over medium heat until mixture is thick and smooth. Add white sauce to stew mixture. Continue cooking for several minutes, stirring until mixture is thick.
Preparation time = 10 minutes. Cooking time = 20 minutes.

Nutrition Facts
Serving size = 1 1/2 cup • Servings per recipe = 8 • Calories = 159 • Calories from fat = 8

% Daily Value
Total fat 2 gm. = 2% • Saturated fat < 1 gm. = 1% • Cholesterol = 0 • Sodium 127 mg. = 4% • Total carbohydrate 36 gm. = 12% • Dietary fiber 7 gm. = 28% (High in Fiber) • Protein 7 gm. = 12% • Calcium 156 mg. = 20% (High in calcium)

Exchange Values: 1 1/2 fruit, 3 vegetable

CHEESY VEGETABLE SOUP

1 c. diced potatoes
1/2 c. diced carrots
1/2 c. diced celery
1/2 c. chopped onion
1 chicken bouillon cube
2 c. water
10 oz. frozen mixed vegetables
10 oz. frozen chopped broccoli
13-oz. can Campbell's® Healthy Request
cream of chicken soup
1 1/2 c. water
4 oz. Velveeta® Light processed cheese, cubed

Combine potatoes, carrots, celery, onion, and bouillon with 2 cups of water in a stockpot. Bring to a boil, and then reduce heat; simmer for 20 minutes. Add frozen mixed vegetables, frozen broccoli, chicken soup, and 1 1/2 cups of water. Bring to a boil and stir in cheese. *Preparation time = 15 minutes. Cooking time = 20 minutes.*

Nutrition Facts
Serving size = 1 1/2 cup • Servings per recipe = 8 • Calories = 131 • Calories from fat = 35

% Daily Value
Total fat 5 gm. = 7% • Saturated fat 3 gm. = 12% • Cholesterol 12 mg. = 4% • Sodium 455 mg. = 15% • Total carbohydrate 19 gm. = 6% • Dietary fiber 3 gm. = 12% • Protein 6 gm. = 11% • Calcium 122 mg. = 15%

Exchange Values: 2 vegetable, 1 fat, 1/2 bread/starch

CHILI CORN STEW

1 tsp. vegetable oil
1 green pepper, cut into strips
1/2 tsp. oregano
2 14-oz. cans Healthy Choice® chili beef soup
1 medium zucchini, halved lengthwise and sliced
1 c. dry elbow macaroni
1/2 c. frozen corn

In a stockpot, sauté green pepper in oil with oregano until pepper is tender. Stir in remaining ingredients. Bring to a boil, reduce heat, and simmer for 8 minutes or until macaroni is tender.
Preparation time = 10 minutes. Cooking time = 10 minutes.

Nutrition Facts
Serving size = 1 cup • Servings per recipe = 4 • Calories = 211 • Calories from fat = 36

% Daily Value
Total fat 4 gm. = 7% • Saturated fat 2 gm. = 8% • Cholesterol 6 mg. = 2% • Sodium 459 mg. = 16% • Total carbohydrate 37 gm. = 12% • Dietary fiber 0.5 gm. = 2% • Protein 8 gm. = 14% • Calcium 31 mg. = 4%
Exchange Values: 1 lean meat, 2 bread/starch

CHILLED CARROT SOUP

1 lb. carrots, peeled and chopped
1/2 c. water
14 1/2-oz. can chicken broth
1/4 tsp. ground ginger
1/4 tsp. white pepper
4 oz. Land 'O Lakes® nonfat sour cream

In a large stockpot, cook carrots in 1/2 c. water for 15 minutes or until tender. Drain and place carrots in a blender. Cover and blend until carrots are smooth. Turn carrots into a large mixing bowl. Stir in the chicken broth, ginger, and white pepper. Cover and chill in the refrigerator for 30 minutes. Just before serving, stir in sour cream. Garnish with celery leaves or green carrot tops.
Preparation time = 20 minutes. Chilling time = 30 minutes.

Nutrition Facts

Serving size = 1 1/2 cup • Servings per recipe = 4 • Calories = 87 •
Calories from fat = 18

% Daily Value

Total fat 2 gm. = 3% • Saturated fat = 0 • Cholesterol = 0 • Sodium 670 mg.
= 22% • Total carbohydrate 15 gm. = 5% • Dietary fiber 4 gm. = 16% •
Protein 4 gm. = 6% • Calcium 112 mg. = 14%

Exchange Values: 1 bread/starch

CREAM OF
CANTALOUPE SOUP

1 large ripe cantaloupe
2 Tbsp. sugar
2 Tbsp. orange juice
8 oz. Land 'O Lakes® nonfat sour cream

Optional garnish:

1 tsp. chopped nuts

Remove peeling and seeds from cantaloupe. Slice into 1-inch
chunks and place in a blender container. Add sugar and orange
juice. Blend until smooth. Transfer to a large bowl. Allow sour
cream to soften to room temperature. This may also be accom-
plished by microwave defrosting for 1 minute. Using a whisk,
blend the softened sour cream into the cantaloupe mixture, stirring
for 2 minutes to break up small lumps. Chill until serving time.
Garnish with chopped nuts. *Preparation time = 15 minutes.*

Nutrition Facts

Serving size = 1 1/2 cup • Servings per recipe = 4 • Calories = 117 •
Calories from fat = 6

% Daily Value

Total fat < 1 gm. = 1% • Saturated fat = 0 • Cholesterol 2 mg. = 1% • Sodium
78 mg. = 3% • Total carbohydrate 24 gm. = 8% • Dietary fiber 1 gm. = 4% •
Protein 6 gm. = 10% • Calcium 183 mg. = 23% (High in calcium)

Exchange Values: 1 fruit, 1/2 skim milk

Fish and Mixed Vegetable Stew

Use any firm white fish in this stew.

1 lb. cod or haddock
1 medium onion, chopped
1 tsp. vegetable oil
28-oz. can whole tomatoes
2 medium potatoes, peeled and diced
1/2 tsp. basil
1/4 tsp. pepper
1/2 tsp. sugar
16 oz. Bird's Eye® frozen mixed vegetables

Cut fish into bite-sized chunks and set aside.

Sauté onion in oil until tender in a 4-quart saucepan. Stir in tomatoes. Add potatoes, basil, pepper, and sugar and cook over high heat until boiling. Reduce heat to low. Cover and simmer for another 15 minutes, or until potatoes are tender. Stir occasionally. Add fish and frozen vegetables to tomato mixture and heat just until boiling. Reduce heat to low. Cover, and simmer for 5 minutes or until vegetables are tender and fish flakes when tested with a fork. *Preparation time = 15 minutes. Cooking time = 20 minutes.*

Nutrition Facts
Serving size = 1 1/2 cup • Servings per recipe = 8 • Calories = 158 • Calories from fat = 18

% Daily Value
Total fat 2 gm. = 2% • Saturated fat = 0 • Cholesterol 32 mg. = 11% • Sodium 397 mg. = 13% • Total carbohydrate 22 gm. = 7% • Dietary fiber 3 gm. = 12% • Protein 16 gm. = 28% • Calcium 63 mg. = 8%

Exchange Values: 1 lean meat, 1 bread/starch, 1 vegetable

FISH STEW WITHOUT TOMATOES

1 1/2 lb. Alaskan pollock
3/4 c. chopped carrots
1/2 c. chopped green pepper
1/2 c. chopped celery
1 c. chopped onion
1/4 tsp. garlic powder
1 Tbsp. margarine
1/4 tsp. tarragon
1/4 tsp. basil
1/4 tsp. oregano
1 c. water
1/2 c. Chablis wine
1 Tbsp. Wyler's® instant chicken bouillon

Cut fish into chunks and set aside. In a stockpot sauté all vegetables in margarine until tender-crisp, about 5 minutes. Add remaining ingredients, except fish. Heat mixture over medium flame for 5 minutes until boiling. Add fish; then reduce heat to a simmer, and continue cooking just until fish is opaque, about 8 minutes. Add fresh parsley to bowls of stew to garnish. *Preparation time = 15 minutes. Cooking time = 18 minutes.*

Nutrition Facts
Serving size = 1 1/2 cup • Servings per recipe = 4 • Calories = 282 •
Calories from fat = 45

% Daily Value
Total fat 5 gm. = 8% • Saturated fat 1 gm. = 4% • Cholesterol 164 mg. = 55% • Sodium 264 mg. = 9% • Total carbohydrate 11 gm. = 4% • Dietary fiber 3 gm. = 12% • Protein 41 gm. = 71% • Calcium 45 mg. = 6%

Exchange Values: 2 vegetable, 4 lean meat

GAZPACHO

The secret to success is the quality of the cucumber. Choose a firm, dark cucumber that is slender and well-shaped.

2 14-oz. cans Del Monte® diced tomatoes
1 1/2 c. tomato juice
1 large cucumber, peeled, seeded, and chopped
1/4 c. finely chopped green pepper
1/4 c. finely chopped green onion
1 Tbsp. vegetable oil
2 Tbsp. white-wine vinegar
1 tsp. Lawry's® seasoned salt
1/2 tsp. dried oregano

Garnish
Freshly ground pepper
Hot pepper sauce (optional)

Combine all ingredients in a large bowl. Blend well, cover, and refrigerate until chilled. Garnish bowls of soup with freshly ground pepper. For more spice, pass around the bottle of hot pepper sauce. *Preparation time = 15 minutes.*

Nutrition Facts
Serving size = 1 cup • Servings per recipe = 8 • Calories = 58 •
Calories from fat = 18

% Daily Value
Total fat 2 gm. = 3% • Saturated fat = 0 • Cholesterol = 0 • Sodium 673 mg.
= 23% • Total carbohydrate 10 gm. = 4% • Dietary fiber 0.5 gm. = 2% •
Protein 2 gm. = 3% • Calcium 45 gm. = 6%

Exchange Values: 2 vegetable

Harvest Pepper Squash Stew

Garlic lovers unite!

1/2 c. chopped onion
1 Tbsp. margarine
1/2 c. white cooking wine or any white wine
2/3 c. julienned red bell pepper
1 small yellow pepper, chopped
1 jalapeño pepper, minced
4 c. fresh zucchini, sliced 1/4-inch thick
10 oz. Green Giant® frozen whole-kernel corn
1 c. skim milk
2 oz. part-skim Monterey Jack cheese, shredded
Sprinkles of garlic powder

Sauté onion in margarine in a 2-quart saucepan, stirring frequently until tender. Stir in cooking wine, peppers, zucchini, and corn. Heat to boiling; reduce heat and cover. Simmer for 5 minutes until vegetables are tender. Stir in milk and cheese. Heat through just until cheese melts. Garnish each bowl of stew with a scant sprinkle of garlic powder as it is served. *Preparation time = 15 minutes. Cooking time = 15 minutes.*

Nutrition Facts
Serving size = 1 cup • Servings per recipe = 8 • Calories = 103 • Calories from fat = 27

% Daily Value
Total fat 3 gm. = 4% • Saturated fat 1 gm. = 5% • Cholesterol 6 mg. = 2% • Sodium 146 mg. = 5% • Total carbohydrate 15 gm. = 5% • Dietary fiber 0.5 gm. = 2% • Protein 6 gm. = 11% • Calcium 126 mg. = 16%

Exchange Values: 1 bread/starch, 1/2 fat

HONEYDEW-LIME SOUP

1/2 of a ripe medium honeydew melon
1/2 c. water
1/3 c. Minute Maid® frozen limeade concentrate
8 oz. nonfat vanilla yogurt

Remove and discard seeds from melon half. Scoop melon pulp into a blender or food processor. Add water and limeade. Cover and blend or puree until smooth. Pour mixture into a large mixing bowl. Whisk in yogurt until mixture is completely smooth. Cover and refrigerate until chilled.
Preparation time = 20 minutes. Chilling time = 30 minutes.

Nutrition Facts
Serving size = 1 cup • Servings per recipe = 4 • Calories = 130 •
Calories from fat = 0

% Daily Value
Total fat 1 gm. = 2% • Saturated fat = 0 • Cholesterol 4 mg. = 1% • Sodium
115 mg. = 4% • Total carbohydrate 30 gm. = 10% • Dietary fiber = 0 •
Protein 3 gm. = 5% • Calcium 65 mg. = 8%

Exchange Values: 1 fruit, 1 skim milk

ITALIAN VEGETABLE SOUP

1 lb. lean ground beef
1 medium onion, chopped
1 pkg. Hamburger Helper® mix for lasagna
5 c. water
10 oz. frozen whole-kernel corn
2 small zucchini, chopped
2 Tbsp. Parmesan cheese

Cook ground beef and onion in a 4-quart Dutch oven, stirring frequently, until beef is browned; drain. Stir in Hamburger Helper sauce mix, water, and tomatoes. Heat to boiling, stirring constantly. Then reduce heat, cover, and simmer for at least 5 minutes. Add corn, macaroni, and chopped zucchini to the simmering mixture. Continue to simmer 8 minutes. Then ladle into bowls and garnish with Parmesan cheese. *Preparation time = 20 minutes.*

Nutrition Facts

Serving size = 1 1/2 cup • Servings per recipe = 8 • Calories = 186 • Calories from fat = 27

% Daily Value

Total fat 3 gm. = 5% • Saturated fat 1 gm. = 4% • Cholesterol 10 mg. = 4% • Sodium 74 mg. = 3% • Total carbohydrate 32 gm. = 11% • Dietary fiber 4 gm. = 16% • Protein 11 gm. = 19% • Calcium 85 mg. = 11%

Exchange Values: 1 lean meat, 2 vegetable, 1 bread/starch

MANHATTAN CLAM CHOWDER

1 pkg. Knorr® vegetable soup and recipe mix
16-oz. can whole tomatoes with juice
2 c. water
6-oz. can minced clams with juice

Combine ingredients in a 2-quart saucepan. Bring mixture to a boil over medium-high heat. Stir to break up tomatoes. Simmer for 10 minutes and serve. *Preparation time = 15 minutes*

Nutrition Facts

Serving size = 1 1/2 cup • Servings per recipe = 4 • Calories = 112 • Calories from fat = 18

% Daily Value

Total fat 2 gm. = 3% • Saturated fat < 1 gm. = 2% • Cholesterol 29 mg. = 10% • Sodium 732 mg. = 24% (To reduce sodium, use half of soup mix.) • Total carbohydrate 11 gm. = 4% • Dietary fiber = 0 • Protein 13 gm. = 23% • Calcium 70 mg. = 9%

Exchange Values: 2 vegetable, 1 lean meat

NEW ENGLAND
CLAM CHOWDER

1 pkg. Knorr® vegetable soup and recipe mix
1 1/2 c. water
1 medium potato, peeled and cut
   into 1/2-inch cubes
6-oz. can minced clams with juice
14-oz. can evaporated skim milk
1 tsp. margarine.

Combine first four ingredients in a 2-quart saucepan. Bring the mixture to a boil over medium-high heat. Reduce heat. Simmer, patially covered, for 10 minutes. Stir in evaporated skim milk and margarine. Heat through, but do not boil.
Preparation time = 30 minutes.

Nutrition Facts
Serving size = 1 1/2 cup • Servings per recipe = 4 • Calories = 200 •
Calories from fat = 18

% Daily Value
Total fat 2 gm. = 3% • Saturated fat < 1 gm. = 3% • Cholesterol 32 mg. =
11% • Sodium 675 mg. = 23% (To reduce sodium, use half of soup mix.) •
Total carbohydrate 24 gm. = 8% • Dietary fiber 0.5 gm. = 2% • Protein 20 gm.
= 35% • Calcium 328 mg. = 41% (High in calcium)

Exchange Values: 1 1/2 bread/starch, 1 1/2 lean meat

OLD-FASHIONED CREAM OF VEGETABLE STEW

1/2 c. water
4 c. cubed turnips (3 large)
5 carrots, scrubbed and sliced thin
1 c. chopped cabbage
1 c. chopped onion
1 Tbsp. margarine
1 Tbsp. flour
1/4 tsp. salt
1 c. skim milk
1 tsp. Tone's® curry powder

Steam turnips, carrots, cabbage, and onions in a stockpot with 1/2 cup water for 10 minutes. Meanwhile, melt margarine in a small saucepan. Blend in flour, salt, and curry powder until smooth. Stir cold milk gradually into the flour mixture, continuing to stir until thick. Add white sauce to cooked vegetables in their juice. *Preparation time = 20 minutes.*

Nutrition Facts
Serving size = 1 cup • Servings per recipe = 8 • Calories = 100 •
Calories from fat = 9

% Daily Value
Total fat 1 gm. = 2% • Saturated fat = 0 • Cholesterol = 0 • Sodium 193 mg.
= 7% • Total carbohydrate 20 gm. = 7% • Dietary fiber 5.0 gm. = 20% (High in fiber) • Protein 4 gm. = 6% • Calcium 96 mg. = 12%

Exchange Values: 1 bread/starch, 1 vegetable

ONE-POT JAMBALAYA STEW

1/2 lb. low-fat ground turkey sausage, browned
1 1/2 tsp. vegetable oil
2 c. chopped onion
1 c. sliced celery
3/4 tsp. garlic powder
1 3/4 c. Minute® Rice
2 14-1/2 oz. cans diced tomatoes in juice
2 c. chicken broth
8-oz. can tomato sauce
1 tsp. dried thyme
1 tsp. dried oregano
1/2 tsp. pepper
1/2 tsp. hot pepper sauce
2 bay leaves
1 lb. medium-sized fresh or frozen shrimp,
    peeled and deveined

Brown turkey sausage in a large stockpot. Allow sausage to drain for 5 minutes in a colander. Heat oil in the stockpot. Add onion, celery, and garlic powder, sautéing for 3 minutes or until vegetables are tender. Add browned sausage, rice, tomatoes, broth, tomato sauce, and seasonings. Bring to a boil and cook for 7 minutes. Stir in shrimp. Bring to a boil. Reduce heat and simmer for 1 minute. Serve.

Preparation time = 25 minutes.

Nutrition Facts
Serving size = 1 1/2 cup • Servings per recipe = 8 • Calories = 234 • Calories from fat = 63

% Daily Value
Total fat 7 gm. = 11% • Saturated fat 2 gm. = 6% • Cholesterol 116 mg. = 39% • Sodium 902 mg. = 30% • Total carbohydrate 21 gm. = 7% • Dietary fiber 2 gm. = 8% • Protein 22 gm. = 39% • Calcium 97 mg. = 12%

Exchange Values: 2 lean meat, 2 vegetable, 1 bread/starch

PRIZE-WINNING CHILI

1 lb. ground turkey
1 tsp. pepper
1 large red onion, chopped
2 24-oz. cans Del Monte® stewed tomatoes
1 large green pepper, chopped
8 oz. fresh mushrooms, sliced
4 stalks celery, chopped
1 small can diced green chilis
16 oz. tomato sauce
2 tsp. chili powder
1 tsp. allspice
1/4 tsp. cinnamon
1/2 tsp. garlic powder
2 16-oz. cans hot chili beans
1 c. brown or wild rice

Brown turkey in a large stockpot. Add black pepper. If necessary, pour off excess fat when done. Add remaining ingredients and bring to a boil. Reduce heat to a simmer and continue cooking for 25 minutes or until rice is tender. *Preparation time = 35 minutes.*

Nutrition Facts
Serving size = 1 1/2 cup • Servings per recipe = 12 • Calories = 288 • Calories from fat = 54

% Daily Value
Total fat 6 gm. = 10% • Saturated fat 2 gm. = 10% • Cholesterol 38 mg. = 12% • Sodium 564 mg. = 19% • Total carbohydrate 42 gm. = 14% • Dietary fiber 3 gm. = 12% • Protein 10 gm. = 33% • Calcium 77 mg. = 9%

Exchange Values: 2 bread/starch, 2 vegetable, 1 1/2 lean meat

SALMON CHOWDER

3 c. water
1 small onion, diced
3 medium potatoes, unpeeled and diced
2 stalks celery, chopped
2 carrots, sliced
6 whole allspice
1 tsp. dill weed
1/2 tsp. white pepper
2 cans Carnation® evaporated skimmed milk
2 Tbsp. flour
16-oz. can salmon
1 tsp. margarine

Combine water, onions, potatoes, celery, carrots, allspice, dill weed, and white pepper in a stockpot. Cover and simmer for 15 minutes. Add 1 can of milk and salmon to vegetables. Blend flour with remaining can of milk, whisking until smooth. Slowly stir flour and milk mixture into chowder. Simmer for 10 minutes. Add margarine before serving. *Preparation time = 35 minutes.*

Nutrition Facts
Serving size = 1 1/2 cup • Servings per recipe = 8 • Calories = 183 • Calories from fat = 27

% Daily Value
Total fat 3 gm. = 6% • Saturated fat < 1 gm. = 1% • Cholesterol 23 mg. = 8% • Sodium 348 mg. = 12% • Total carbohydrate 21 gm. = 7% • Dietary fiber 1.5 gm. = 6% • Protein 17 gm. = 30% • Calcium 277 mg. = 35% (High in calcium)

Exchange Values: 1 bread/starch, 1 vegetable, 1 1/2 lean meat

SLOW-COOK SOUP MIX

Mix:

14-oz. pkg. dry green split peas
12-oz. pkg. Quaker® pearl barley
14-oz. alphabet macaroni
12-oz. pkg. lentils
1 1/2 c. brown rice
1/4 c. dry onion

Combine ingredients in a large airtight container. Stir well. Store in a cool, dry place for up to 6 months. Shake before using. Makes 12 1/2 cups of soup mix. *Preparation time = 20 minutes.*

SOUP FOR THE DAY IN THE SLOW COOKER

8 c. water
1 1/2 c. Slow-Cook Soup Mix (above)
1/2 tsp. salt
2 carrots, sliced
2 stalks celery, chopped
1 c. chopped cabbage
6-oz. can tomato paste
1 lb. cooked ground beef or cooked roast beef

Combine all ingredients in a crockpot and cook on high for 4 to 6 hours or on low for 8 to 10 hours. *Slow-cooker time = 4 to 6 hours on low heat or 8 to 10 hours on high heat.*

Nutrition Facts

Serving size = 1 1/2 cup of soup • Servings per recipe = 8 • Calories = 175 • Calories from fat = 9

% Daily Value

Total fat 1 gm. = 2% • Saturated fat = 0 • Cholesterol 8 mg. = 3% • Sodium 181 mg. = 6% • Total carbohydrate 29 gm. = 10% • Dietary fiber 2 gm. = 8% • Protein 15 gm. = 26% • Calcium 46 mg. = 6%

Exchange Values: 1 bread/starch, 2 vegetable, 1 lean meat

Southwestern Vegetable Soup

4 strips bacon, diced fine
1 c. chopped onion
1/4 tsp. garlic powder
2 c. chicken broth
2 medium red-skinned potatoes, cubed
2 medium carrots, thinly sliced
1 tsp. hot pepper sauce
16-oz. can Del Monte® diced tomatoes

In a 3-quart microwave-safe casserole, microwave bacon on high for 2 minutes or until crisp. Remove bacon, crumble, and set aside. Drain bacon fat from the casserole dish and add onion and garlic to pan. Microwave on high for 5 minutes. Add broth, potatoes, carrots, and pepper sauce. Cover loosely with plastic wrap, microwave on high for 15 minutes or until vegetables are tender. Stir in tomatoes and bacon, and microwave again on high power for 5 minutes. *Preparation time = 30 minutes.*

Nutrition Facts
Serving size = 1 cup • Servings per recipe = 8 • Calories = 82 •
Calories from fat = 27

% Daily Value
Total fat 3 gm. = 4% • Saturated fat < 1 gm. = 3% • Cholesterol 3 mg. = 1% •
Sodium 480 mg. = 16% • Total carbohydrate 13 gm. = 4% • Dietary fiber
2 gm. = 8% • Protein 3 gm. = 5% • Calcium 27 mg. = 4%

Exchange Values: 2 vegetable, 1/2 fat

SPANISH SOUP WITH OKRA

1 tsp. vegetable oil
1/2 tsp. garlic powder
1/2 tsp. dried thyme leaves, crushed
1 19-oz. can Campbell's® chunky
    chicken rice soup
1 c. frozen cut okra
1/8 tsp. dried red pepper flakes
8 oz. shrimp, cooked, peeled, and deveined

In a 2-quart saucepan over medium heat, cook garlic powder and thyme in hot oil, stirring constantly. Add soup, okra, and pepper. Heat to boiling and then reduce heat to low. Cook for 5 minutes until okra is tender. Stir in shrimp and heat through, stirring constantly. *Preparation time = 15 minutes.*

Nutrition Facts
Serving size = 1 1/2 cup • Servings per recipe = 4 • Calories = 167 • Calories from fat = 36

% Daily Value
Total fat 4 gm. = 6% • Saturated fat < 1 gm. = 4% • Cholesterol 94 mg. = 31% • Sodium 614 mg. = 20% • Total carbohydrate 12 gm. = 4% • Dietary fiber = 0 • Protein 19 gm. = 34% • Calcium 105 mg. = 13%

Exchange Values: 2 lean meat, 1/2 bread/starch, 1 vegetable

SQUASH AND BEAN SOUP

I know this combination sounds strange,
but our gourmet club gave this soup a "thumbs up"!

1 lb. beef stew meat, cut into 3/4-inch cubes
2 c. water
1 tsp. salt
1/4 tsp. ground ginger
1/4 tsp. dried red pepper flakes
10 oz. Bird's Eye® frozen butternut squash
2 fresh tomatoes, chopped
10 oz. Bird's Eye® frozen lima beans

Heat beef, water, salt, ginger, and red pepper to boiling in a stock-pot. Reduce heat and cover. Simmer until beef is tender, a minimum of 10 minutes. Add squash, tomatoes, and beans. Heat to boiling. Reduce heat and simmer uncovered for 10 minutes. *Preparation time = 25 minutes.*

Nutrition Facts

Serving size = 1 cup • Servings per recipe = 8 • Calories = 133 • Calories from fat = 7

% Daily Value

Total fat 1 gm. = 2% • Saturated fat = 0 • Cholesterol 8 mg. = 3% • Sodium 283 mg. = 10% • Total carbohydrate 23 gm. = 8% • Dietary fiber 6 gm. = 24% (High in fiber) • Protein 10 gm. = 17% • Calcium 41 mg. = 5%

Exchange Values: 1 bread/starch, 1 lean meat

STRAWBERRY SOUP

2 c. fresh ripe strawberries, cold
1 c. Kemp's® low-fat buttermilk
1 Tbsp. plus 1 tsp. sugar

Blend all ingredients in a food processor. Serve immediately or chill in the refrigerator. Garnish with mint leaves. May substitute raspberries, cantaloupe, honeydew melon, or nectarine for strawberries. *Preparation time = 10 minutes.*

Nutrition Facts
Serving size = 1 cup • Servings per recipe = 4 • Calories = 62 • Calories from fat = 3

% Daily Value
Total fat < 1 gm. = 1% • Saturated fat < 1 gm. = 2% • Cholesterol 2 mg. = 1% • Sodium 62 mg. = 2% • Total carbohydrate 12 gm. = 4% • Dietary fiber 2 gm. = 8% • Protein 2 gm. = 4% • Calcium 82 mg. = 10%

Exchange Values: 1 fruit

SWISS BROCCOLI SOUP

16 oz. frozen chopped broccoli
1 Tbsp. water
2 Tbsp. minced onion
1 Tbsp. margarine
12 oz. Heinz® HomeStyle chicken gravy
1 1/2 c. skim milk
1 c. reduced-fat Swiss cheese, shredded

Steam broccoli with 1 Tbsp. water in a covered microwave-safe dish, cooking on high power for 4 minutes. Drain. Meanwhile, in a 2-quart saucepan, sauté onion in margarine until tender. Stir in gravy, milk, and broccoli. Heat slowly, stirring occasionally. Add cheese, and heat until cheese is melted. *Preparation time = 10 minutes.*

Nutrition Facts
Serving size = 1 cup • Servings per recipe = 8 • Calories = 124 •
Calories from fat = 48

% Daily Value
Total fat 5 gm. = 9% • Saturated fat 2 gm. = 9% • Cholesterol 17 mg. = 6% •
Sodium 711 mg. = 23% • Total carbohydrate 10 gm. = 3% • Dietary fiber = 0 •
Protein 10 gm. = 17% • Calcium 295 mg. = 37% (High in calcium)

Exchange Values: 1 fat, 1 skim milk

THREE-INGREDIENT VEGETABLE SOUP

16 oz. Bird's Eye® frozen mixed vegetables
46-oz. can tomato juice
3 oz. ramen oriental noodles with beef flavoring.

Mix vegetables and tomato juice in a 5-quart pan. Heat to boiling. Add noodles and flavor packet. Simmer for 15 minutes, stirring occasionally. *Preparation time = 20 minutes.*

Nutrition Facts

Serving size = 1 cup • Servings per recipe = 8 • Calories = 122 •
Calories from fat = 9

% Daily Value

Total fat 1 gm. = 1% • Saturated fat = 0 • Cholesterol = 0 • Sodium 910 mg.
= 30% (To reduce sodium, choose reduced sodium tomato juice.) • Total carbohydrate 25 gm. = 9% • Dietary fiber 3.6 gm. = 14% • Protein 5 gm. = 9% •
Calcium 32 mg. = 10%

Exchange Values: 1 bread/starch, 2 vegetable

THREE MELON SUMMER SOUP

1 c. Minute Maid® orange juice
1 1/2 c. each cubed cantaloupe and honeydew
1/3 c. fresh lime juice
1/4 c. honey
2 Tbsp. sugar
1 c. watermelon, diced very fine
2 c. chilled sparkling wine or sparkling
   white grape juice

Purée orange juice, cantaloupe, honeydew, lime juice, honey, and
sugar in a blender or food processor. Pour into a bowl. Stir in
watermelon and wine. Chill for at least 1 hour before serving.
Preparation time = 10 minutes. Chilling time = 1 hour.

Nutrition Facts

Serving size = 1 cup • Servings per recipe = 8 • Calories = 129 •
Calories from fat = 7

% Daily Value

Total fat < 1 gm. = 1% • Saturated fat = 0 • Cholesterol = 0 • Sodium 12 mg. =
1% • Total carbohydrate 24 gm. = 8% • Dietary fiber 0.4 gm. = 2% • Protein
1 gm. = 2% • Calcium 18 mg. = 2%

Exchange Values: 1 1/2 fruit

WILD RICE SOUP

1 c. wild rice, uncooked
1 onion, chopped fine
1 carrot, grated
1 Tbsp. margarine
1 10-oz. can Campbell's® Healthy Request
    cream of chicken soup
1 10-oz. can Campbell's® Healthy Request
    cream of mushroom soup
1 10-oz. can chicken broth
3 c. water
1 c. white cooking wine

Steam the wild rice until tender, following package directions. Meanwhile in a stockpot, cook onion and carrot in 1 Tbsp. margarine until tender. Add remaining ingredients including cooked rice. Heat through. *Preparation time = 25 minutes.*

Nutrition Facts
Serving size = 1 cup • Servings per recipe = 8 • Calories = 96 •
Calories from fat = 36

% Daily Value
Total fat 4 gm. = 6% • Saturated fat 1 gm. = 4% • Cholesterol 2 mg. = 1% •
Sodium 337 mg. = 11% • Total carbohydrate 10 gm. = 4% • Dietary fiber
0.5 gm. = 2% • Protein 2 gm. = 4% • Calcium 22 mg. = 3%

Exchange Values: 1 bread/starch, 1/2 fat

Main-Dish Salads

Beefy Broccoli Mandarin Salad

1 lb. cold roast beef, cut in thin strips
2 Tbsp. honey
1/8 tsp. salt
1/4 tsp. ginger
1/4 tsp. nutmeg
1/8 tsp. anise seed, crushed (optional)
1/2 c. orange juice
1 Tbsp. vinegar
1 Tbsp. vegetable oil
3 c. broccoli florets
1 apple, cored and sliced
1 medium onion, sliced thin
8-oz. can Geisha Girl® mandarin orange sections, drained
2 Tbsp. toasted slivered almonds
Fresh greens

Combine honey, salt, ginger, nutmeg, and anise in small saucepan; add orange juice, vinegar, and oil. Simmer 2 to 3 minutes, stirring to blend; cool. Place beef strips in a bowl or plastic bag. Add half of the marinade, turning beef strips to coat. Cover bowl or tie bag securely. Marinate in refrigerator at least 30 minutes. Place broccoli, apple, onion, mandarin oranges, and almonds in a salad bowl. Drain most of the marinade from the beef and then toss with remaining half of marinade and all other ingredients. Serve on fresh greens with hot breadsticks. *Preparation time = 10 minutes. Marinating time = 30 minutes.*

Nutrition Facts
Serving size = 1 cup • Servings per recipe = 8 • Calories = 201 • Calories from fat = 72

% Daily Value
Total fat 8 gm. = 12% • Saturated fat 4 gm. = 19% • Cholesterol 49 mg. = 16% • Sodium 93 mg. = 3% • Total carbohydrate 18 gm. = 6% • Dietary fiber 4 gm. = 15% • Protein 17 gm. = 29% • Calcium 73 mg. = 9%

Exchange Values: 2 lean meat, 2 vegetable, 1/2 fruit

BLACK BEAN CHILI SALAD

16-oz. can black beans
2 c. chopped onion, divided
1 tsp. garlic powder, divided
20-oz. can Del Monte® whole tomatoes,
 chopped, drained
1 lb. lean ground beef
1 green pepper, chopped
1/4 c. raisins
1/8 tsp. salt
1/2 tsp. black pepper
2 Tbsp. chili powder
1 Tbsp. cumin
1/8 tsp. crushed red pepper (optional)
8 c. fresh greens

Accompaniments:

Doritos® Light tortilla chips
1/2 c. Kraft® Healthy Favorites cheddar cheese,
 shredded
1 c. thinly sliced lettuce

Drain the beans well. In a microwave-safe bowl, combine beans, 1 1/2 cup onions, 1/2 teaspoon garlic powder, and tomatoes. Cover and cook at 70% power for 6 minutes or until onions are tender. Meanwhile, brown the ground beef in a skillet with remaining onion and garlic powder, raisins, green pepper, salt, pepper, chili powder, cumin, and red pepper. Drain the browned beef mixture very well. Fold meat mixture into beans and tomatoes. Serve hot or cold on individual plates lined with greens. Garnish with accompaniments. *Preparation time = 10 minutes.*

Nutrition Facts
Serving size = 1 cup • Servings per recipe = 8 • Calories = 225 •
Calories from fat = 27

% Daily Value
Total fat 3 gm. = 5% • Saturated fat 1 gm. = 4% • Cholesterol 30 mg. = 10% •
Sodium 295 mg. = 10% • Total carbohydrate 30 gm. = 10% • Dietary fiber
2.3 gm. = 10% • Protein 23 gm. = 40% • Calcium 96 mg. = 12%

Exchange Values: 1 vegetable, 1 bread/starch, 2 lean meat

CHICKEN AND PASTA SALAD

1 envelope Good Seasons® Italian salad
  dressing mix
1/4 c. wine vinegar
2 Tbsp. water
1 Tbsp. vegetable oil
2 c. shell pasta, uncooked
16 oz. Bird's Eye® Farm-Fresh broccoli,
  green beans, pearl onions, and red peppers
1 c. cooked chicken, diced
1 Tbsp. grated Parmesan cheese

Prepare salad dressing mix with wine vinegar, water, and oil in a shaker container and set aside. Cook pasta as directed on the package and drain. Rinse with cold water and drain again. Run cold tap water over vegetables in a strainer to thaw completely. Drain well. Combine pasta, vegetables, chicken, and cheese in a large bowl. Toss with salad dressing. Chill or serve immediately.
Preparation time = 20 minutes.

Nutrition Facts
Serving size = 1 cup • Servings per recipe = 8 • Calories = 190 •
Calories from fat = 36

% Daily Value
Total fat 4 gm. = 6% • Saturated fat 1 gm. = 4% • Cholesterol 26 mg. = 9% •
Sodium 265 mg. = 9% • Total carbohydrate 25 gm. = 8% • Dietary fiber 2 gm.=
8% • Protein 16 gm. = 27% • Calcium 60 mg. = 8%

Exchange Values: 1 bread/starch, 2 vegetable, 1 lean meat

CHINESE CHICKEN SALAD

Dressing:
3 1/2 Tbsp. LaChoy® soy sauce
2 Tbsp. vinegar
1 Tbsp. vegetable oil
1 Tbsp. sugar
1/2 tsp. garlic powder
1/2 tsp. pepper

Salad:
2 c. torn lettuce
1 1/2 c. chopped cooked chicken
8-oz. can sliced water chestnuts, drained
1/2 c. julienne carrots
1/4 c. diagonally sliced green onions
1/4 c. chopped red cabbage
5 oz. chow mein noodles

In a small bowl, whisk together dressing ingredients; set aside. In a large bowl, combine remaining salad ingredients, except chow mein noodles. Just before serving, toss salad with dressing and top with chow mein noodles. *Preparation time = 15 minutes.*

Nutrition Facts
Serving size = 1 cup • Servings per recipe = 4 • Calories = 294 •
Calories from fat = 81

% Daily Value
Total fat 9 gm. = 14% • Saturated fat 1 gm. = 7% • Cholesterol 72 mg. = 24% • Sodium 1020 mg. = 34% (To reduce sodium, choose reduced sodium soy sauce.) • Total carbohydrate 22 gm. = 7% • Dietary fiber 4 gm. = 16% • Protein 31 gm. = 53% • Calcium 58 mg. = 7%

Exchange Values: 3 lean meat, 1 bread/starch, 2 vegetable

DELI SALAD

8-oz. package Creamette® rainbow rotini
9 oz. frozen artichoke hearts, cooked and drained
4 oz. lean ham, shredded
1 c. sliced fresh cauliflowerets
1 c. small fresh broccoli florets
1/2 c. Kraft® Healthy Favorites Monterey Jack
    cheese, shredded
1/2 c. sliced green onions
1 Tbsp. vegetable oil
1 Tbsp. water
1 tsp. sugar
1/4 c. red wine vinegar
1/2 tsp. basil
1/2 tsp. oregano

Prepare rotini according to package directions; drain. Meanwhile, measure remaining ingredients into a large salad bowl, add rotini and toss to mix. Cover and chill or serve immediately.
Preparation time = 20 minutes.

Nutrition Facts
Serving size = 1 cup • Servings per recipe = 8 • Calories = 154 •
Calories from fat = 72

% Daily Value
Total fat 7 gm. = 10% • Saturated fat 2 gm. = 11% • Cholesterol 28 mg. = 9% • Sodium 331 mg. = 11% • Total carbohydrate 15 gm. = 5% • Dietary fiber 2 gm. = 8% • Protein 11 gm. = 19% • Calcium 157 mg. = 20% (High in calcium)

Exchange Values: 2 vegetable, 1 lean meat, 1 fat

Grilled Chicken Salad

1 lb. chicken breasts, boneless, skinless
2 large tomatoes, coarsely chopped
1 medium zucchini, halved lengthwise and
    thinly sliced crosswise
1 c. frozen whole-kernel corn, thawed
1/3 c. green onion with tops
1/2 c. Chi Chi's® salsa
1 Tbsp. lemon juice
1/4 tsp. garlic powder
1/2 tsp. cumin
Lettuce leaves

Grill or broil the chicken until cooked through; slice crosswise. Combine chicken and vegetables in a large bowl. Combine remaining ingredients in a small bowl and mix well. Pour dressing over the salad. Mix gently. Chill, then stir gently again and serve on lettuce-lined plates. *Preparation time = 20 minutes. Chilling time = 30 minutes.*

Nutrition Facts
Serving size = 1 cup • Servings per recipe = 4 • Calories = 263 • Calories from fat = 45

% Daily Value
Total fat 5 gm. = 7% • Saturated fat 1 gm. = 6% • Cholesterol 96 mg. = 32% • Sodium 418 mg. = 14% • Total carbohydrate 18 gm. = 6% • Dietary fiber 1 gm. = 4% • Protein 38 gm. = 66% • Calcium 33 mg. = 4%

Exchange Values: 2 vegetable, 4 lean meat

HIDDEN VALLEY®
CLUB SALAD

When assembled and served in a clear glass bowl,
this salad can serve as the centerpiece!

3 c. shredded lettuce
1 c. Hidden Valley® Light low-fat dressing, divided
2 strips bacon, cooked and crumbled
10 cherry tomatoes, halved
4 oz. lean ham, cubed
4 oz. reduced-fat Monterey Jack cheese, cubed
4 oz. cooked turkey, cubed

In a 3-quart salad bowl, carefully layer lettuce, 1/2 c. dressing, bacon, tomatoes, ham, cheese, and turkey. Pour remaining dressing over the top. May be assembled ahead of time and refrigerated overnight. Serve with crunchy breadsticks. *Preparation time = 20 minutes.*

Nutrition Facts
Serving size = 2 cup • Servings per recipe = 4 • Calories = 267 •
Calories from fat = 126

% Daily Value
Total fat 14 gm. = 22% • Saturated fat 4 gm. = 20% • Cholesterol 71 mg. = 24% • Sodium 1001 mg. = 33% (To reduce sodium, omit bacon and substitute lean roast beef for ham.) • Total carbohydrate 7 gm. = 2% • Dietary fiber 3 gm. = 12% • Protein 29 gm. = 49% • Calcium 324 mg. = 45% (High in calcium)

Exchange Values: 3 lean meat, 2 vegetable, 1 fat

LAYERED SEAFOOD SALAD

1 medium head lettuce, chopped
8 imitation crab sticks, sliced diagonally
1/4 c. diced onion
1 c. diced celery
1 c. Kraft® Healthy Favorites reduced-fat
   mozzarella cheese
10 oz. frozen peas, thawed

Dressing:

1/2 c. Hellmann's® reduced-fat
   mayonnaise
1 Tbsp. Dijon mustard

Garnish: 1 large tomato

Layer lettuce, crab, onion, celery, cheese, and peas in a salad bowl.
Combine mayonnaise and mustard in a small bowl. Pour over salad.
Garnish with tomato wedges. *Preparation time = 20 minutes.*

Nutrition Facts
Serving size = 2 cup • Servings per recipe = 8 • Calories = 171 •
Calories from fat = 9

% Daily Value
Total fat 4 gm. = 6 % • Saturated fat < 1 gm. = 2% • Cholesterol 40 mg. =
14% • Sodium 600 mg. = 20% • Total carbohydrate 12 gm. = 4% • Dietary
fiber 0.5 gm. = 2% • Protein 23 gm. = 40% • Calcium 249 mg. = 31%
(High in calcium)

Exchange Values: 2 vegetable, 2 lean meat

LOBSTER SALAD ON FRENCH BREAD

8 oz. Louis Kemp® Lobster Delights
  (salad style), thawed
4 fresh mushrooms, sliced
1 Tbsp. olive oil
1/2 tsp. dried Italian seasoning

Serve with:
Crusty French bread
4 wedges fresh lemon
Grated Parmesan cheese
4 lettuce leaves

Mix lobster, mushrooms, olive oil, and Italian seasoning. Serve on crusty French bread. Top with a squeeze of fresh lemon, grated Parmesan, and lettuce. *Preparation time = 15 minutes.*

Nutrition Facts
Serving size = 3/4 cup (salad only) • Servings per recipe = 4 • Calories =92 • Calories from fat = 36 •

% Daily Value
Total fat 4 gm. = 6% • Saturated fat < 1 gm. = 2% • Cholesterol 54 mg. = 18% • Sodium 75 mg. = 3% • Total carbohydrate 3 gm. = 1% • Dietary fiber = 0 • Protein 11 gm. = 19% • Calcium 5 mg. = 1%

Exchange Values: 1 lean meat, 2 vegetable

NECTARINE PASTA SALAD

1 Tbsp. vegetable oil
1/2 c. white wine vinegar
3 Tbsp. fresh chives or 1 Tbsp. dried chives
1/8 tsp. salt
1 1/2 tsp. dry mustard
1/2 tsp. pepper
3 c. cooked pork or beef, cut in julienne strips
3 c. Creamette® cooked pasta (seashell or rotelle)
   (start out with 1 1/2 c. dry pasta and cook for 7
   minutes in boiling water)
3 fresh nectarines, sliced
1 small cucumber, sliced
Lettuce

In a large bowl, whisk together oil, vinegar, chives, salt, mustard, and pepper. Add pork, pasta, nectarines, and cucumber. Toss gently. Cover and chill 30 minutes to blend flavors, stirring occasionally. Arrange lettuce on serving plates. Spoon meat mixture in equal portions onto lettuce. Serve with corn muffins.
Preparation time = 20 minutes. Chilling time = 30 minutes.

Nutrition Facts
Serving size = 1 1/2 cup • Servings per recipe = 8 • Calories = 300 • Calories from fat = 63

% Daily Value
Total fat 7 gm. = 11% • Saturated fat 2 gm. = 9% • Cholesterol 88 mg. = 29% • Sodium 92 mg. = 3% • Total carbohydrate 28 gm. = 10% • Dietary fiber 1 gm. = 4% • Protein 30 gm. = 52% • Calcium 18 mg. = 2%

Exchange Values: 1/2 bread/starch, 1 fruit, 1 vegetable,

3 lean meat

PEPPER CHICKEN TORTELLINI SALAD

2 whole medium chicken breasts,
    skinned, boned, and cut into bite-size strips
4 oz. cheese-filled egg tortellini
4 c. fresh spinach
1 sweet red pepper, cut into bite-size strips
1 can jalapeño peppers, seeded and chopped

Marinade:
1/2 tsp. finely shredded lime peel
3 Tbsp. ReaLime® lime juice
1 Tbsp. cooking oil
1 tsp. chili powder
1/8 tsp. salt

Marinate chicken in marinade for 30 minutes at room temperature. Meanwhile, cook tortellini according to package directions. Cook until tender but still slightly firm. Drain and keep warm in a salad bowl. Drain chicken, reserving marinade. In a skillet, heat oil over high heat. Stir-fry chicken 3 to 4 minutes or until done. Add to warm tortellini. Add reserved marinade to skillet and cook over high heat for 1 minute. Remove from heat. Add spinach and peppers to skillet. Toss 1 minute or until spinach wilts slightly. Add spinach mixture to tortellini and chicken. Toss and serve immediately. *Preparation time = 25 minutes. Marinating time = 30 minutes.*

Nutrition Facts
Serving size = 1 cup • Servings per recipe = 8 • Calories = 235 •
Calories from fat = 81

% Daily Value
Total fat 9 gm. = 14% • Saturated fat 3 gm. = 13% • Cholesterol 49 mg. = 17% • Sodium 389 mg. = 13% • Total carbohydrate 18 gm. = 6% • Dietary fiber 4 gm. = 16% • Protein 23 gm. = 39% • Calcium 226 mg. = 29% (High in calcium)

Exchange Values: 1 bread/starch, 3 lean meat

PIZZA RICE SALAD

1 1/2 c. Minute® rice
4 oz. reduced-fat mozzarella cheese, shredded
4 oz. lean ham or roast beef, sliced paper thin
1 large tomato, diced
2 c. sliced raw vegetables
   (create a combination of green pepper, mushroom,
   celery, and green onions)
1/2 c. Kraft Free® Italian dressing

Prepare rice as directed on the package and cool. Lightly toss rice with remaining ingredients, except dressing, in a large salad bowl. Add the dressing just before serving.
Preparation time = 20 minutes.

Nutrition Facts
Serving size = 2 cup • Servings per recipe = 4 • Calories = 273 • Calories from fat = 126

% Daily Value
Total fat 14 gm. = 22% • Saturated fat 4 gm. = 20% • Cholesterol 26 mg. = 9% • Sodium 685 mg. = 23% • Total carbohydrate 21 gm. = 7% • Dietary fiber 2 gm. = 8% • Protein 16 gm. = 27% • Calcium 257 mg. = 32% (High in calcium)

Exchange Values: 2 vegetable, 1 lean meat, 1 bread/starch, 2 fat

RICE, ALMOND, AND CHICKEN SALAD

1 c. Uncle Ben's® brown rice
1/2 tsp. salt
1/2 c. chopped green onions
1/2 c. chopped red pepper
1/2 c. finely sliced celery
2 Tbsp. slivered almonds
2 c. cooked chicken, cubed
1/2 c. plain nonfat yogurt
1/4 c. reduced-fat mayonnaise
1/4 tsp. garlic powder
1/4 tsp. black pepper
1 Tbsp. lemon juice

Cook rice with salt according to package directions; drain and cool. Add onions, pepper, celery, almonds, and chicken to the rice in a large salad bowl. Mix yogurt, mayonnaise, garlic powder, pepper and lemon juice in a glass cup. Fold dressing into salad and serve. *Preparation time = 30 minutes.*

Nutrition Facts
Serving size = 1 cup • Servings per recipe = 8 • Calories = 167 •
Calories from fat = 45

% Daily Value
Total fat 5 gm. = 7% • Saturated fat 1 gm. = 4% • Cholesterol 49 mg. = 16% • Sodium 308 mg.= 10% • Total carbohydrate 11 gm. = 4% • Dietary fiber 1 gm. = 4% • Protein 20 gm. = 35% • Calcium 59 mg. = 8%

Exchange Values: 1/2 bread/starch, 1 vegetable, 2 lean meat

Roast Beef Dinner Salad

1 1/2 c. Minute® rice
15-oz. can three-bean salad
1 Tbsp. vegetable oil
1/4 tsp. salt
1/8 tsp. pepper
2 drops hot pepper sauce
2 green onions, sliced
2 oz. Kraft® Healthy Favorites reduced-fat
   cheddar cheese, shredded
2 tsp. vinegar
Lettuce leaves
2 tomatoes, cut in wedges
8 oz. cooked roast beef, sliced into strips

Prepare rice following package directions. Drain bean salad, reserving 1/2 cup of the marinade. For dressing, combine reserved marinade, oil, salt, black pepper, and pepper sauce in a glass cup. Combine drained bean-salad, rice, onion, and cheese in a bowl. Add dressing and vinegar to the bean-salad and rice mixture and chill. To serve, place lettuce on plates. Top with bean-salad and rice mixture, followed by wedges of tomato and slices of beef. *Preparation time = 25 minutes.*

Nutrition Facts
Serving size = 1/2 cup • Servings per recipe = 8 • Calories = 182 • Calories from fat = 54

% Daily Value
Total fat 6 gm. = 9% • Saturated fat 2 gm. = 8% • Cholesterol 27 mg. = 9% • Sodium 366 mg. = 12% • Total carbohydrate 18 gm. = 6% • Dietary fiber 0.7 gm. = 3% • Protein 15 gm. = 25% • Calcium 69 mg. = 9%

Exchange Values: 1 1/2 lean meat, 1 bread/starch, 1 vegetable

SALMON PASTA SALAD

1 1/2 c. canned salmon
1 1/2 c. dry shell macaroni
1 c. frozen stir-fry blend vegetables
1/4 c. Hellmann's® reduced-fat mayonnaise
1/4 c. plain nonfat yogurt
1 tsp. lemon juice
1/8 tsp. black pepper
1/8 tsp. dill weed

Prepare macaroni according to package directions. Cook, drain, and combine with all ingredients. Chill or serve immediately. *Preparation time = 20 minutes.*

Nutrition Facts
Serving size = 1 1/2 cup • Servings per recipe = 4 • Calories = 349 • Calories from fat = 23

% Daily Value
Total fat 6 gm. = 10% • Saturated fat 1 gm. = 6% • Cholesterol 33 mg. = 11% • Sodium 611 mg. = 20% • Total carbohydrate 45 gm. = 15% • Dietary fiber = 0 • Protein 30 gm. = 51% • Calcium 240 mg. = 30% (High in calcium)

Exchange Values: 3 lean meat, 2 bread/starch, 1 vegetable

Shrimp and Rice Salad with Soy-Sauce Dressing

1 lb. shrimp, cooked, and drained
1 c. rice, uncooked
2/3 c. celery, finely chopped
1/4 c. green onion, finely chopped
1/4 c. green pepper, finely chopped
8-oz. can sliced water chestnuts, cut into halves
10 oz. frozen sugar snap peas
1/2 c. reduced-fat mayonnaise
4 tsp. La Choy® soy sauce
1/2 tsp. curry powder (optional)

Cook shrimp if necessary, drain, and dice. Cook 1 cup dry rice according to package directions to yield approximately 3 cups of cooked rice. Measure onion, pepper, water chestnuts, and peas into a large salad bowl. Combine mayonnaise, soy sauce, and curry powder in a small bowl. Add cooked rice and shrimp to vegetables. Pour dressing over all. Serve hot or cold. *Preparation time = 25 minutes.*

Nutrition Facts
Serving size = 1 cup • Servings per recipe = 8 • Calories = 195 •
Calories from fat = 9

% Daily Value
Total fat 1 gm. = 2% • Saturated fat 2 gm. = 10% • Cholesterol 92 mg. = 31% • Sodium 340 mg. = 12% • Total carbohydrate 28 gm. = 9% • Dietary fiber 3 gm. = 12% • Protein 15 gm. = 26% • Calcium 59 mg. = 8%

Exchange Values: 1 bread/starch, 2 vegetable, 1 lean meat

SMOKED TURKEY AND SLAW SALAD

1 package Dole® Fresh coleslaw mix
  (from the produce section)
10 radishes, cleaned and sliced thin
1 lb. smoked turkey, sliced into strips
2 oz. slivered almonds
1/2 c. reduced-fat bottled salad dressing
  (Excellent with blue cheese, ranch, or
  1000-Island varieties)

Layer coleslaw mix, radishes, turkey, and almonds on eight salad plates. Top with dressing of choice. *Preparation time = 15 minutes.*

Nutrition Facts

Serving size = 2 cup (salad only) • Servings per recipe = 4 • Calories = 150 • Calories from fat = 45

% Daily Value

Total fat 5 gm. = 9% • Saturated fat < 1 gm. = 4% • Cholesterol 40 mg. = 13% • Sodium 50 mg. = 2% • Total carbohydrate 5 gm. = 2% • Dietary fiber 1.6 gm. = 6% • Protein 20 gm. = 34% • Calcium 65 mg. = 8%

Exchange Values: 1 vegetable, 2 meat

SPRINGTIME CHICKEN AND ASPARAGUS SALAD

1 cup dry corkscrew macaroni
4 stalks of fresh asparagus
1 Tbsp. water
2 5-oz. cans of Swanson® chunk chicken
   white and dark, drained
1/2 c. wine vinegar
2 Tbsp. vegetable oil
1/2 c. sliced green onions
1 tsp. dried dill weed
Lettuce
Cherry tomatoes for garnish

Cook macaroni according to package directions. Do not overcook. Drain well and cool. Dice asparagus into a microwave-safe dish. Sprinkle with 1 Tbsp. water, cover, and microwave on high power for 3 minutes. Drain. In a small bowl, combine cooled rice and asparagus with all ingredients except lettuce and cherry tomatoes. Toss lightly. Chill, then serve salad on lettuce. Garnish with cherry tomatoes. *Preparation time = 20 minutes.*

Nutrition Facts
Serving size = 1 1/2 cup • Servings per recipe = 4 • Calories = 222 • Calories from fat = 81

% Daily Value
Total fat 9 gm. = 15% • Saturated fat 2 gm. = 9% • Cholesterol 54 mg. = 18% • Sodium 50 mg. = 2% • Total carbohydrate 10 gm. = 3% • Dietary fiber 0.6 gm. = 2% • Protein 21 gm. = 38% • Calcium 15 mg. = 2%

Exchange Values: 2 lean meat, 1/2 bread/starch, 1 fat,

1 vegetable

TURKEY-APPLE SALAD

2 5-oz. cans Swanson® Premium turkey, drained
1 1/2 c. chopped apple
1 c. diced celery
1/4 c. raisins
1/3 c. reduced-fat Italian dressing
2 Tbsp. brown sugar

In medium bowl, gently stir together turkey, apple, celery, and raisins. In a cup, stir together dressing and brown sugar. Pour over turkey and toss gently to coat. Serve on lettuce leaves.
Preparation time = 15 minutes.

Nutrition Facts
Serving size = 1 1/2 cup • Servings per recipe = 4 • Calories = 229 • Calories from fat = 27

% Daily Value
Total fat 3 gm. = 4% • Saturated fat < 1 gm. = 2% • Cholesterol 61 mg. = 20% • Sodium 238 mg. = 8% • Total carbohydrate 31 gm. = 10% • Dietary fiber 3 gm. = 12% • Protein 22 gm. = 38% • Calcium 46 mg. = 6%

Exchange Values: 2 fruit, 1 1/2 lean meat

Turkey with Green Bean and Tomato Salad

2 Tbsp. vegetable oil
1/4 c. wine vinegar
1 Tbsp. prepared Dijon mustard
1 tsp. dried basil leaves, crushed
2 c. cooked turkey, diced
10 oz. Bird's Eye® frozen green beans,
   thawed and drained
1 fresh tomato, peeled, seeded, and chopped fine
1 Tbsp. dry-roasted sunflower seeds

To prepare dressing, mix oil, vinegar, mustard, and basil in a small bowl and set aside. In another bowl, combine turkey with half of the dressing. Toss gently. Toss beans with remaining dressing. To serve, layer turkey, green beans, and chopped tomato on four small plates. Garnish with sunflower seeds. *Preparation time = 15 minutes.*

Nutrition Facts
Serving size = 1 cup • Servings per recipe = 4 • Calories = 258 •
Calories from fat = 90

% Daily Value
Total fat 10 gm. = 16% • Saturated fat 1 gm. = 4% • Cholesterol 95 mg. = 32% • Sodium 116 mg. = 4% • Total carbohydrate 5 gm. = 2% • Dietary fiber 0.4 gm. = 2% • Protein 36 gm. = 62% • Calcium 42 mg. = 5%

Exchange Values: 1 vegetable, 4 lean meat

CASSEROLES

CHEESEBURGER PIE

1 lb. lean ground beef
1 1/2 c. chopped onion
1/8 tsp. salt
1/4 tsp. pepper
1 c. Kraft® Healthy Favorites
   cheddar cheese, shredded
1 1/2 c. skim milk
3/4 c. Bisquick® Light baking mix
3 eggs or 3/4 c. liquid egg substitute

Preheat oven to 400° F. Spray a pie pan with Pam®. Brown ground beef with onion in a skillet and drain well. Stir in salt and pepper and spread in the pie plate. Sprinkle with cheese. Beat remaining ingredients until smooth (15 seconds in a blender on high speed or 1 minute with a hand beater). Pour the batter into the pie plate. Bake about 30 minutes or until golden brown and knife inserted in the center comes out clean. Let stand 5 minutes before cutting. *Preparation time = 15 minutes. Baking time = 30 minutes.*

Nutrition Facts
Serving size = 1 slice • Servings per recipe = 8 • Calories = 280 • Calories from fat = 108

% Daily Value
Total fat 12 gm. = 11% • Saturated fat 5 gm. = 25% • Cholesterol 50 mg. = 17% with egg substitute • Cholesterol 130 mg. = 43% with real egg • Sodium 198 mg. = 7% • Total carbohydrate 15 gm. = 5% • Dietary fiber 0.5 gm. = 2% • Protein 27 gm. = 46% • Calcium 332 mg. = 42% (High in calcium)

Exchange Values: 3 lean meat, 1 bread/starch, 1 fat

CHEESY BROCCOLI AND TUNA BAKE

12 oz. Reames® Home-Style frozen egg noodles
11-oz. can cheddar cheese soup
5 oz. evaporated skim milk
1 tsp. dried onion
12 1/2-oz. can tuna packed in water, drained
4 oz. mushroom pieces, drained
16 oz. frozen chopped broccoli, thawed

Optional garnish: chopped pimiento

Preheat oven to 350° F. Meanwhile in a 3-quart saucepan, cook noodles in boiling water for 20 minutes. In a small bowl, blend soup and milk into a smooth sauce. Add onions and mushrooms. Drain noodles. Layer 1 1/2 c. noodles, 1/3 c. tuna, and 1 c. broccoli in a 2-quart. casserole dish. Pour in 1 cup of sauce. Repeat layers and garnish top of casserole with pimiento, if desired. Bake for 20 minutes. *Preparation time = 25 minutes (including cooking of noodles). Baking time = 20 minutes.*

Microwave Method: Once noodles are cooked and casserole assembled, microwave on high power for 8 minutes, then reduce power to 50% and cook for 5 more minutes. *Preparation time = 15 minutes. Microwave cooking time = 13 minutes.*

Nutrition Facts
Serving size = 1 1/2 cup • Servings per recipe = 8 • Calories = 303 • Calories from fat = 63

% Daily Value
Total fat 7 gm. = 10% • Saturated fat 5 gm. = 12% • Cholesterol 24 mg. = 8% • Sodium 529 mg. = 18% (To reduce sodium, use reduced-sodium tuna.) • Total carbohydrate 40 gm. = 13% • Dietary fiber = 0 • Protein 23 gm. = 39% • Calcium 150 mg. = 19%

Exchange Values: 2 vegetable, 1 bread/starch, 3 lean meat

CRUNCHY ORIENTAL PORK CASSEROLE

A great second meal from a pork roast!

1 c. diced cooked pork
10 3/4-oz. can Campbells® Healthy Request
cream of mushroom soup
1/4 c. skim milk
1 tsp. soy sauce
1 c. thinly sliced celery
6-oz. can water chestnuts, drained and sliced
3-oz. can chow mein noodles
1/4 c. scallions, chopped or sliced

Preheat oven to 375° F. Combine soup, milk, and soy sauce; mix well. Add cooked pork, celery, water chestnuts, 1 cup noodles, and scallions, stir lightly. Spoon into a shallow 1 1/2 quart casserole. Sprinkle with remaining noodles. Bake in a 375° oven until thoroughly heated (about 20 minutes). *Preparation time = 15 minutes. Conventional baking time = 20 minutes.*

Microwave Method: Once casserole is assembled, microwave at 70% power for 12 minutes. *Microwave cooking time = 12 minutes.*

Nutrition Facts
Serving size = 1 cup • Servings per recipe = 4 • Calories = 244 •
Calories from fat = 108

% Daily Value
Total fat 12 gm. = 19% • Saturated fat 4 gm. = 14% • Cholesterol 61 mg. = 20% • Sodium 376 mg. = 13% • Total carbohydrate 13 gm. = 4% • Dietary fiber 2 gm. = 8% • Protein 19 gm. = 34% • Calcium 77 mg. = 10%

Exchange Values: 1 bread/starch, 3 lean meat

Do-Ahead Brunch Casserole

Going to a potluck brunch? This is a winner!

8 squares Ore Ida® frozen hash browns
1 1/4 c. Kraft® Healthy Favorites cheddar cheese,
    shredded and divided
8 oz. lean ham, sliced into thin strips
4 eggs or 1 c. liquid egg substitute
2 1/4 c. skim milk
3/4 tsp. dry mustard
1/4 tsp. pepper
10 3/4-oz. can Campbells'® Healthy Request
    cream of mushroom soup
1/2 c. skim milk

Begin preparing the night before by placing frozen hash browns on the bottom of a 9-x-13 pan that has been sprayed with Pam®. (If using microwave method, use a microwave-safe baking dish.) Top hash browns with 1 cup of shredded cheese and slivered lean ham. Beat together eggs, milk, mustard, and pepper in a bowl. Pour over ham. Cover with foil and refrigerate until morning.

Before baking, dilute 1 can Campbell's® Healthy Request cream of mushroom soup with 1/2 cup skim milk. Pour over casserole, sprinkle with 1/4 cup cheese and bake for 45 minutes in a preheated oven at 400° F. *Preparation time = 15 minutes. Baking time = 45 minutes.*

Microwave Method: Once casserole is assembled, microwave at 70% power for 18 minutes, rotating baking dish at least three times during cooking. *Preparation time = 15 minutes. Microwave cooking time = 18 minutes.*

Nutrition Facts
Serving size = approx. 3x5 square • Servings per recipe = 8 • Calories = 340 • Calories from fat = 21

% Daily Value
Total fat 17 gm. = 26% • Saturated fat 8 gm. = 38% • Cholesterol 36 mg. = 12% with egg substitute • Cholesterol 142 mg. = 47% with real egg • Sodium 789 mg. = 27% • Total carbohydrate 21 gm. = 7% • Dietary fiber 2 gm. = 8% • Protein 25 gm. = 46% • Calcium 453 mg. = 57% (High in calcium)

Exchange Values: 3 lean meat, 1 bread/starch, 2 fat

FLUFFY OVEN-EGGS AND BACON

4 strips bacon, cooked crisp and crumbled
1/2 c. chopped onion
1/2 c. Bisquick® Light baking mix
3 eggs or 3/4 c. liquid egg substitute
1 1/4 c. skim milk
1/8 tsp. pepper
1/2 c. Kraft® Healthy Favorites Monterey Jack
cheese, shredded

Preheat oven to 375° F. Spray a 1 1/2 quart. casserole dish with Pam®. Sprinkle crumbled bacon and onion in bottom of casserole. In a small bowl, beat eggs, milk and pepper until smooth. Pour over bacon. Sprinkle with cheese. Bake uncovered until a knife inserted in the center comes out clean (about 35 minutes).
Preparation time = 10 minutes. Baking time = 35 minutes.

Microwave Method: Once casserole is assembled, microwave at 70% power for 18 minutes. *Preparation time = 10 minutes. Microwave cooking time = 18 minutes.*

Nutrition Facts
Serving size = 3/4 cup • Servings per recipe = 4 • Calories = 67 • Calories from fat = 117

% Daily Value
Total fat 13 gm. = 19% • Saturated fat 1 gm. = 6% • Cholesterol 6 mg. = 2% with egg substitute • Cholesterol 161 mg. = 53% with real egg • Sodium 351 mg. = 12% • Total carbohydrate 18 gm. = 6% • Dietary fiber 0.5 gm. = 2% • Protein 18 gm. = 32% • Calcium 337 mg. = 42% (High in calcium)

Exchange Values: 2 lean meat, 1 fat, 1 1/2 bread/starch

GARDEN TUNA CASSEROLE

8 oz. large bow-tie pasta, cooked and drained
1/3 c. Miracle Whip® Light dressing
1/4 c. flour
1 tsp. dill weed
1 tsp. dried onion
1/8 tsp. salt
1/2 tsp. black pepper
1 c. skim milk
1 c. Kraft® Healthy Favorites
   cheddar cheese, shredded and divided
2 6 1/2-oz. cans tuna packed in water,
   drained and flaked
16-oz. pkg. frozen chopped broccoli,
   thawed and drained
1/2 c. chopped red bell pepper

Preheat oven to 350° F. Boil water in a large pot and cook pasta according to package directions, being careful not to overcook. Mix dressing, flour, and seasonings in a large saucepan. Gradually add milk. Cook, stirring constantly, over low heat until thick. Add 1/2 cup cheese, pasta, and remaining ingredients. Mix lightly. Spoon into a 1 1/2-quart casserole dish and sprinkle with remaining cheese. Bake 25 minutes or until heated through. *Preparation time = 20 minutes. Baking time = 25 minutes.*

Microwave Method: Once casserole is assembled, microwave at 70% power for 15 minutes. *Microwave cooking time = 15 minutes.*

Nutrition Facts
Serving size = 1 1/2 cup • Servings per recipe = 8 • Calories = 255 • Calories from fat = 81

% Daily Value
Total fat 9 gm. = 13% • Saturated fat 4 gm. = 18% • Cholesterol 39 mg. = 13% • Sodium 369 mg. = 13% • Total carbohydrate 22 g. = 7% • Dietary fiber 0.2 gm. = 1% • Protein 25 gm. = 43% • Calcium 327 mg. = 41% (High in calcium)

Exchange Values: 1 vegetable, 1 bread/starch, 3 lean meat

HAM-AND-CHEESE BRUNCH TARTS

8 oz. lean ham, cut into very thin strips
1 1/4 c. Bisquick® Light baking mix
2 Tbsp. margarine
2 Tbsp. boiling water
1/2 c. evaporated skim milk
1 egg
2 Tbsp. thinly sliced green onions
1/2 c. Kraft® Healthy Favorites
    Swiss cheese, shredded

Heat oven to 375° F. Spray 12 muffin cups with Pam®. Cut margarine into baking mix using a fork or pastry cutter. Add boiling water and stir vigorously until a soft dough forms. Press 1 tablespoonful of dough on bottoms and sides of each muffin cup. Divide ham evenly among cups. Beat milk and egg and stir in onions. Spoon about 1 tablespoon of egg batter into each cup; sprinkle cheese over tops. Bake until edges are golden brown and centers are set, about 25 minutes. *Preparation time = 20 minutes. Baking time = 25 minutes.*

Nutrition Facts
Serving size = 1 tart • Servings per recipe = 12 • Calories = 146 •
Calories from fat = 8

% Daily Value
Total fat 6 gm. = 9% • Saturated fat 2 gm. = 10% • Cholesterol 19 mg. =
6% with egg substitute • Cholesterol 36 mg. = 12% with real egg • Sodium
302 mg. = 10% • Total carbohydrate 11 gm. = 4% • Dietary fiber = 0 •
Protein 9 gm. = 16% • Calcium 117 mg. = 15%

Exchange Values: 1 1/2 lean meat, 1 bread/starch

JAMBALAYA

1/2 c. chopped onion
1/2 c. chopped green pepper
1/4 tsp. garlic powder
1 Tbsp. oil
1 c. diced lean ham
28-oz. can chunky tomatoes
1 1/2 c. water
1/2 tsp. dried thyme
1/8 tsp. salt
1/8 tsp. pepper
1 bay leaf
1 c. Minute® rice, uncooked
2 c. (10-oz. pkg.) frozen cooked shrimp

In a large stockpot, sauté onion, green pepper, and garlic powder in oil. Stir in ham, tomatoes, water, seasonings, and rice. Heat to boiling. Reduce heat and boil gently, uncovered for 10 minutes. Add shrimp. Return to a boil and boil for 1 minute. Remove bay leaf. Serve with crusty French bread. *Preparation time = 15 minutes. Cooking time = 10 minutes.*

Nutrition Facts
Serving size = 2 cup • Servings per recipe = 4 • Calories = 237 • Calories from fat = 54

% Daily Value
Total fat 6 gm. = 8% • Saturated fat 1 gm. = 5% • Cholesterol 103 mg. = 34% • Sodium 174 mg. = 22% • Total carbohydrate 26 gm. = 8% • Dietary fiber 1 gm. = 4% • Protein 20 gm. = 35% • Calcium 66 mg. = 8%

Exchange Values: 1 bread/starch, 2 lean meat, 2 vegetable

MAKE-YOUR-OWN RAGU®

28-oz. can Hunt's® whole tomatoes, cut up
6-oz. can tomato paste
1 bay leaf
1/2 tsp. salt
1/2 tsp. sugar
1/2 tsp. fennel seed, crushed
1/2 tsp. basil
1/4 tsp. marjoram
1/4 tsp. thyme
1/8 tsp. oregano
1/8 tsp. crush red pepper

Combine all ingredients in a large stockpot. Bring to a boil, then reduce heat to a simmer and continue cooking for 10 minutes. Use as a sauce for lasagna, spaghetti, or other favorite pasta. This keeps in the refrigerator for 1 week or freezes well for future use. If you like the chunky variety of sauce, add chopped onion, pepper, carrots, zucchini, or celery to the pot. *Preparation time = 20 minutes.*

Nutrition Facts
Serving size = 1/2 cup • Servings per recipe = 8 • Calories = 39 •
Calories from fat = 2

% Daily Value
Total fat < 1 gm. = 1% • Saturated fat = 0 • Cholesterol = 0 • Sodium 309 mg. = 11% • Total carbohydrate 9 gm. = 3% • Dietary fiber 1 gm. = 4% • Protein 2 gm. = 3% • Calcium 35 mg. = 5%

Exchange Values: 1/2 fruit

Microwave Fiesta Pie

3 eggs or 3/4 c. liquid egg substitute
3/4 c. skim milk
2 c. Stove Top® chicken flavor stuffing mix
1 1/2 c. cubed cooked chicken
1 large tomato, chopped
3 Tbsp. chopped green onion
3 Tbsp. chopped green chilies

Accompaniments:

Salsa
Land 'O Lakes® nonfat sour cream
Shredded lettuce
Chopped tomato

Beat eggs in a large bowl; stir in milk. Add remaining ingredients. Mix well. Pour mixture into a glass pie pan that has been sprayed with Pam®. Cover loosely with wax paper. Microwave on high power for 5 minutes. Stir edges of mixture into the center, and from center to outside edges, smoothing out surface. Cover. Microwave 4 minutes or until center is no longer wet. Remove from microwave oven. Let stand for 5 minutes and serve immediately with accompaniments. *Preparation time = 10 minutes.*

Nutrition Facts

Serving size = 1/4 pie • Servings per recipe = 4 • Calories = 270 • Calories from fat = 45

% Daily Value

Total fat 5 gm. = 7% • Saturated fat 1 gm. = 4% • Cholesterol 73 mg. = 24% with egg substitute • Cholesterol 233 mg. = 78% with real egg • Sodium 173 mg. = 6% • Total carbohydrate 16 gm. = 6% • Dietary fiber 0.5 gm. = 2% • Protein 34 gm. = 59% • Calcium 99 mg. = 12%

Exchange Values: 3 lean meat, 1 bread/starch, 1 vegetable

PIZZA CUPS

1 lb. lean ground beef
6-oz. can Hunt's® tomato paste
1 Tbsp. dried onion
1/2 tsp. basil
1/2 tsp. oregano
10-oz. can refrigerated biscuits (12 biscuits)
1/2 c. shredded part-skim mozzarella cheese

Preheat oven to 400° F. Brown ground beef and drain well. Return drained beef to the skillet, then stir in tomato paste, onion, and seasonings. Cook 5 minutes to heat through. Place biscuits in muffin tins sprayed with Pam®, pressing to cover bottom and sides. Spoon about 1/3 cup of meat mixture into each biscuit and sprinkle with cheese. Bake for 12 minutes, or until golden brown.
Preparation time = 15 minutes. Baking time = 12 minutes.

Nutrition Facts
Serving size = 1 pizza cup • Servings per recipe = 12 • Calories = 219 • Calories from fat = 108

% Daily Value
Total fat 12 gm. = 19% • Saturated fat 5 gm. = 22% • Cholesterol 35 mg. = 12% • Sodium 357 mg. = 12% • Total carbohydrate 14 gm. = 5% • Dietary fiber 1 gm. = 4% • Protein 13 gm. = 23% • Calcium 75 mg. = 9%

Exchange Values: 1 vegetable, 1 bread/starch, 2 lean meat

POTATO FLAN OLÉ

1 1/2 c. instant mashed potato flakes
1 c. skim milk
1 c. boiling water
1 egg or 1/4 c. liquid egg substitute
1/2 c. flour
1/4 c. cornmeal
1/4 tsp. garlic powder
1/4 tsp. salt
1/2 tsp. black pepper
2 Tbsp. vegetable oil
1 c. Chi Chi's® medium salsa
1 c. cubed cooked chicken
1/2 c. part-skim Monterey Jack cheese
1 Tbsp. chopped fresh parsley

Preheat oven to 375° F. Spray an 11-inch tart pan or 9-inch round baking dish with Pam®. Mix potato flakes, skim milk, boiling water, and egg in a large bowl until smooth. Add flour, cornmeal, garlic, pepper, and oil. Stir until well mixed. Press mixture evenly into the bottom and sides of prepared pan. Bake crust in a preheated oven for 15 minutes. Spread salsa over the bottom of the crust. Arrange chicken over salsa. Sprinkle cheese and parsley over the top. Continue baking for 20 minutes or until the cheese is melted and lightly browned. Cut into wedges and serve with a slice of fresh avocado as a garnish. *Preparation time = 20 minutes. Baking time = 35 minutes.*

Nutrition Facts
Serving size = 1/8 of pie • Servings per recipe = 8 • Calories = 280 • Calories from fat = 108

% Daily Value
Total fat 12 gm. = 19% • Saturated fat 2 gm. = 10% • Cholesterol 31 mg. = 10% with egg substitute • Cholesterol 58 mg. = 19% with real egg • Sodium 660 mg. = 22% (To reduce sodium, reduce amount of salsa and omit salt.) • Total carbohydrate 28 gm. = 10% • Dietary fiber 0.4 gm. = 2% • Protein 18 gm. = 31% • Calcium 179 mg. = 23% (High in calcium)

Exchange Values: 2 lean meat, 2 bread/starch

PUFFED-UP PIZZA

1 lb. lean ground beef
15-oz. can Hunt's® tomato sauce
1 c. finely chopped onion
1 c. finely chopped green pepper
1/2 c. water
1 1/2-oz. pkg. dry spaghetti-sauce mix
1 c. skim milk
2 tsp. oil
2 eggs or 1/2 c. liquid egg substitute
1 c. flour
4 oz. part-skim mozzarella cheese, shredded
1/4 c. Parmesan cheese

In a skillet, brown the ground beef and drain. Stir in the tomato sauce, onion, pepper, water, and spaghetti sauce mix. Reduce heat and simmer covered for 10 minutes. Meanwhile, in a small bowl, beat milk, oil, and eggs for 1 minute. Add flour and beat 2 minutes longer. Spread meat mixture in a 9-by-13-inch pan that has been sprayed with Pam®. Sprinkle with mozzarella. Top with flour mixture. Sprinkle with Parmesan. Bake at 400° F. for 30 minutes or until puffed and golden. Let stand for 10 minutes before serving. *Preparation time = 15 minutes. Baking time = 30 minutes.*

Nutrition Facts
Serving size = approx. 3x5 square • Servings per recipe = 8 • Calories = 274 • Calories from fat = 108

% Daily Value
Total fat 12 gm. = 18% • Saturated fat 5 gm. = 22% • Cholesterol 40 mg. = 15% with egg substitute • Cholesterol 93 mg. = 31% with real egg • Sodium 188 mg. = 6% • Total carbohydrate 28 gm. = 10% • Dietary fiber 2 gm. = 8% • Protein 19 gm. = 33% • Calcium 178 mg. = 22% (High in calcium)

Exchange Values: 2 lean meat, 2 bread/starch

Seafood Enchiladas in the Microwave

10 3/4-oz. can Campbell's® Healthy Request
  cream of mushroom soup
1/2 c. chopped onion
3 drops hot pepper sauce
Dash of ground nutmeg
Dash of black pepper
10-oz. pkg. frozen chopped spinach,
  thawed and drained
8 oz. frozen mock crab, thawed and chopped
1 c. shredded reduced-fat Monterey Jack cheese
8 corn tortillas
1 c. skim milk

In a mixing bowl, stir together soup, onion, hot pepper sauce, nutmeg, and dash of black pepper. In another bowl, stir together half of the soup mixture, spinach, crab, and 1/2 cup of the cheese; set aside. Wrap tortillas in paper towels; microwave at 100% power for 30 seconds. Place 1/3 cup of crab mixture on each tortilla; roll up. Place seam side down in a 12-by-7-inch baking dish that has been sprayed with Pam®. Stir milk into the reserved soup mixture; pour over the enchiladas. Cover and cook on high power for 14 minutes. Sprinkle with remaining cheese. Let stand for 10 minutes. Garnish with fresh cilantro, if desired. *Preparation time 20 minutes. Microwave cooking time = 14 minutes. Standing time = 10 minutes.*

Nutrition Facts

Serving size = 2 tortillas • Servings per recipe = 8 • Calories = 243 • Calories from fat = 108

% Daily Value

Total fat 12 gm. = 18% • Saturated fat 2 gm. = 9% • Cholesterol 18 mg. = 6% • Sodium 654 mg. = 21% • Total carbohydrate 21 gm. = 7% • Dietary fiber 2 gm. = 8% • Protein 14 gm. = 24% • Calcium 365 mg. = 46% (High in calcium)

Exchange Values: 2 lean meat, 1 1/2 bread/starch

SHEPHERD'S PIE

1 tsp. vegetable oil
1 large onion, chopped
1/3 c. chopped sweet red pepper
1/4 tsp. garlic powder
1/2 lb. lean ground beef
1 c. shredded zucchini
1/2 c. shredded reduced-fat cheddar cheese
1/4 tsp. salt
1 tsp. basil
1/4 tsp. pepper
2 c. water
1/2 c. skim milk
2 c. French's® Idaho instant mashed potato flakes
1 egg, beaten or 1/4 c. liquid egg substitute
1 Tbsp. Parmesan cheese

Heat oil in a large no-stick skillet over medium heat. Sauté onion, red pepper, and garlic for 3 minutes. Add ground beef. Continue to cook mixture for 4 minutes or until beef is browned. Drain well and return to skillet. Add zucchini, half of the shredded cheese, salt, basil, and pepper, and set aside.

Preheat oven to 450° F. Spray a 9-inch pie plate with Pam®. Bring water and milk to a boil in a saucepan. Stir in potato flakes, then beat in egg and remaining half of cheese. Remove from heat. Spread about half of the potato mixture in the bottom on the pan. Spoon meat over potatoes. Spoon remaining potatoes on top. Sprinkle with Parmesan cheese. Bake for 15 minutes. Let stand for 5 minutes before cutting. *Preparation time = 20 minutes. Baking time = 15 minutes. Standing time = 5 minutes.*

Nutrition Facts
Serving size = 1/8 pie • Servings per recipe = 8 • Calories = 218 • Calories from fat = 108

% Daily Value
Total fat 12 gm. = 18% • Saturated fat 6 gm. = 27% • Cholesterol 41 mg. = 14% with egg substitute • Cholesterol 68 mg. = 23% with real egg • Sodium 356 mg. = 12% • Total carbohydrate 14 gm. = 5% • Dietary fiber 0.5 gm. = 2% • Protein 15 gm. = 26% • Calcium 216 mg. = 27% (High in calcium)

Exchange Values: 2 lean meat, 1 bread/starch, 1 vegetable

Shrimp and Feta Cheese on Vermicelli

1 lb. medium shrimp, peeled and deveined
Pinch of dried red pepper flakes
1 Tbsp. vegetable oil, divided
1/3 c. feta cheese, crumbled
1/2 tsp. garlic powder
14-oz. can Del Monte® tomato wedges
1/4 c. dry white wine
3/4 tsp. basil
1/2 tsp. oregano
1/4 tsp. salt
1/4 tsp. pepper
8 oz. vermicelli, uncooked

Sauté shrimp and red pepper in oil in a large skillet for 2 minutes or until shrimp are pink. Arrange shrimp in a 10-by-6-inch baking dish. Sprinkle with feta cheese and set aside. Add remaining oil to skillet and sauté garlic over low heat. Add tomatoes and juice. Cook for 1 minute. Stir in wine and seasonings. Simmer uncovered for 10 minutes. Spoon tomato mixture over shrimp. Bake uncovered at 400° for 10 minutes. Meanwhile, cook vermicelli according to package directions, being careful not to overcook. Drain and serve shrimp over vermicelli. *Preparation time = 15 minutes. Baking time = 10 minutes.*

Nutrition Facts
Serving size = 1 1/2 cup • Servings per recipe = 4 • Calories = 379 • Calories from fat = 90

% Daily Value
Total fat 10 gm. = 15% • Saturated fat 3 gm. = 17% • Cholesterol 191 mg. = 64% • Sodium 675 mg. = 22% • Total carbohydrate 6 gm. = 2% • Dietary fiber = 0 • Protein 31 gm. = 55% • Calcium 181 mg. = 23% (High in calcium)

Exchange Values: 4 lean meat, 1 vegetable, 2 bread/starch

SKILLET CHICKEN

1 1/2 c. cubed chicken
1/3 c. flour
1 Tbsp. chopped parsley
1 tsp. basil
1 Tbsp. vegetable oil
1/4 tsp. garlic powder
10-oz. can Progresso® vegetable soup
1/2 c. sliced mushrooms
1/2 c. chopped green onions
3/4 c. halved cherry tomatoes
1/2 c. sliced zucchini

In a small bowl, toss chicken in flour, parsley and basil until well coated. Heat oil and garlic in a large skillet. Add chicken and cook until lightly browned and no longer pink. Pour in soup, mushrooms, green onions, tomatoes, and zucchini. Stir over medium heat until heated through, about 10 minutes. *Preparation time = 15 minutes. Cooking time = 15 minutes.*

Nutrition Facts
Serving size = 1 1/2 cup • Servings per recipe = 4 • Calories = 288 • Calories from fat = 96

% Daily Value
Total fat 8 gm. = 12% • Saturated fat 1 gm. = 6% • Cholesterol 72 mg. = 24% • Sodium 325 mg. = 11% • Total carbohydrate 27 gm. = 9% • Dietary fiber 2 gm. = 8% • Protein 31 gm. = 53% • Calcium 31 mg. = 4%

Exchange Values: 3 lean meat, 1 bread/starch, 2 vegetable

SOUTHWESTERN BEEF HASH

1 lb. lean ground beef
1 small onion, chopped
3 c. frozen Ore' Ida® Potatoes O'Brien
1/4 tsp. salt
1 c. salsa
Chopped green onion and chopped ripe olives
    as garnish

Brown ground beef and onion in a large skillet over medium heat for 8 minutes. Drain well. Stir in potatoes, salt, and pepper. Cook over medium heat for 5 minutes, stirring occasionally. Stir in salsa. Continue cooking for 8 minutes or until potatoes are lightly browned, stirring occasionally. Garnish with green onion and ripe olive slices, if desired. *Preparation time = 25 minutes.*

Nutrition Facts
Serving size = 1 1/2 cup • Servings per recipe = 4 • Calories = 287 • Calories from fat = 117

% Daily Value
Total fat 13 gm. = 20% • Saturated fat 5 gm. = 24% • Cholesterol 34 mg. = 11% • Sodium 1312 mg. = 46% (To reduce sodium, use fresh tomatoes instead of salsa.) • Total carbohydrate 27 gm. = 9% • Dietary fiber 0.6 gm. = 2% • Protein 15 gm. = 26% • Calcium 124 mg. = 16%

Exchange Values: 2 bread/starch, 1 vegetable, 2 lean meat

STUFFED SHELLS PICANTÉ

12 pasta stuffing shells, cooked and drained
1 lb. lean ground beef
1 c. Chi Chi's® medium salsa
1/2 c. water
8-oz. can tomato sauce
4-oz. can chopped green chilies, drained
1 c. shredded reduced-fat cheddar cheese

Start pasta cooking according to package directions. *Do not over-cook.* Preheat oven to 350° F. Meanwhile, brown the ground beef in a small skillet and drain well. Combine salsa, water, and tomato sauce in a small bowl. Stir 1/2 cup of this mixture into the ground beef, along with the chilies and 1/2 c. of cheese. Mix well. Pour 1/2 cup of sauce mixture on the bottom of an 8-by-12 baking dish. Stuff cooked shells with ground beef mixture. Arrange shells in the baking dish. Pour remaining sauce over the shells. Sprinkle remaining cheese on top and bake, uncovered for 15 minutes. *Preparation time = 15 minutes. Baking time = 15 minutes.*

Nutrition Facts
Serving size = 1 1/2 shells • Servings per recipe = 8 • Calories = 248 •
Calories from fat = 108

% Daily Value
Total fat 12 gm. = 48% • Saturated fat 11 gm. = 52% • Cholesterol 54 mg. =
18% • Sodium 1670 mg. = 56% (To reduce sodium, substitute fresh tomatoes
for salsa.) • Total carbohydrate 15 gm. = 5% • Dietary fiber 0.8 gm. = 3% •
Protein 22 gm. = 38% • Calcium 251 mg. = 31% (High in calcium)

Exchange Values: 3 lean meat, 1 bread/starch

THREE-CHEESE BROCCOLI PIE

1/2 c. cornmeal
1/2 c. flour
2 tsp. baking powder
1/4 tsp. salt
1/2 c. skim milk
1 egg, beaten or 1/4 c. liquid egg substitute
1/4 c. finely chopped onion
4 eggs, slightly beaten or 1 c. liquid egg substitute
10-oz. pkg. frozen Bird's Eye® chopped broccoli, thawed and drained
1/2 c. low-fat cottage cheese
1/2 c. shredded reduced-fat cheddar cheese
1/2 c. shredded reduced-fat Monterey Jack cheese

Heat oven to 350° F. Spray a 9-inch pie plate with Pam®. (If using microwave method, use a glass pan.) Combine cornmeal, flour, baking powder, and salt. Combine milk, egg, and onion and add to cornmeal mixture, mixing well. Pour into prepared pie plate, spreading evenly. Bake for 10 minutes, then set aside. Mix remaining 4 eggs, broccoli, and cheese. Spoon evenly over cornmeal base. Bake for 45 minutes or until a knife inserted in the center comes out clean. Let stand for 5 minutes before serving.
Preparation time = 20 minutes. Baking time = 55 minutes.

Microwave Method: Bake crust in conventional oven, following the directions above. Spoon broccoli mixture over baked crust and microwave on high power for 15 minutes. Let stand for 5 minutes before serving. *Preparation time = 20 minutes. Conventional baking time = 10 minutes. Microwave time = 15 minutes in microwave.*

Nutrition Facts
Serving size = 1/8 pie • Servings per recipe = 8 • Calories = 244 • Calories from fat = 63

% Daily Value
Total fat 7 gm. = 11% • Saturated fat 4 gm. = 17% • Cholesterol 22 mg. = 7% with egg substitute • Cholesterol 48 mg. = 16% with real egg • Sodium 433 mg. = 15% • Total carbohydrate 29 gm. = 10% • Dietary fiber 2 gm. = 7% • Protein 20 gm. = 35% • Calcium 372 mg. = 47% (High in calcium)

Exchange Values: 2 lean meat, 2 vegetable, 1 bread/starch

TORTILLA-BLACK BEAN CASSEROLE

2 c. chopped onion
1 1/3 c. chopped green pepper
14-oz. can chunky tomatoes
3/4 c. salsa
1/2 tsp. garlic
2 tsp. cumin
2 15-oz. cans black beans, drained
8 Aztec® corn tortillas
1 1/2 c. shredded reduced-fat
    Monterey Jack cheese

In a large skillet over medium heat, combine first six ingredients, bringing the mixture to a boil. Reduce heat and simmer uncovered for 5 minutes. Stir in beans. Coat the bottom of a 13-by-9 pan with Pam®. Spread one-third of the bean mixture over the bottom. Top with half of the tortillas, overlapping as necessary and half of the cheese. Add another third of the bean mixture, then remaining tortillas and bean mixture. Cover and bake in a 350° F. oven for 30 minutes or until heated through. Sprinkle with remaining cheese. Let stand for 10 minutes. Garnish with shredded lettuce.
Preparation time = 15 minutes. Baking time = 30 minutes. Standing time = 10 minutes.

Microwave Method: Microwave on 70% power for 12 minutes. Let stand for 5 minutes. Garnish with shredded lettuce.
Preparation Time = 15 minutes. Microwave cooking time = 12 minutes. Standing time = 5 Minutes.

Nutrition Facts
Serving size = 1 cup • Servings per recipe = 8 • Calories = 326 •
Calories from fat = 45

% Daily Value
Total fat 5 gm. = 8% • Saturated fat 2 gm. = 12% • Cholesterol 15 mg. = 5% • Sodium 1150 mg. = 38% (To reduce sodium, reduce salsa.) • Total carbohydrate 48 gm. = 16% • Dietary fiber 3 gm. = 12% • Protein 19 gm. = 33% • Calcium 357 mg. = 33% (High in calcium)

Exchange Values: 2 lean meat, 2 vegetable, 2 bread/starch

TURKEY BROCCOLI DIVINE

16 oz. frozen broccoli spears
8 slices cooked turkey breast
1 10-oz. can Campbell's® Healthy Request
cream of chicken soup
1/2 c. skim milk
1/2 c. Hellmann's® reduced-fat mayonnaise
1 tsp. lemon juice
3/4 tsp. curry powder
1/2 c. shredded reduced-fat cheddar cheese

Place broccoli in a microwave-safe dish. Cover and microwave on high power for 7 minutes. Drain brocolli and top with turkey slices. Combine soup, milk, mayonnaise, juice, and curry. Pour over turkey and top with cheese. Bake at 350° F. for 20 minutes or microwave on high power for 8 minutes.

Preparation time = 15 minutes. Conventional baking time = 20 minutes. Microwave cooking time = 8 minutes.

Nutrition Facts

Serving size = 1 cup • Servings per recipe = 8 • Calories = 189 • Calories from fat = 90

% Daily Value

Total fat 10 gm. = 15% • Saturated fat 3 gm. = 15% • Cholesterol 34 mg. = 11% • Sodium 1004 mg. = 34% (To reduce sodium, use Campbell's® low-sodium cream of chicken soup.) • Total carbohydrate 10 gm. = 3% • Dietary fiber = 0 • Protein 19 gm. = 32% • Calcium 207 mg. = 26% (High in calcium)

Exchange Values: 3 lean meat, 1 vegetable

TURKEY-TORTILLA CASSEROLE

1 tsp. vegetable oil
1 small onion, chopped fine
1/2 tsp. garlic powder
1 lb. ground turkey
2 tsp. chili powder
1/2 tsp. cumin
1/4 tsp. cayenne pepper
1 1/2 tsp. dried oregano
1 Tbsp. vinegar
15-oz. can black beans, rinsed and drained
12-oz. jar of mild or medium-hot salsa
3/4 c. chicken broth
8 Aztec® flour tortillas, cut into 1-inch strips
1/2 c. shredded reduced-fat Monterey Jack cheese
1/3 c. plain nonfat yogurt

Heat oven to 325° F. Heat oil over medium heat in a large nonstick skillet. Cook onion and garlic until softened, about 5 minutes. Add turkey, chili powder, cumin, cayenne, oregano, and vinegar; cook until turkey is no longer pink. Stir in black beans and remove from heat. Combine salsa and chicken broth and spread a thin layer of the salsa mixture in the bottom of a 2-quart baking dish. Top with half of the tortilla strips, half of the turkey mixture, and half of the remaining salsa mixture. Repeat the layers and sprinkle with cheese. Bake until bubbly hot, about 25 minutes, or microwave on 70% power for 15 minutes. Top each serving with a spoon of yogurt.

Preparation time = 15 minutes. Conventional baking time = 25 minutes. Microwave cooking time = 15 minutes.

Nutrition Facts
Serving size = 1 cup • Servings per recipe = 8 • Calories = 389 • Calories from fat = 63

% Daily Value
Total fat 7 gm. = 11% • Saturated fat 2 gm. = 8% • Cholesterol 47 mg. = 16% • Sodium 1903 mg. = 63% (To reduce sodium, use fresh tomatoes instead of salsa.) • Total carbohydrate 48 gm. = 16% • Dietary fiber 1 gm. = 4% • Protein 29 gm. = 50% • Calcium 375 mg. = 47% (High in calcium)

Exchange Values: 2 1/2 bread/starch, 3 lean meat, 1 vegetable

VEGETABLE SEAFOOD CASSEROLE

8 mock crab sticks, sliced
16 oz. California-blend frozen vegetables, thawed
4 oz. sliced mushrooms
1 c. Campbell's® cheddar cheese soup
1/2 c. skim milk
1 large tomato, cut into wedges

Preheat oven to 350° F. In a 2-quart baking dish, layer vegetables, crab, and mushrooms. In a small bowl, mix soup with milk. Pour cheese sauce over the crab and vegetables. Bake for 20 minutes or microwave on 70% high power for 12 minutes. Garnish with tomato wedges. *Preparation time = 10 minutes. Conventional baking time = 20 minutes. Microwave cooking time = 12 minutes.*

Nutrition Facts
Serving size = 1 1/2 cup • Servings per recipe = 4 • Calories = 273 • Calories from fat = 14

% Daily Value
Total fat 7 gm. = 10% • Saturated fat 3 gm. = 15% • Cholesterol 75 mg. = 25% • Sodium 1592 mg. = 53% (To reduce sodium, reduce soup.) • Total carbohydrate 24 gm. = 8% • Dietary fiber 4 gm. = 16% • Protein 30 gm. = 52% • Calcium 226 mg. = 28% (High in calcium)

Exchange Values: 3 lean meat, 1 1/2 bread/starch

Grain-Based Side Dishes

Apricot Pilaf

Dress up white rice with this recipe

1 Tbsp. margarine
1 medium onion, chopped
1 c. rice, uncooked
1/4 tsp. salt
2 1/2 c. water
17-oz. can Del Monte® apricot halves,
   drained and quartered
1/4 c. chopped fresh parsley

Melt margarine in saucepan. Add onion and sauté over medium heat, stirring until tender. Add rice and sauté until rice is golden. Stir in salt and water. Bring mixture to a boil, then reduce heat and simmer, covered, for 20 minutes. Gently fold in apricots and parsley, and continue to heat through. *Preparation time = 30 minutes.*

Nutrition Facts
Serving size = 1/2 cup • Servings per recipe = 8 • Calories = 157 •
Calories from fat = 9

% Daily Value
Total fat 1 gm. = 2% • Saturated fat < 1 gm. = 1% • Cholesterol = 0 • Sodium
86 mg. = 3% • Total carbohydrate 36 gm. = 12% • Dietary fiber 2 gm. = 8% •
Protein 2 gm. = 4% • Calcium 13 mg. = 2%

Exchange Values: 1 fruit, 1 bread/starch

Barley Pilaf

2 Tbsp. margarine
1 small onion, chopped
2 ribs celery, sliced
4-oz. can mushroom pieces, drained
1 c. Quaker® pearl barley
1 1/2 tsp. chicken-flavored bouillon granules
3 1/4 c. water
1/4 tsp. poultry seasoning

Melt margarine in a large saucepan. Stir in onion, celery, and mushrooms; sauté until tender. Stir in barley and cook, stirring frequently, until browned. Add bouillon, water, and poultry seasoning. Bring mixture to a boil, then reduce heat to simmer, covered, for 20 minutes. *Preparation time = 30 minutes.*

Nutrition Facts

Serving size = 1/2 cup • Servings per recipe = 8 • Calories = 184 • Calories from fat = 18

% Daily Value

Total fat 2 gm. = 4% • Saturated fat 1 gm. = 2% • Cholesterol = 0 • Sodium 320 mg. = 11% • Total carbohydrate 35 gm. = 12% • Dietary fiber 4 gm. = 16% • Protein 6 gm. = 11% • Calcium 24 mg. = 3%

Exchange Values: 2 bread/starch, 1 vegetable

BARLEY WITH CORN AND RED PEPPER

1/2 c. reduced-fat Italian salad dressing
1 medium red pepper, chopped
1/2 c. chopped onion
1 c. Quaker® pearl barley
1 1/2 c. chicken broth
1 1/4 c. water
1 Tbsp. lime juice
1/8 tsp. cumin
1/4 tsp. pepper
10 oz. frozen whole-kernel corn

Heat Italian dressing in a large saucepan. Add red pepper and onion and cook over medium heat, stirring occasionally, for 5 minutes or until vegetables are tender. Stir in barley and cook, stirring constantly for 1 minute. Add broth, water, lime juice, cumin, and pepper. Cover and continue to simmer mixture for 20 minutes. Add frozen corn and continue heating just until corn is tender. *Preparation time = 30 minutes.*

Nutrition Facts
Serving size = 3/4 cup • Servings per recipe = 8 • Calories = 86 •
Calories from fat = 18

% Daily Value
Total fat 2 gm. = 4% • Saturated fat < 1 gm. = 1% • Cholesterol 1 mg. = 1% •
Sodium 362 mg. = 12% • Total carbohydrate 16 gm. = 6% • Dietary fiber
6 gm. = 24% (High in fiber) • Protein 2 gm. = 4% • Calcium 8 mg. = 1%

Exchange Values: 1 bread/starch

BLACK BEAN RELISH

A spicy bold side dish for grilled meats.

> 15-oz. can black beans, rinsed and drained
> 1 medium tomato, finely chopped
> 1 /2 c. chopped red pepper
> 1/4 c. chopped red onion
> 4-oz. can Old El Paso® chopped green chilies
> 2 Tbsp. vinegar
> 1 Tbsp. vegetable oil
> 1/4 tsp. salt

Combine all ingredients in a medium bowl; stir to blend. Cover and refrigerate until chilled, about 1 hour. *Preparation time = 10 minutes. Chilling time = 1 hour.*

Nutrition Facts
Serving size = 1/2 cup • Servings per recipe = 8 • Calories = 82 • Calories from fat = 18

% Daily Value
Total fat 2 gm. = 3% • Saturated fat < 1 gm. = 1% • Cholesterol = 0 • Sodium 69 mg. = 3% • Total carbohydrate 13 gm. = 4% • Dietary fiber 6 gm. = 24% (High in fiber) • Protein 4 gm. = 7% • Calcium 17 mg. = 2%

Exchange Values: 1 bread/starch

CHEESY GRITS AND VEGETABLES

1 c. quick-cooking grits
2 oz. Velveeta® Light processed cheese, shredded
1 Tbsp. margarine
2 eggs, beaten, or 1/2 c. liquid egg substitute
10 oz. frozen mixed vegetables, thawed

Prepare grits as directed on the package. Add cheese and margarine, stirring until melted. Beat eggs in a small bowl. Stir a small amount of the hot mixture into eggs, then combine eggs with hot mixture, mixing well. Fold in thawed mixed vegetables. Pour mixture into a lightly greased 2-quart casserole. Microwave on high power for 12 to 15 minutes or until thoroughly heated, turning dish twice during cooking. Let stand for 5 minutes before serving. To heat in conventional oven, bake at 350° for 1 hour. *Preparation time = 10 minutes. Microwave cooking time = 15 minutes. Conventional baking time = 1 hour.*

Nutrition Facts
Serving size = 3/4 cup • Servings per recipe = 8 • Calories = 71 •
Calories from fat = 18

% Daily Value
Total fat 2 gm. = 3% • Saturated fat < 1 gm. = 3% • Cholesterol 2 mg. =
1% with egg substitute • Cholesterol 55 mg. = 18% with real egg • Sodium
87 mg. = 3% • Total carbohydrate 9 gm. = 3% • Dietary fiber 4 gm. = 16% •
Protein 5 gm. = 9% • Calcium 55 mg. = 7%

Exchange Values: 1 bread/starch

Classic Spanish Rice

1 1/2 c. Original Minute® rice
1 onion, cut into thin wedges
1/4 tsp. garlic powder
2 Tbsp. margarine
1 1/2 c. water
1 small green pepper, diced
1/4 tsp. salt
1/2 tsp. prepared mustard

Optional garnish: 4 stuffed green olives, sliced

In a large skillet over medium heat, cook and stir rice, onion, and garlic in margarine. Stir in remaining ingredients except olives. Bring to a full boil. Cover and then remove from heat. Allow to stand 5 minutes. Transfer to a serving bowl and garnish with olives. *Preparation time = 10 minutes.*

Nutrition Facts
Serving size = 1 cup • Servings per recipe = 8 • Calories = 151 •
Calories from fat = 18

% Daily Value
Total fat 2 gm. = 3% • Saturated fat < 1 gm. = 2% • Cholesterol = 0 • Sodium 160 mg. = 5% • Total carbohydrate 106 mg. = 4% • Dietary fiber 4 gm. = 16% • Protein 3 gm. = 5% • Calcium 9 mg. = 1%

Exchange Values: 2 bread/starch

CONFETTI RICE I

3 c. water
1 pkg. Knorr® vegetable soup mix
1 Tbsp. margarine
1 1/2 c. uncooked rice

In a 2-quart saucepan, bring water and soup mix to a boil over medium heat. Add margarine and rice. Reduce heat, cover, and simmer for 20 minutes or until rice is tender. *Preparation time = 25 minutes.*

Nutrition Facts
Serving size = 1 cup • Servings per recipe = 8 • Calories = 150 •
Calories from fat = 18
% Daily Value
Total fat 2 gm. = 2% • Saturated fat < 1 gm. = 1% • Cholesterol = 0 • Sodium 186 mg. = 6% • Total carbohydrate 31 gm. = 10% • Dietary fiber 4 g. = 16% • Protein 3 gm. = 5% • Calcium 8 mg. = 1%
Exchange Values: 2 bread/starch

CONFETTI RICE II

2 c. tomato juice
10 oz. Bird's Eye® frozen mixed vegetables,
    broken apart
1 1/2 c. instant rice uncooked
1/8 tsp. pepper

Combine tomato juice and mixed vegetables in a medium saucepan; bring to a boil. Stir in rice and pepper. Cover, turn off heat, and allow to stand 6 minutes. *Preparation time = 10 minutes.*

Nutrition Facts
Serving size = 1 cup • Servings per recipe = 8 • Calories = 160 •
Calories from fat = 8

% Daily Value
Total fat < 1 gm. = 1% • Saturated fat = 0 • Cholesterol = 0 • Sodium 220 mg. = 8% • Total carbohydrate 36 gm. = 12% • Dietary fiber 4 gm. = 16% • Protein 4 gm. = 7% • Calcium 17 mg. = 2%

Exchange Values: 2 bread/starch

Couscous Pilaf

1 c. chopped fresh broccoli (about 1 large stalk)
1 Tbsp. vegetable oil
1 medium onion, chopped
1 red bell pepper, chopped
1 1/2 c. water
1/4 tsp. salt
1/8 tsp. pepper
1/2 c. Campbell's® Healthy Request
    cream of chicken soup
1 c. couscous

Heat oil in a large nonstick stillet over medium heat. Sauté broccoli, onion, and red bell pepper for 3 minutes. Add water, salt, pepper, and soup. Bring to boiling. Stir in couscous. Remove from heat; cover and let stand for 5 minutes. Serve.
Preparation time = 15 minutes.

Nutrition Facts
Serving size = 1 cup • Servings per recipe = 8 • Calories = 132 •
Calories from fat = 7

% Daily Value
Total fat 3 gm. = 4% • Saturated fat < 1 gm. = 2% • Cholesterol < 1 mg. =
1% • Sodium 139 mg. = 5% • Total carbohydrate 24 gm. = 8% • Dietary fiber
4 gm. = 16% • Protein 5 gm. = 8% • Calcium 28 mg. = 4%

Exchange Values: 1 bread/starch, 2 vegetable

EASY MIDEASTERN PILAF

1 1/2 c. beef broth
1 medium onion, chopped
1/4 c. raisins
1 Tbsp. margarine
1 1/2 c. Original Minute® rice, uncooked
2 Tbsp. sliced almonds
2 Tbsp. chopped fresh parsley or
   1 Tbsp. dried parsley

Combine broth, onion, raisins, and margarine in medium saucepan and bring to full boil. Stir in rice. Cover and remove from heat. Let stand for 5 minutes. Stir in almonds and serve.

Preparation time = 10 minutes.

Nutrition Facts

Serving size = 1 cup • Servings per recipe = 8 • Calories = 184 • Calories from fat = 9

% Daily Value

Total fat 3 gm. = 5% • Saturated fat < 1 gm. = 2% • Cholesterol = 0 • Sodium = 0 • Total carbohydrate 35 gm. = 12% • Dietary fiber 4 gm. = 16% • Protein 4 gm. = 7% • Calcium 18 mg. = 2%

Exchange Values: 2 bread/starch, 1 vegetable

Fruit and Barley

1/2 c. Quaker® pearl barley, uncooked
2 1/2 c. water
1/2 c. golden raisins
1/2 c. finely chopped prunes
1/2 c. finely chopped dried apricots
1 Tbsp. brown sugar
1 Tbsp. lemon juice

Combine barley and water in a medium saucepan. Bring mixture to a boil, cover, and simmer for 20 minutes. Add fruit and simmer for 5 more minutes. Just before serving, add brown sugar and lemon juice. *Preparation time = 25 minutes.*

Nutrition Facts
Serving size = 1/2 cup • Servings per recipe = 8 • Calories = 85 • Calories from fat = 4

% Daily Value
Total fat < 1 gm. = 1% • Saturated fat = 0 • Cholesterol = 0 • Sodium = 0 • Total carbohydrate 22 gm. = 8% • Dietary fiber 4 gm. = 16% • Protein 1 gm. = 2% • Calcium 14 mg. = 2%

Exchange Values: 1 bread/starch

GRITS FLORENTINE

2 c. water
2/3 c. Quaker® Quick grits, uncooked
2 slices bacon, diced and cooked crisp
14-oz. can chopped spinach, drained
1/2 c. thinly sliced green onions
2 oz. reduced-fat cheddar cheese, shredded
1/4 tsp. pepper
1/4 tsp. nutmeg
1/4 tsp. salt
1/2 c. reduced-fat sour cream

Bring water to a boil in a saucepan. Slowly stir in grits and salt. Reduce heat and simmer 2 to 4 minutes or until thick. Meanwhile, dice bacon, fry until crisp, and drain well. Measure remaining ingredients into a soufflé dish and stir to mix. Spoon hot grits and drained bacon into other ingredients, gently folding mixture. Microwave for 8 minutes or until cheese is melted. *Preparation time = 20 minutes.*

Nutrition Facts
Serving size = 3/4 cup • Servings per recipe = 8 • Calories = 69 • Calories from fat = 4

% Daily Value
Total fat 3 gm. = 4% • Saturated fat 1 gm. = 6% • Cholesterol 6 mg. = 3% • Sodium 143 mg. = 5% • Total carbohydrate 7 gm. = 3% • Dietary fiber 5 gm. = 20 % (High in fiber) • Protein 6 gm. = 10% • Calcium 169 mg. = 21%

Exchange Values: 1/2 bread/starch, 1 vegetable

HIDDEN VALLEY® PASTA PRIMAVERA

1 c. carrots, cut in 1/4-inch diagonal slices
1 c. fresh broccoli florets
10 oz. frozen pea pods
8 oz. fettuccine
3 14 1/2-oz. cans chicken broth
1 Tbsp. basil
2/3 c. Hidden Valley Ranch® Low-fat Original
  ranch dressing
2 Tbsp. grated Parmesan cheese

Combine carrots, broccoli, and pea pods in a microwave-safe dish. Cover and microwave on high power for 5 minutes. Drain. Meanwhile, bring chicken broth to a boil and add fettuccine. Cook for 7 minutes and drain. Combine vegetables and pasta. In a small cup, stir basil into dressing. Pour over pasta and vegetables and sprinkle with Parmesan cheese. Serve hot, cold, or just warm. *Preparation time = 15 minutes.*

Nutrition Facts
Serving size = 1 cup • Servings per recipe = 8 • Calories = 192 • Calories from fat = 63

% Daily Value
Total fat 7 gm. = 11% • Saturated fat < 1 gm. = 1% • Cholesterol 8 mg. = 3% • Sodium 1130 mg. = 38% (To reduce sodium, use no-added-salt chicken broth.) • Total carbohydrate 27 gm. = 9% • Dietary fiber 2 gm. = 8% • Protein 6 gm. = 10% • Calcium 38 mg. = 5%

Exchange Values: 2 bread/starch, 1 fat

INDIAN CHICKPEAS

2 15-oz. cans chickpeas
  (also called garbanzo beans)
1 tsp. margarine
1 1/2 c. chopped onion
1 1/2 tsp. turmeric
1/4 tsp. crushed red pepper
14-oz. can Del Monte® diced tomatoes
1/4 tsp. salt
2 Tbsp. minced fresh parsley
1/4 tsp. powdered ginger

Drain chickpeas. Melt the margarine in a skillet, add onion, and sauté for 10 minutes. Mix in the turmeric, ginger, crushed red pepper, and chickpeas. Cook over low heat for 5 minutes. Add tomatoes and salt. Cook uncovered over low heat for 10 minutes. Sprinkle with parsley. *Preparation time = 25 minutes.*

Nutrition Facts
Serving size = 3/4 cup • Servings per recipe = 8 • Calories = 130 • Calories from fat = 9

% Daily Value
Total fat 1 gm. = 2% • Saturated fat = 0 • Cholesterol = 0 • Sodium 420 mg. = 14% • Total carbohydrate 25 gm. = 8% • Dietary fiber 8 gm. = 32% (High in fiber) • Protein 5 gm. = 9% • Calcium 48 mg. = 6%

Exchange Values: 1 bread/starch, 2 vegetable

Oven-Baked Lentils and Rice with Herbs

3 c. chicken broth
3/4 c. lentils, uncooked
3/4 c. chopped onion
1/2 c. Uncle Ben's® brown rice, uncooked
1/4 c. white wine
1 tsp. basil
1/4 tsp. oregano
1/4 tsp. thyme
1/4 tsp. garlic powder
1/8 tsp. pepper

Preheat oven to 350° F. In a 2 1/2-quart casserole, combine broth, lentils, onion, rice, wine, basil, oregano, thyme, and garlic powder. Cover and bake at 350° for 2 hours or until lentils are tender. Add more liquid if mixture becomes dry. *Preparation time = 10 minutes. Baking time = 2 hours.*

Nutrition Facts
Serving size = 3/4 cup • Servings per recipe = 8 • Calories = 135 • Calories from fat = 7

% Daily Value
Total fat 2 gm. = 3% • Saturated fat = 0 • Cholesterol = 0 • Sodium 498 mg. = 17% (To reduce sodium, use no-added-salt chicken broth.) • Total carbohydrate 23 gm. = 8% • Dietary fiber 8 gm. = 32% (High in fiber) • Protein 7 gm. = 12% • Calcium 18 mg. = 2%

Exchange Values: 1 1/2 bread/starch

LOW-FAT MACARONI AND CHEESE

This recipe reduces the fat in this kid favorite by 75%!

1 pkg. Kraft® macaroni and cheese dinner
4 c. water
1 Tbsp. margarine
1/3 c. skim milk

Bring water to a boil in a medium saucepan. Stir in noodles. Reduce heat to medium-low and cook for 8 minutes. Drain noodles and return to the saucepan or a serving bowl. Stir in contents of cheese packet, margarine, and milk. Serve. *Preparation time = 15 minutes.*

Nutrition Facts
Serving size = 3/4 cup • Servings per recipe = 4 • Calories = 210 • Calories from fat = 27

% Daily Value
Total fat 3 gm. = 5% • Saturated fat 1 gm. = 2% • Cholesterol 6 mg. = 2% • Sodium 460 mg. = 15% • Total carbohydrate 37 gm. = 12% • Dietary fiber 1 gm. = 4% • Protein 11 gm. = 19% • Calcium 120 mg. = 15%

Exchange Values: 2 bread/starch, 1 fat

NUTS AND RICE DRESSING

1 bag Success® rice
1/2 c. chopped onion
1/2 c. chopped celery
1 Tbsp. margarine
1/4 c. sliced almonds
1 Tbsp. chopped fresh parsley
1/4 tsp. poultry seasoning
1/2 tsp. salt
1/2 tsp. pepper
1/4 c. chicken broth

Cook rice according to package directions. While rice is cooking, sauté onion and celery in margarine in a skillet. Add nuts, parsley, poultry seasoning, salt, and pepper. Fold in cooked rice. Add chicken broth. Serve. *Preparation time = 15 minutes.*

Nutrition Facts
Serving size = 3/4 cup • Servings per recipe = 8 • Calories = 190 • Calories from fat = 12

% Daily Value
Total fat 5 gm. = 8% • Saturated fat < 1 gm. = 3% • Cholesterol = 0 • Sodium 208 mg. = 7% • Total carbohydrate 30 gm. = 14% • Dietary fiber 4 gm. = 16% • Protein 5 gm. = 9% • Calcium 28 mg. = 4%
Exchange Values: 2 bread/starch, 1/2 fat

ORANGE RICE WITH CARROTS

1 1/2 c. sliced fresh carrots
1 c. orange juice
1/2 c. raisins
1 c. Original Minute® rice
1/2 tsp. grated orange rind

Place carrots in a microwave-safe dish with 1/4 cup water. Cover and microwave on high power for 5 minutes. Drain carrots, reserving liquid. Combine liquid from carrots with orange juice and raisins in a medium saucepan. Bring to a boil. Stir in rice and orange rind. Cover and remove from heat. Let stand 5 minutes. Stir in carrots. *Preparation time = 15 minutes.*

Nutrition Facts
Serving size = 3/4 cup • Servings per recipe = 8 • Calories = 148 • Calories from fat = 6

% Daily Value
Total fat < 1 gm. = 1% • Saturated fat < 1 gm. = 1% • Cholesterol = 0 • Sodium 18 mg. = 1% • Total carbohydrate 35 gm. = 12% • Dietary fiber 4 gm. = 16% • Protein 3 gm. = 5% • Calcium 23 mg. = 3%

Exchange Values: 1 1/2 bread/starch, 1 vegetable

ORZO PRIMAVERA

1 c. orzo
16 oz. Bird's Eye® California blend vegetables
1 Tbsp. water
1/4 tsp. salt
1/4 tsp. oregano
1 tsp. vegetable oil
2 Tbsp. Parmesan cheese

Prepare orzo in a medium saucepan according to package directions and drain. Meanwhile, in a microwave-safe dish, combine vegetables with 1 tablespoon of water. Cover and microwave on high power for 5 minutes. Drain well. Return drained orzo, drained vegetables, and all remaining ingredients to the medium saucepan and stir to mix. Serve. *Preparation time = 15 minutes.*

Nutrition Facts
Serving size = 3/4 cup • Servings per recipe = 8 • Calories = 139 • Calories from fat = 18

% Daily Value
Total fat 2 gm. = 3% • Saturated fat < 1 gm. = 4% • Cholesterol 3 mg. = 1% • Sodium 149 mg. = 5% • Total carbohydrate 27 gm. = 9% • Dietary fiber 4 gm. = 16% • Protein 5 gm. = 8% • Calcium 61 mg. = 8%

Exchange Values: 1 1/2 bread/starch, 1 vegetable

QUICK RISOTTO

2 1/4 c. chicken broth, divided
1 c. uncooked rice
1/2 c. thinly sliced carrots
1/2 c. thinly sliced yellow squash
1/2 c. thinly sliced zucchini
1/4 c. dry white wine
1/2 c. Kraft® Parmesan cheese
1/4 tsp. white pepper

Combine 1 3/4 cup broth and rice in a 3-quart saucepan. Bring this mixture to a boil, stirring once or twice. Reduce heat, cover, and simmer 15 minutes or until rice is tender and liquid is absorbed. Spray a large skillet with Pam® and place over medium-high heat until hot. Cook carrots, squash, and zucchini 2 to 3 minutes or until tender crisp. Add wine and cook for 2 more minutes. Set aside and cover to keep warm. Add remaining 1/2 cup broth to hot rice. Stir over medium-high heat until broth is absorbed. Stir in cheese, pepper, and vegetables. Serve immediately. *Preparation time = 25 minutes.*

Nutrition Facts
Serving size = 3/4 cup • Servings per recipe = 8 • Calories = 172 •
Calories from fat = 45

% Daily Value
Total fat 5 gm. = 8% • Saturated fat 3 gm. = 12% • Cholesterol 15 mg. = 5% • Sodium 241 mg. = 8% • Total carbohydrate 22 gm. = 8% • Dietary fiber 4 gm. = 16% • Protein 9 gm. = 15% • Calcium 216 mg. = 27% (High in calcium)
Exchange Values: 1 bread/starch, 1 vegetable, 1 fat

Rice with Spinach and Water Chestnuts

1/4 c. chopped onion
1 Tbsp. margarine
1 cup brown rice, uncooked
3 c. water
10 oz. frozen chopped spinach
6-oz. can La Choy® sliced water chestnuts, drained
1/4 tsp. salt
2 Tbsp. Parmesan cheese

In a medium skillet, sauté onion in margarine until tender. Stir in rice and water. Bring to a boil, then reduce heat and simmer for 20 minutes. Meanwhile, thaw spinach by running package under warm water until spinach is easy to break apart. Open package and drain spinach well. When rice is done, add water chestnuts, salt, spinach, and Parmesan to the skillet. Heat through and serve. *Preparation time = 25 minutes.*

Nutrition Facts

Serving size = 3/4 cup • Servings per recipe = 8 • Calories = 144 • Calories from fat = 21

% Daily Value

Total fat 3 gm. = 4% • Saturated fat 1 gm. = 4% • Cholesterol 4 mg. = 2% • Sodium 171 mg. = 6% • Total carbohydrate 27 gm. = 9% • Dietary fiber 4 gm. = 16% • Protein 5 gm. = 9% • Calcium 101 mg. = 13%

Exchange Values: 1 bread/starch, 1 vegetable, 1/2 fat

SPICY THAI RICE

*These spices may be out of the ordinary,
but this dish is extraordinary!*

2 c. water
1 c. Original Minute® rice
1/4 c. chopped green onions
2 fresh red chilies, seeded and chopped
1 Tbsp. chopped fresh cilantro
1 Tbsp. margarine
1 tsp. minced fresh ginger root
1/4 tsp. salt
1/8 tsp. turmeric
2 tsp. lime juice
Crushed red pepper for garnish

Combine rice, water, and onions in a microwave-safe dish. Cover and microwave on high power for 5 minutes. Stir in all remaining ingredients. Replace cover on mixture and allow to stand for 5 more minutes. Transfer to a serving bowl and garnish with crushed red pepper. *Preparation time = 15 minutes.*

Nutrition Facts
Serving size = 3/4 cup • Servings per recipe = 8 • Calories = 109 •
Calories from fat = 9%

% Daily Value
Total fat 1 gm. = 2% • Saturated fat < 1 gm. = 1% • Cholesterol = 0 • Sodium 85 mg. = 3% • Total carbohydrate 22 gm. = 7% • Dietary fiber 4 gm. = 16% • Protein 2 gm. = 4% • Calcium 7 mg. = 1%

Exchange Values: 1 1/2 bread/starch

VEG-ALL® SEVEN VEGETABLE MUSHROOM RICE

2 16-oz. cans of veg-all® mixed vegetables,
   well drained
1 c. brown rice, uncooked
5-oz. can sliced mushrooms, drained well
1/2 c. grated green onion

Cook brown rice according to package directions. Drain vegetables and mushrooms and add cooked rice along with grated green onion. Heat through and serve. *Preparation time = 25 minutes.*

Nutrition Facts
Serving size = 1 cup • Servings per recipe = 8 • Calories = 163 • Calories from fat = 8

% Daily Value
Total fat 1 gm. = 2% • Saturated fat < 1 gm. = 1% • Cholesterol = 0 • Sodium 170 mg. = 6% • Total carbohydrate 35 gm. = 12% • Dietary fiber 4 gm. = 16% • Protein 6 gm. = 10% • Calcium 43 mg. = 6%

Exchange Values: 1 1/2 bread/starch, 2 vegetable

WILD RICE CASSEROLE

1 c. Uncle Ben's® brown and wild rice, uncooked
1/2 c. white rice, uncooked
1 beef bouillon cube
3 c. boiling water
2 strips bacon, diced and cooked crisp
1 c. chopped onion
3 c. chopped celery
1/4 c. chopped nuts

Combine wild rice, white rice, bouillon cube, and boiling water in a medium saucepan. Bring to a boil, then reduce heat and simmer for 25 minutes or until rice is tender. Meanwhile, dice bacon and cook crisp in a small skillet; then drain. Add onion and celery to the skillet and sauté until tender. Add bacon, onion and celery and nuts to the cooked rice and serve. *Preparation time = 30 minutes.*

Nutrition Facts
Serving size = 3/4 cup • Servings per recipe = 8 • Calories = 134 • Calories from fat = 7

% Daily Value
Total fat 5 gm. = 7% • Saturated fat 1 gm. = 4% • Cholesterol 2 mg. = 1% • Sodium 167 mg. = 6% • Total carbohydrate 21 gm. = 7% • Dietary fiber 4 gm. = 16% • Protein 5 gm. = 8% • Calcium 45 mg. = 6%

Exchange Values: 1 bread/starch, 1 vegetable, 1 fat

LOW- OR NO-MEAT ENTREES

BAKED RICE-STUFFED PEPPERS

1 c. Minute® rice, uncooked
2 c. boiling water
1 small zucchini cut into 1/4-inch cubes
3 oz. lean ham, finely chopped
1/4 c. finely chopped red onion
2 Tbsp. chopped fresh parsley
1 c. shredded part-skim mozzarella cheese
4 large sweet red or yellow peppers

Preheat oven to 400° F. Boil water in a medium saucepan and add rice. Cover and simmer over low heat for 10 minutes. Combine rice, zucchini, ham, onion, parsley, and half of the cheese in a bowl. Cut peppers in half lengthwise; core and seed. Place peppers, cut-side up in a 13-by-9 inch baking dish. Fill each pepper half with rice mixture. Sprinkle the tops of the peppers with remaining mozzarella. Cover dish loosely with foil. Bake at 400° F. for 25 minutes. (I do not recommend microwave cooking for this recipe.)
Preparation time = 15 minutes. Baking time = 25 minutes.

Nutrition Facts
Serving size = 2 stuffed pepper halves • Servings per recipe = 4 •
Calories = 158 • Calories from fat = 36

% Daily Value
Total fat 4 gm. = 6% • Saturated fat 2 gm. = 9% • Cholesterol 19 mg. = 6% • Sodium 324 mg. = 11% • Total carbohydrate 20 gm. = 7% • Dietary fiber 4 gm. = 16% • Protein 10 gm. = 18% • Calcium 111 mg. = 14%

Exchange Values: 1 vegetable, 1 bread/starch, 1 lean meat

BUFFET BEAN BAKE

4 slices bacon
1/3 c. brown sugar
1/4 c. vinegar
1 Tbsp. French's® America's Favorite mustard
16-oz. can butter beans, drained
16-oz. can French-cut green beans, drained
16-oz. can pork and beans, drained
16-oz. can lima beans, drained
15-oz. can kidney beans, drained.

Optional: Beano®

Preheat oven to 350° F. Dice bacon and fry crisp. Drain on a paper towel and pat to remove grease. In a large baking dish, stir brown sugar, vinegar, and mustard until smooth. Fold in bacon and drained beans. Bake uncovered at 350° F. for 30 minutes.

Beano® is a liquid product available at most large grocery stores and pharmacies that can be added to reduce the gas-producing effects of dried beans, peas and lentils. I recommend its use for people who are just adding beans to their routine diet and are sensitive to gas-producing foods. The gastrointestinal tract eventually adapts to a high-fiber diet and gas production lessens as dried beans, peas, and lentils become part of the routine diet.
Preparation time = 15 minutes. Baking time = 30 minutes.

Nutrition Facts
Serving size = 3/4 cup • Servings per recipe = 8 • Calories = 250 •
Calories from fat = 27

% Daily Value
Total fat 3 gm. = 5% • Saturated fat < 1 gm. = 4% • Cholesterol 5 mg. = 2% •
Sodium 768 mg. = 26% • Total carbohydrate 45 gm. = 15% • Dietary fiber
8 gm. = 32% (High in fiber) • Protein 13 gm. = 23% • Calcium 88 mg. = 11%

Exchange Values: 3 bread/starch

CHALUPA

This is sometimes known as Mexican-American Chili.

1 lb. pinto beans
1/2 lb. lean uncooked pork roast,
    cubed into 1/2-inch pieces
7 c. water
1/2 c. onion
1/2 tsp. garlic powder
1 tsp. salt
2 Tbsp. chili powder
1 Tbsp. cumin
1 tsp. oregano
4-oz. can Old El Paso® chopped green chilies

Optional: Beano®

Optional toppings: Chopped fresh tomato,
    avocado, green onion, or taco sauce

Put all ingredients in a crockpot. Cover and cook on high for 5 hours or until beans are tender. Serve this hot dish with toppings such as chopped fresh tomato, chopped avocado, chopped green onion, or taco sauce.

Beano® is a liquid product available at most large grocery stores and pharmacies that can be added to reduce the gas-producing effects of dried beans, peas, and lentils. I recommend its use for people who are just adding beans to their routine diet and are sensitive to gas-producing foods. The gastrointestinal tract eventually adapts to a high-fiber diet and gas production lessens as dried beans, peas, and lentils become part of the routine diet.
Preparation time = 15 minutes. Crockpot time = 5 hours.

Nutrition Facts
Serving size = 1 1/2 cup • Servings per recipe = 8 • Calories = 246 • Calories from fat = 13

% Daily Value
Total fat 5 gm. = 8% • Saturated fat 2 gm. = 8% • Cholesterol 27 mg. = 9% • Sodium 293 mg. = 10% • Total carbohydrate 33 gm. = 11% • Dietary fiber 18 gm. = 72% (High in fiber) • Protein 19 gm. = 32% • Calcium 66 mg. = 8%

Exchange Values: 2 bread/starch, 1 vegetable, 1 lean meat

Chilies, Cheese, and Rice

3 c. cooked rice
1/2 tsp. garlic powder
4-oz. can chopped green chilies
2 tsp. chili powder
1/2 tsp. salt
15-oz. can red kidney beans, rinsed and drained
1 medium onion, chopped fine
2 tsp. cumin
1 tsp. oregano
1 tsp. Cajun-blend seasoning, optional
2 oz. Kraft® Healthy Favorites cheddar cheese, shredded

Preheat oven to 350° F. In a 2-quart casserole dish, combine all ingredients except cheese. Sprinkle cheese on top. Cover and bake for 25 minutes. Uncover and bake for 10 more minutes. *Preparation time = 15 minutes. Baking time = 35 minutes.*

Nutrition Facts
Serving size = 3/4 cup • Servings per recipe = 8 • Calories = 184 • Calories from fat = 18

% Daily Value
Total fat 2 gm. = 3% • Saturated fat 1 gm. = 4% • Cholesterol 1 mg. = 1% • Sodium 158 mg. = 5% • Total carbohydrate 30 gm. = 23% • Dietary fiber 6 gm. = 24% (High in fiber) • Protein 11 gm. = 19% • Calcium 90 mg. = 11%

Exchange Values: 2 bread/starch, 1/2 lean meat

COUNTRY BEAN BARBEQUE

4 slices bacon, diced
16-oz. can lima beans, well drained
1/2 c. diced onion
1/2 c. diced celery
1/4 tsp. garlic powder
1/2 c. catsup
16-oz. can red kidney beans, drained
1/2 tsp. Tabasco® sauce

Optional: Beano®

In a large skillet cook diced bacon until crisp . Drain well. Return bacon to the skillet and add all remaining ingredients. Heat over medium heat for 20 minutes.

Beano® is a liquid product available at most large grocery stores and pharmacies that can be added to reduce the gas-producing effects of dried beans, peas, and lentils. I recommend its use for people who are just adding beans to their routine diet and are sensitive to gas-producing foods. The gastrointestinal tract eventually adapts to a high-fiber diet and gas production lessens as dried beans, peas, and lentils become part of the routine diet.
Preparation time = 15 minutes. Cooking time = 20 minutes.

Nutrition Facts
Serving size = 1 cup • Servings per recipe = 4 • Calories = 227 •
Calories from fat = 36

% Daily Value
Total fat 4 gm. = 21% • Saturated fat < 1 gm. = 3% • Cholesterol 3 mg. =
1% • Sodium 1159 mg. = 39% (To reduce sodium, cut bacon to 2 slices.) •
Total carbohydrate 38 gm. = 13% • Dietary fiber 12 gm. = 20% (High in fiber) •
Protein 12 gm. = 21% • Calcium 79 mg. = 10%
Exchange Values: 2 bread/starch, 1 lean meat

FAMILY-STYLE BAKED PASTA

8 oz. macaroni or mastacholi noodles
4 qts. water
1/2 lb. lean ground beef
3/4 tsp. garlic powder
3/4 c. Ragu® spaghetti sauce
3/4 c. canned brown gravy
1/2 c. evaporated skim milk
2 Tbsp. Parmesan cheese
1 tsp. oregano
1/2 tsp. rosemary
1/4 tsp. black pepper

Preheat oven to 350° F. Bring 4 quarts of water to a boil. Add pasta to the boiling water. Boil for 7 minutes and then drain immediately. Do not overcook. Meanwhile, brown ground beef with garlic in a medium skillet. Drain well. In a large baking dish, mix remaining ingredients with browned meat and cooked pasta. Bake uncovered for 25 minutes.

Preparation time = 15 minutes. Baking time = 25 minutes.

Nutrition Facts

Serving size = 1 cup • Servings per recipe = 8 • Calories = 245 • Calories from fat = 81

% Daily Value

Total fat 9 gm. = 13% • Saturated fat 3 gm. = 14% • Cholesterol 30 mg. = 10% • Sodium 273 mg. = 8% • Total carbohydrate 27 gm. = 9% • Dietary fiber 4 gm. = 16% • Protein 15 gm. = 26% • Calcium 122 mg. = 15%

Exchange Values: 2 lean meat, 1 1/2 bread/starch, 1 vegetable

GOULASH WITH BEANS AND BACON

4 slices bacon, diced
1 small onion, diced
1/4 c. chopped celery
1/4 c. chopped carrot
16-oz. can Del Monte® diced tomatoes, with juice
16-oz. can great northern beans
4 c. chicken broth
1/2 tsp. salt
1/4 tsp. pepper
2 oz. elbow macaroni

Dice bacon and cook crisp. Drain well and pat with a paper towel to remove all grease. In a Dutch oven, combine bacon with all remaining ingredients, except macaroni. Bring mixture to a boil. Reduce heat and simmer for at least 15 minutes. Add macaroni to mixture and boil in mixture for 8 minutes only and then serve.
Preparation time = 30 minutes.

Nutrition Facts
Serving size = 1 cup • Servings per recipe = 8 • Calories = 125 •
Calories from fat = 36

% Daily Value
Total fat 4 gm. = 6% • Saturated fat < 1 gm. = 2% • Cholesterol 3 mg. = 1% •
Sodium 994 mg. = 33% (To reduce sodium, use no-added-salt chicken broth.) •
Total carbohydrate 18 gm. = 6% • Dietary fiber 6 gm. = 24% (High in fiber) •
Protein 6 gm. = 11% • Calcium 50 mg. = 7%

Exchange Values: 1 bread/starch, 1 vegetable, 1/2 fat

HAMBURGER HOT DISH

1/2 lb. lean ground beef
4 potatoes
15-oz. can Del Monte® diced tomatoes, in juice
15-oz. can cut green beans, drained well
8-oz. can tomato sauce
1 onion, chopped
1 green pepper, chopped
1 Tbsp. sugar
1 Tbsp. basil

In a large skillet, brown ground beef and drain well. Peel and dice potatoes, then boil in a medium saucepan for 5 to 10 minutes. Drain potatoes and add to the skillet along with the browned ground beef and the remaining ingredients. Cook over low heat for about 15 minutes to heat through. *Preparation time = 15 minutes. Cooking time = 15 minutes.*

Nutrition Facts
Serving size = 1 1/2 cup • Servings per recipe = 8 • Calories = 186 • Calories from fat = 45

% Daily Value
Total fat 5 gm. = 8% • Saturated fat 2 gm. = 9% • Cholesterol 24 mg. = 8% • Sodium 458 mg. = 15% (To reduce sodium, use no-added-salt tomatoes.) • Total carbohydrate 28 gm. = 9% • Dietary fiber 3 gm. = 12% • Protein 10 gm. = 18% • Calcium 51 gm. = 7%

Exchange Values: 1 lean meat, 2 vegetable, 1 bread/starch

Manicotti Supreme

8 manicotti shells, dry
8 oz. part-skim mozzarella cheese, shredded
1/4 c. grated parmesan cheese
1 Tbsp. chopped fresh parsley
1/4 tsp. seasoned salt
1/4 tsp. pepper
1/4 tsp. garlic powder
1 1/2 c. Chi Chi's® Salsa
1/2 c. water
1/2 c. red wine

Preheat oven to 400° F. Place manicotti shells in a 7-by-12 inch baking dish and cover with boiling water. Let stand for 5 minutes, then drain and rinse in cold water and drain well again. Combine next six ingredients in a small bowl, and mix well. Fill drained manicotti shells with the mixture of cheeses and seasonings. Return filled shells to the baking dish. Combine salsa with water and red wine and pour over manicotti. Cover and bake for 30 minutes. Serve with additional Parmesan cheese on the side. *Preparation time = 15 minutes. Baking time = 30 minutes.*

Nutrition Facts
Serving size = 1 filled shell • Servings per recipe = 8 • Calories = 130 • Calories from fat = 7

% Daily Value
Total fat 7 gm. = 11% • Saturated fat 4 gm. = 20% • Cholesterol 24 mg. = 8% • Sodium 676 mg. = 23% (To reduce sodium, substitute chopped fresh tomatoes for salsa.) • Total carbohydrate 5 gm. = 2% • Dietary fiber 0.2 gm. = 1% • Protein 10 gm. = 17% • Calcium 284 mg. = 36% (High in calcium)

Exchange Values: 1/2 bread/starch, 1 lean meat, 1 fat

MUSHROOM SKILLET RICE

2/3 c. chopped onion
3/4 c. Uncle Ben's® rice, uncooked
1 Tbsp. margarine
1 c. sliced fresh mushrooms
10-oz. can chicken broth
1 c. water
1 medium tomato, peeled and diced
1 1/2 tsp. chili powder
1/2 tsp. salt
1/2 tsp. marjoram, crumbled
1 c. diced cooked lean ham
1/4 c. chopped fresh parsley

In a large skillet, sauté onion and rice in margarine for 5 minutes. Add mushrooms, broth, water, tomato, chili powder, salt, marjoram, and ham to the skillet. Bring to a boil and cover the skillet tightly. Simmer for 20 minutes. Stir in parsley. Serve.
Preparation time = 10 minutes.

Nutrition Facts
Serving size = 3/4 cup • Servings per recipe = 8 • Calories = 137 •
Calories from fat = 7

% Daily Value
Total fat 4 gm. = 6% • Saturated fat 1 gm. = 5% • Cholesterol 12 mg. = 4% •
Sodium 466 mg. = 16% (To reduce sodium, omit salt.) • Total carbohydrate
18 gm. = 6% • Dietary fiber 2 gm. = 8% • Protein 9 gm. = 15% • Calcium
12 mg. = 2%

Exchange Values: 1/2 lean meat, 1 bread/starch, 1 vegetable

Rice and Beans
with Toppings

1 c. instant rice
1 c. water
15-oz. can Healthy Choice® chili
8 oz. tomato juice
16 oz. frozen mixed vegetables, thawed and drained

Toppings:
Sliced green onions
Nonfat sour cream
Reduced-fat shredded cheddar cheese

Cook rice with water according to package directions. In a large saucepan, combine chili, tomato juice, and mixed vegetables. Bring to a boil, cover, and simmer over medium heat for 4 minutes. Serve over rice and top with onions, sour cream, or cheddar cheese. *Preparation time = 15 minutes.*

Nutrition Facts
Serving size = 1 1/2 cup • Servings per recipe = 4 • Calories = 202 • Calories from fat = 36

% Daily Value
Total fat 4 gm. = 6% • Saturated fat 2 gm. = 8% • Cholesterol 11 mg. = 4% • Sodium 559 mg. = 19% • Total carbohydrate 35 gm. = 12% • Dietary fiber 7 gm. = 28% (High in fiber) • Protein 8 gm. = 14% • Calcium 67 mg. = 8%

Exchange Values: 1/2 lean meat, 1 vegetable, 2 bread/starch

SPAGHETTI PIE

6 oz. spaghetti, uncooked
2 eggs or 1/2 c. liquid egg substitute
1/2 c. grated Parmesan cheese, divided
1 Tbsp. vegetable oil
1 c. grated reduced-fat part-skim mozzarella cheese
1 1/2 tsp. Italian seasoning blend
1/2 c. chopped green pepper
1 c. Ragu® Today's Recipe spaghetti sauce

Preheat oven to 350° F. Lightly spray a 12-inch pizza pan with Pam®. Set aside. Cook spaghetti as directed on package. Drain well, rinse with cold water and drain again. In a medium bowl, beat eggs well; then add cooked spaghetti, 1/2 c. Parmesan, and oil. Toss until spaghetti is well coated. Spread spaghetti evenly onto the prepared pizza pan and bake until spaghetti crust is firm (about 20 minutes). Remove from oven and set aside. In a small bowl, combine mozzarella cheese, Italian seasoning, and remaining 1/4 cup Parmesan cheese. Sprinkle 1 cup cheese mixture on spaghetti crust. Top with spaghetti sauce and chopped green pepper. Sprinkle with remaining cheese mixture. Bake until the cheese is melted, about 10 minutes. *Preparation time = 15 minutes. Baking time = 30 minutes.*

Nutrition Facts

Serving size = 1/8 pie • Servings per recipe = 8 • Calories = 240 • Calories from fat = 99

% Daily Value

Total fat 11 gm. = 17% • Saturated fat < 1 gm. = 20% • Cholesterol 23 mg. = 7% with egg substitute • Cholesterol 76 mg. = 25% with real egg • Sodium 317 mg. = 11% • Total carbohydrate 20 gm. = 7% • Dietary fiber 8 gm. = 24% (High in fiber) • Protein 14 gm. = 25% • Calcium 311 mg. = 39%

Exchange Values: 1 bread/starch, 2 lean meat, 1 fat

Spaghetti with Zucchini Sauce

1 medium onion, sliced
1 Tbsp. vegetable oil
2 medium zucchini, sliced thin
2 c. diced tomatoes
1/2 tsp. salt
1 bay leaf
1/4 tsp. pepper
1/4 tsp. basil
1/4 tsp. oregano
6 oz. spaghetti
1/4 c. Kraft® Parmesan cheese

In a large skillet or pot, sauté onion in hot oil until tender-crisp. Add zucchini, tomatoes, salt, bay leaf, pepper, basil, and oregano. Simmer uncovered for 15 minutes. Discard bay leaf. Meanwhile, cook spaghetti as directed on package and drain well. Serve spaghetti topped with zucchini sauce. Sprinkle 2 Tbsp. Parmesan cheese on top of each serving. *Preparation time = 20 minutes.*

Nutrition Facts
Serving size = 1 1/2 cup • Servings per recipe = 4 • Calories = 316 • Calories from fat = 90

% Daily Value
Total fat 9 gm. = 14% • Saturated fat 3 gm. = 14% • Cholesterol 15 mg. = 5% • Sodium 230 mg. = 8% • Total carbohydrate 47 gm. = 16% • Dietary fiber 4 gm. = 16% • Protein 13 gm. = 23% • Calcium 221 mg. = 28% (High in calcium)

Exchange Values: 3 bread/starch, 1 vegetable, 1 fat

Spanish Rice and Beans

1 tsp. vegetable oil
3 medium onions, coarsely chopped
2 tsp. chili powder
1 tsp. oregano, crumble
1 c. Uncle Ben's® brown rice
3/4 c. water
2 Tbsp. vinegar
1/2 tsp. salt
2 green peppers, coarsely chopped
15-oz. can black beans, rinsed and drained

Optional: Beano®

Heat oil in a Dutch oven over medium heat. Add chopped onion and cook, covered, for 6 minutes or until softened, stirring occasionally. Stir in chili powder and oregano and cook for 1 minute. Stir in rice, water, vinegar, and salt. Bring to a boil. Reduce heat to simmer. Sprinkle peppers on top of the rice. Cover and cook for 15 more minutes. Fold in beans. Serve.

Beano® is a liquid product available at most large grocery stores and pharmacies that can be added to reduce the gas-producing effects of dried beans, peas, and lentils. I recommend its use for people who are just adding beans to their routine diet and are sensitive to gas-producing foods. The gastrointestinal tract eventually adapts to a high-fiber diet and gas production lessens as dried beans, peas, and lentils become part of the routine diet.
Preparation time = 25 minutes.

Nutrition Facts
Serving size = 1 cup • Servings per recipe = 8 • Calories = 204 • Calories from fat = 8

% Daily Value
Total fat 2 gm. = 4% • Saturated fat < 1 gm. = 1% • Cholesterol = 0 • Sodium 135 mg. = 95% • Total carbohydrate 42 mg. = 15% • Dietary fiber 4 gm. = 16% • Protein 7 gm. = 12% • Calcium 44 mg. = 5%

Exchange Values: 2 bread/starch, 2 vegetables

Speedy "Baked" Ziti

1 large (26 oz.) jar of Ragu® Healthy Choice
    spaghetti sauce
1/2 c. reduced-fat ricotta cheese
1/4 tsp. crushed red-pepper
1 lb. ziti
3 Tbsp. grated Parmesan cheese

Start cooking ziti according to package directions. Meanwhile, combine 1 1/2 cup of spaghetti sauce, the ricotta, and crushed red pepper in a blender, blending until smooth (about 1 minute). Preheat broiler. When ziti is drained well, transfer it to a broiler-proof 13-by-9 inch baking dish that has been sprayed with Pam®. Add the ricotta, mixture to the baking dish and stir to combine. Spoon the remaining spaghetti sauce on top and sprinkle with Parmesan cheese. Broil on low for 10 minutes or until mixture is heated through.
Preparation time = 15 minutes. Broiling time = 10 minutes.

Nutrition Facts
Serving size = 1 1/2 cup • Servings per recipe = 8 • Calories = 302 •
Calories from fat = 72

% Daily Value
Total fat 8 gm. = 12% • Saturated fat 2 gm. = 9% • Cholesterol 11 mg. = 4% •
Sodium 118 mg. = 4% • Total carbohydrate 45 gm. = 15% • Dietary fiber
8 gm. = 32% (High in fiber) • Protein 13 gm. = 23% • Calcium 158 mg. = 20%

Exchange Values: 1 lean meat, 1 vegetable, 3 bread/starch

SPICY RED BEANS AND RICE

2 15-oz. cans Del Monte®
   red kidney beans, drained
2 tsp. paprika
1/2 tsp. cayenne pepper
1 tsp. black pepper
2 bay leaves
1 tsp. ground cumin
1 qt. water
4 oz. lean ham
1 1/2 c. chopped celery
1 1/2 c. chopped onion
1/2 tsp. garlic powder
1/2 tsp. hot pepper sauce
3 Tbsp. minced fresh parsley
6 cups of cooked rice
   (prepare according to package directions)

Optional: Beano®

Rinse beans. In a large Dutch oven or kettle, place all ingredients except parsley and rice. Bring to a boil, then simmer, covered for at least 20 minutes. Just before serving, remove bay leaves and stir in parsley. Serve 1 cup of bean mixture over 3/4 cup cooked rice.

Beano® is a liquid product available at most large grocery stores and pharmacies that can be added to reduce the gas-producing effects of dried beans, peas, and lentils. I recommend its use for people who are just adding beans to their routine diet and are sensitive to gas-producing foods. The gastrointestinal tract eventually adapts to a high-fiber diet and gas production lessens as dried beans, peas, and lentils become part of the routine diet.
Preparation time = 30 minutes.

Nutrition Facts
Serving size = 1 3/4 cup • Servings per recipe = 8 • Calories = 345 •
Calories from fat = 18

% Daily Value
Total fat 2 gm. = 3% • Saturated fat < 1 gm. = 2% • Cholesterol 6 mg. = 3% • Sodium 599 mg. = 20% • Total carbohydrate 62 gm. = 22% • Dietary fiber 8 gm. = 32% (High in fiber) • Protein 14 gm. = 25% • Calcium 75 mg. = 9%

Exchange Values: 3 bread/starch, 1 lean meat, 2 vegetable

Spinach Pasta Casserole

8 oz. spinach noodles, dry
1 c. sliced onion
1/2 c. chopped green pepper
1 Tbsp. vegetable oil
1 1/2 c. Kemps® low-fat cottage cheese
1/2 c. plain nonfat yogurt
1 1/2 Tbsp. Worcestershire sauce
1/4 tsp. pepper
1/4 tsp. garlic powder
1 c. shredded part-skim mozzarella cheese

Preheat oven to 400° F. Cook noodles according to package directions. Drain and set aside. In a small skillet, sauté onion and green pepper in oil until onion is tender and golden. In a large bowl, combine noodles, onion, green pepper, cottage cheese, yogurt, Worcestershire sauce, pepper, garlic powder, and cheese. Toss to mix. Transfer to a 2-quart baking dish that has been sprayed with Pam®. Cover and bake for 15 minutes. Remove cover and bake an additional 5 minutes.
Preparation time = 15 minutes. Baking time = 20 minutes.

Nutrition Facts
Serving size = 1 1/2 cup • Servings per recipe = 8 • Calories = 152 • Calories from fat = 54

% Daily Value
Total fat 6 gm. = 8% • Saturated fat 3 gm. = 16% • Cholesterol 25 mg. = 8% • Sodium 346 mg. = 12% • Total carbohydrate 11 gm. = 4% • Dietary fiber 2 gm. = 8% • Protein 15 gm. = 25% • Calcium 248 mg.= 31%

Exchange Values: 1 bread/starch, 1 lean meat, 1 vegetable

Spinach Quiche

4 eggs, slightly beaten or 1 c. liquid egg substitute
1 1/2 c. skim milk
1 c. reduced-fat shredded Swiss cheese
1/2 pkg. Knorr® vegetable soup mix
10 oz. frozen chopped spinach, thawed dried
1 9-inch frozen deep-dish pie crust.

Preheat oven to 400° F. In a large bowl, combine eggs, milk, cheese, soup mix, and spinach. Spoon into the pie crust. Bake for 40 minutes or until a knife inserted halfway between center and edge comes out clean. *Preparation time = 10 minutes. Baking time = 40 minutes.*

Nutrition Facts
Serving size = 1/8 pie • Servings per recipe = 8 • Calories = 220 • Calories from fat = 90

% Daily Value
Total fat 10 gm. = 15% • Saturated fat 3 gm. = 14% • Cholesterol 17 mg. = 6% with egg substitute • Cholesterol 124 mg. = 41% with real egg • Sodium 750 = 25% (To reduce sodium, use salt-free home-prepared crust.) • Total carbohydrate 19 gm. = 7% • Dietary fiber 0.5 gm. = 2% • Protein 15 gm. = 25% • Calcium 851 mg. = 44% (High in calcium)

Exchange Values: 1 bread/starch, 1 vegetable, 1 fat, 1 1/2 lean meat

Three Beans for Supper

15-oz. can Mrs. Grime's red kidney beans,
    rinsed and drained
15-oz. can garbanzo beans, rinsed and drained
16-oz. can lima beans, rinsed and drained
1/2 lb. lean ground beef
1 large onion, chopped
1/4 tsp. garlic powder
1/4 c. packed brown sugar
1/4 tsp. salt
1/4 tsp. black pepper
2 Tbsp. prepared mustard
1/2 c. catsup
1 tsp. ground cumin
1/4 c. water
1 Tbsp. vinegar

Optional: Beano®

If using a conventional oven, preheat oven to 350° F. In a 2 1/2-quart casserole dish, combine drained beans and set aside. In a skillet, cook ground beef, onion, and garlic until beef is no longer pink. Drain well. Return meat to skillet; add all remaining ingredients to the skillet and mix well. Stir beef mixture into the beans and bake for at least 30 minutes. To microwave, cover and cook on 70% power for 15 minutes, stirring mixture twice during cooking.

Beano® is a liquid product available at most large grocery stores and pharmacies that can be added to reduce the gas-producing effects of dried beans, peas, and lentils. I recommend its use for people who are just adding beans to their routine diet and are sensitive to gas-producing foods. The gastrointestinal tract eventually adapts to a high-fiber diet and gas production lessens as dried beans, peas and lentils become part of the routine diet.

Preparation time = 15 minutes. Conventional baking time = 30 minutes. Microwave Cooking time = 15 minutes.

Nutrition Facts
Serving size = 1 cup • Servings per recipe = 8 • Calories = 270 • Calories from fat = 63

% Daily Value
Total fat 7 gm. = 7% • Saturated fat 2 gm. = 7% • Cholesterol 21 mg. = 7% • Sodium 814 mg. = 27% (To reduce sodium, omit salt.) • Total carbohydrate 41 gm. = 14% • Dietary fiber 12 gm. = 48% (High in fiber) • Protein 17 gm. = 28% • Calcium 75 mg. = 9%

Exchange Values: 2 bread/starch, 1 lean meat, 2 vegetable

UP-SIDE DOWN VEGETABLE LASAGNA

1 pkg. Chef Boy-Ar-Dee® lasagna dinner
16 oz. Bird's Eye® San Fransisco Blend frozen
    vegetables, thawed and drained
2 c. part-skim ricotta cheese
1 egg, beaten
Dash nutmeg
1/4 tsp. basil
1/4 tsp. oregano
4-oz. part-skim mozzarella cheese, shredded

Preheat oven to 425° F. Prepare lasagna noodles according to package directions and drain well. Meanwhile, drain vegetables well. Spray a 7-by-11 baking dish with Pam®. Sprinkle 1 cup of thawed vegetables over the bottom of the dish. Spoon half of lasagna sauce from package over the vegetables. Place a third of the drained lasagna noodles on top. Combine ricotta, egg, and nutmeg, with cheese from the package. Spread half of this over noodles. Place another third of noodles over the cheese mixture. Sprinkle remaining thawed vegetables over the layer of the noodles. Top with remaining noodles, ricotta, and sauce. Bake for 20 minutes. *Preparation time = 15 minutes. Baking time = 20 minutes.*

Nutrition Facts
Serving size = 3 by 3 inch square • Servings per recipe = 8 •
Calories = 270 • Calories from fat = 81

% Daily Value
Total fat 9 gm. = 14% • Saturated fat 5 gm. = 22% • Cholesterol 27 mg. = 9% with egg substitute • Cholesterol 54 mg. = 18% with real egg • Sodium 212 mg. = 7% • Total carbohydrate 32 gm. = 11% • Dietary fiber 6 gm. = 22% (High in fiber) • Protein 18 gm. = 31% • Calcium 305 mg. = 38% (High in calcium)

Exchange Values: 2 bread/starch, 2 lean meat, 1 vegetable

VEGETARIAN SUPPER

16-oz. can great northern beans
1 c. chopped onion
1 1/2 c. chopped celery
1 Tbsp. vegetable oil
1/4 c. flour
1/2 tsp. salt
1/4 tsp. pepper
3 c. skim milk
14-oz. can Del Monte® chopped tomatoes
16-oz. whole-kernel corn
4 oz. shredded part-skim Monterey Jack cheese

Optional: Beano®

Preheat oven to 375° F. In a 3-quart baking dish, combine all ingredients except cheese. Bake for 20 minutes. Top with cheese. Return to oven for 5 minutes. Serve.

Beano® is a liquid product available at most large grocery stores and pharmacies that can be added to reduce the gas-producing effects of dried beans, peas and lentils. I recommend its use for people who are just adding beans to their routine diet and are sensitive to gas-producing foods. The gastrointestinal tract eventually adapts to a high-fiber diet and gas production lessens as dried beans, peas and lentils become part of the routine diet.
Preparation time = 10 minutes. Chilling time = 25 minutes.

Nutrition Facts
Serving size = 1 cup • Servings per recipe = 8 • Calories = 211 •
Calories from fat = 45

% Daily Value
Total fat 5 gm. = 7% • Saturated fat 2 gm. = 9% • Cholesterol 12 mg. = 4% •
Sodium 430 mg. = 15% • Total carbohydrate 31 gm. = 11% • Dietary fiber
8 gm. = 32% (High in fiber) • Protein 14 gm. = 24% • Calcium 326 mg. =
41% (High in calcium)

Exchange Values: 1 1/2 bread/starch, 2 vegetable, 1 lean meat

Entrees

Almond Fish Fillets

1 lb. cod fillets, frozen
1/4 c. slivered almonds
1 Tbsp. margarine, melted
4 Tbsp. ReaLemon® lemon juice

Preheat oven to 400° F. Place fish fillets in a baking pan. Combine almonds, margarine, and lemon juice in a glass cup and pour over fish. Cover with foil and bake for 45 minutes or until fish tests done. To test fish for doneness, use a fork to flake the middle-most section of the fish. It should be opaque in color and flake apart easily. *Preparation time = 10 minutes. Baking time = 45 minutes.*

Nutrition Facts
Serving size = 4 oz. • Servings per recipe = 4 • Calories = 185 •
Calories from fat = 81

Daily Value
Total fat 9 gm. = 14% • Saturated fat 1 gm. = 6% • Cholesterol 15 mg. = 5% •
Sodium 309 mg. = 10% • Total carbohydrate 3 gm. = 1% • Dietary fiber = 0 •
Protein 22 gm. = 38% • Calcium 72 mg. = 9%

Exchange Values: 3 1/2 lean meat

Baked Salmon Squares with Cheese and Dill

This recipe works with tuna, also.

1 15 - oz. can Humpty Dumpty® pink salmon,
    drained and flaked
1 Tbsp. dried minced onion
2 c. Bisquick® Light baking mix
1/2 c. water
2 oz. part-skim mozzarella cheese
2 Tbsp. Parmesan cheese
10 3/4-oz. can Campbell's® Healthy Request
    cream of celery soup
1/4 c. skim milk
1/2 tsp. dill weed

Preheat oven to 450° F. Combine salmon and onion and set aside. Combine Bisquick and water. Divide dough in half, pressing half of it into an 8-inch square baking dish that has been sprayed with Pam®. Top evenly with salmon mixture, then shredded cheese. Drop remaining dough over cheese and sprinkle with Parmesan. Bake for 15 to 18 minutes or until crust is golden brown. Cut into squares. Make a sauce by combining soup, milk, and dill weed in a glass cup. Heat through and serve on the side.
Preparation time = 15 minutes. Baking time = 30 minutes.

Nutrition Facts
Serving size = 2-x 4-inch pieces • Servings per recipe = 8 • Calories = 330 • Calories from fat = 72

% Daily Value
Total fat 8 gm. = 12% • Saturated fat 3 gm. = 12% • Cholesterol 11 mg. = 4% • Sodium 566 mg. = 19% • Total carbohydrate 56 gm. = 19% • Dietary fiber = 0 • Protein 22 gm. = 38% • Calcium 235 mg. = 30% (High in calcium)

Exchange Values: 2 bread/starch, 3 lean meat

BOURBON-MARINATED SIRLOIN

1 lb. lean sirloin, trimmed and cut into four pieces
1/4 c. high-quality bourbon
1 Tbsp. vegetable oil
2 Tbsp. French's® Worcestershire sauce
1/2 tsp. garlic powder
1/4 tsp. freshly ground pepper

Place the steaks in a flat baking dish. Mix all remaining ingredients in a glass cup and pour over the steaks. Cover and marinate in the refrigerator for at least 30 minutes or up to 4 hours. Grill steaks over a hot fire, 4 minutes on each side for medium doneness. Use remaining marinade to brush on steaks just before removing from the grill. *Preparation time = 10 minutes. Marinating time = 30 minutes. Grilling time = 8 minutes.*

Nutrition Facts
Serving size = 4 oz. • Servings per recipe = 4 • Calories = 174 • Calories from fat = 63

% Daily Value
Total fat 7 gm. = 9% • Saturated fat 2 gm. = 8% • Cholesterol 59 mg. = 20% • Sodium 145 mg. = 5% • Total carbohydrate = 0 • Dietary fiber = 0 • Protein 24 gm. = 42% • Calcium 13 mg. = 2%

Exchange Values: 3 lean meat

Chicken Breasts Stuffed with Veggies and Cheese

1 pkg. Knorr® vegetable soup mix
1 1/2 c. water
1 c. white rice, dry
1/2 medium tomato, coarsely chopped
1 oz. part-skim mozzarella cheese
1/4 c. grated Parmesan cheese
1/4 tsp. garlic powder
4 whole boneless chicken breasts,
skinned and halved

In a medium saucepan, blend vegetable soup mix with water and bring to a boil. Stir in rice and simmer for 15 minutes. Stir in tomato, cheese, and garlic and set aside. Preheat oven to 375° F. Using a sharp knife parallel to the cutting board, made a deep 3-inch-long cut in the center of each chicken breast half to form a pocket. Evenly stuff the pockets with rice and vegetable mixture. Place the stuffed breasts in a baking dish that has been sprayed with Pam®. Bake uncovered, for 35 minutes or until done.

Preparation time = 20 minutes. Baking time = 35 minutes.

Nutrition Facts
Serving size = 1 stuffed breast • Servings per recipe = 4 • Calories = 259 • Calories from fat = 29

% Daily Value
Total fat 9 gm. = 14% • Saturated fat 4 gm. = 21% • Cholesterol 92 mg. = 31% • Sodium 959 mg. = 32% (To reduce sodium, use 1/2 pkg. of soup mix.) • Total carbohydrate 17 gm. = 2% • Dietary fiber 1 gm. = 4% • Protein 6 gm. = 62% • Calcium 264 mg. = 33% (High in calcium)

Exchange Values: 3 lean meat, 1 vegetable, 1 bread/starch

CHICKEN PARMESAN

4 half chicken breasts, skinned and boned
2 14-oz. can Del Monte® Italian style
   stewed tomatoes
2 Tbsp. cornstarch
1/2 tsp. oregano
1/2 tsp. basil
1/4 tsp. hot pepper sauce
1/4 c. grated Parmesan cheese

Place chicken in a baking dish. Cover and bake for 15 minutes in a preheated 425° F. oven. Meanwhile, combine tomatoes, cornstarch, oregano, and pepper sauce in a small saucepan. Cook, stirring constantly until sauce is thickened. Pour heated sauce over the chicken. Top with cheese. Bake for 5 minutes, uncovered. Garnish with parsley. Serve with steamed noodles or rice.
Preparation time = 25 minutes.

Nutrition Facts
Serving size = 1 half breast • Servings per recipe = 4 • Calories = 255 • Calories from fat = 14

% Daily Value
Total fat 8 gm. = 12% • Saturated fat 3 gm. = 16% • Cholesterol 88 mg. = 29% • Sodium 601 mg. = 20% • Total carbohydrate 11 gm. = 5% • Dietary fiber = 0 • Protein 35 gm. = 60% • Calcium 266 mg. = 33%

Exchange Values: 2 vegetable, 4 lean meat

Finger Lickin' Good Spicy Fish

1 Tbsp. margarine, melted
1/2 tsp. rosemary
1/2 tsp. basil
1/4 tsp. salt
1 tsp. black pepper
2 shakes cayenne pepper
1/4 tsp. garlic powder
2 Tbsp. ReaLemon® lemon juice
1 lb. firm whitefish boneless fillets, thawed

Preheat oven to 400° F. Melt margarine in a flat baking dish. Add spices and lemon juice. Stir to evenly coat bottom of dish. Place fish fillets in dish. Bake uncovered for 20 minutes or until fish tests done. Turn fillets once during baking.
Preparation time = 30 minutes.

Nutrition Facts below

Finger Lickin' Good Italian Fish

Combine 2 tsp. Italian blend seasoning with lemon juice and margarine. Baking instructions same as above.
Preparation time = 30 minutes.

Nutrition Facts for both finger lickin' spicy and italian fish
Serving size = 4 oz. • Servings per recipe = 4 • Calories = 92 • Calories from fat = 5

% Daily Value
Total fat 5 gm. = 7% • Saturated fat = 0 • Cholesterol 15 mg. = 5% • Sodium 253 mg. = 8% • Total carbohydrate = 0 • Dietary fiber = 0 • Protein 17 gm. = 29% • Calcium 65 mg. = 8%

Exchange Values: 2 lean meat

FRUITY BAKED CHICKEN

1 Tbsp. lemon juice
2 tsp. soy sauce
1/4 tsp. salt
1/4 tsp. ginger
1/8 tsp. pepper
4 chicken breast halves, boned and skinned
8-oz. can Del Monte® Light pears in juice
8-oz. can Del Monte® Light peaches in juice

Preheat oven to 350° F. Combine lemon juice, soy sauce, salt, ginger, and pepper. Pour over chicken in a shallow baking dish. Bake for 15 minutes. Add drained fruit to pan. Baste fruit with liquid from bottom of pan. Continue baking for 10 more minutes. Serve with brown rice. *Preparation time = 30 minutes.*

Nutrition Facts
Serving size = 1 chicken breast half + 4 oz. fruit • Servings per recipe = 4 •
Calories = 201 • Calories from fat = 10

% Daily Value
Total fat 3 gm. = 5% • Saturated fat 1 gm. = 24% • Cholesterol 36 mg. =
12% • Total carbohydrate 15 gm. = 5% • Dietary fiber 2 gm. = 8% • Protein
28 gm. = 48% • Calcium 24 mg. = 3%

Exchange Values: 1 fruit, 2 1/2 lean meat

Ginger-soy Fish Steaks

4 1-inch thick fish steaks, such as halibut or salmon
1/2 tsp. garlic powder
3 Tbsp. La Choy® soy sauce
1 Tbsp. white-wine vinegar
1 Tbsp. vegetable oil
2 Tbsp. sugar
1 tsp. ground ginger

Place the fish in a glass or ceramic bowl. Mix marinade ingredients and pour over the fish. Cover and refrigerate for at least 30 minutes or up to overnight. Over hot flame, grill fish 6 to 8 minutes on each side, brushing with the remaining marinade.

Marinating time = 30 minutes. Cooking time = 10 minutes.

Nutrition Facts

Serving size = 4 oz. • Servings per recipe = 4 • Calories = 181 • Calories from fat = 54

% Daily Value

Total fat 6 gm. = 9% • Saturated fat < 1 gm. = 3% • Cholesterol 35 mg. = 12% • Sodium 813 mg. = 27% • Total carbohydrate 7 gm. = 2% • Dietary fiber = 0 • Protein 24 gm. = 42% • Calcium 54 mg. = 7%

Exchange Values: 3 lean meat

GLAZED PORK CHOPS

4 3-oz. pork chops, trimmed
1/2 c. Simply Fruit® apricot preserves
1 Tbsp. light corn syrup
3 Tbsp. cider vinegar
1/2 tsp. dry mustard.

Bake, broil, grill, or panbroil chops. Meanwhile, combine apricot preserves, corn syrup, vinegar, and mustard in a small saucepan. Bring mixture to a boil and then reduce heat to simmer, cooking for 3 minutes, until slightly thick. Brush glaze over the chops 2 to 3 times during last few minutes of cooking.
Preparation time = 20 minutes.

Nutrition Facts
Serving size = 4 oz. • Servings per recipe = 4 • Calories = 163 • Calories from fat = 36

% Daily Value
Total fat 4 gm. = 6% • Saturated fat 2 gm. = 8% • Cholesterol 63 mg. = 21% • Sodium 60 mg. = 2% • Total carbohydrate 16 gm. = 5% • Dietary fiber = 0 • Protein 16 gm. = 28% • Calcium 13 mg. = 2%

Exchange Values: 1 fruit, 3 lean meat

GLAZED CHICKEN BREASTS

Substitute 4 boneless, skinless chicken breast halves for pork chops in recipe above. *Preparation time = 10 minutes for glaze only.*

Nutrition Facts
Serving size = 4 oz. • Servings per recipe = 4 • Calories = 217 • Calories from fat = 90

% Daily Value
Total fat 10 gm. = 15% • Saturated fat 4 gm. = 19% • Cholesterol 72 mg. = 24% • Sodium 60 mg. = 2% • Total carbohydrate 16 gm. = 5% • Dietary fiber = 0 • Protein 16 gm. = 28% • Calcium 13 mg. = 2%

Exchange Values: 1 fruit, 3 lean meat

GRILLED FISH
WITH HERBS

1 lb. Gorton's® Freshmarket fresh cod
   (halibut steaks or any firm whitefish will work)
1 Tbsp. vegetable oil
2 Tbsp. vinegar
1 bay leaf
1 Tbsp. chopped parsley
1/4 tsp. salt
1/2 tsp. Worcestershire sauce
1/8 tsp. tarragon
1/8 tsp. pepper

Optional garnish: lime wedges

Thaw fish and then place in an 8-inch square glass dish. Mix remaining ingredients and pour over the fish. Marinate for at least 30 minutes. Grill fish 5 to 7 minutes on each side, or until fish flakes easily with a fork. Baste with marinade while grilling. Garnish with lime wedges. *Preparation time = 5 minutes. Marinating time = 30 minutes. Grilling time = 14 minutes.*

Nutrition Facts

Serving size = 4 oz. • Servings per recipe = 4 • Calories = 190 • Calories from fat = 72

% Daily Value

Total fat 7 gm. = 10% • Saturated fat 1 gm. = 3% • Cholesterol 47 mg. = 16% • Sodium 237 mg. = 7% • Total carbohydrate = 0 • Dietary fiber = 0 • Protein 30 gm. = 52% • Calcium 16 mg. = 2%

Exchange Values: 3 1/2 lean meat

GRILLED ITALIAN PORK CHOPS

4 3-oz. pork chops, well trimmed
1/2 c. Kraft Free® Italian dressing

Marinate pork chops in dressing for at least 30 minutes or up to overnight in the refrigerator. Broil or grill chops about 6 inches from the heat source, turning once, until internal temperature reaches 170° F. (about 10 minutes). Serve with mixed vegetables and a baked potato. *Preparation time = 5 minutes. Marinating time = 30 minutes. Grilling time = 10 minutes.*

Nutrition Facts
Serving size = 1 chop • Servings per recipe = 4 • Calories = 166 • Calories from fat = 90

% Daily Value
Total fat 10 gm. = 35% • Saturated fat 4 gm. = 19% • Cholesterol 72 mg. = 24% • Sodium 461 mg. = 15% • Total carbohydrate 2 gm. = 1% • Dietary fiber = 0 • Protein 16 gm. = 28% • Calcium 9 mg. = 1%

Exchange Values: 3 lean meat

Grilled Pork Kabobs with Orange Sauce

1/2 c. orange juice
2 Tbsp. lime juice
1 tsp. oregano
1 tsp. marjoram
1 tsp. thyme
1/8 tsp. cumin
1 tsp. oil
1/4 tsp. salt
1/2 tsp. pepper
1 lb. pork tenderloin, well trimmed

Orange Sauce:
1/2 c. Land 'O Lakes® nonfat sour cream
1 Tbsp. mayonnaise
1 tsp. lime juice
1 tsp. grated orange peel
3 drops hot pepper sauce

Combine orange and lime juice with spices in a flat shallow baking dish. Cut the tenderloin into 1-inch pieces or thin horizontal slices. Marinate for at least 30 minutes or up to overnight. Place the meat on 4 skewers and grill about 6 inches from the flame until the internal temperature reaches 170° F (6 to 8 minutes). For orange sauce, combine all ingredients in a small glass bowl and serve on the side with pork kabobs. *Preparation time = 15 minutes. Marinating time = 30 minutes. Grilling time = 8 minutes.*

Nutrition Facts
Serving size = 4 oz • Servings per recipe = 4 • Calories = 236 •
Calories from fat = 12

% Daily Value
Total fat 7 gm. = 10% • Saturated fat 2 gm. = 10% • Cholesterol 106 mg. = 35% • Sodium 291 mg. = 10% • Total carbohydrate 7 gm. = 2% • Dietary fiber = 0 • Protein 35 gm. = 60% • Calcium 114 mg. = 14%

Exchange Values: 1/2 fruit, 4 lean meat

GRILLED SHRIMP

2 Tbsp. Heinz® chili sauce
2 tsp. chopped fresh parsley
2 tsp. lemon juice
1 lb. medium shrimp, peeled and deveined

In a small shallow dish, combine chili sauce, parsley, and lemon juice, mixing well. Add shrimp, stirring to coat. Cover and let stand for 10 minutes. Arrange shrimp on metal skewers and grill 4 to 6 inches from medium-high heat. Cook for 4 minutes or until the shrimp turn pink, turning once and brushing with marinade. Serve over rice. *Preparation time = 20 minutes.*

Nutrition Facts
Serving size = 4 oz. • Servings per recipe = 4 • Calories = 129 • Calories from fat = 6

% Daily Value
Total fat 2 gm. = 3% • Saturated fat < 1 gm. = 2% • Cholesterol 174 mg. = 58% • Sodium 259 mg. = 9% • Total carbohydrate 3 gm. = 1% • Dietary fiber = 0 • Protein 23 gm. = 40% • Calcium 62 mg. = 8%

Exchange Values: 2 1/2 lean meat

HONEY-AND-HERB GRILLED PORK

1 lb. pork tenderloin or roast, well trimmed
1/2 c. beer
1/2 c. gingerale
1/4 c. honey
1/4 c. French's® Dijon mustard
1 Tbsp. vegetable oil
1/2 tsp. onion powder
1 tsp. rosemary
1/2 tsp. garlic powder
1/4 tsp. salt
1/4 tsp. ground black pepper

Place tenderloin in a heavy plastic bag. Combine remaining ingredients in a glass cup, mixing well. Pour over the pork and seal the bag. Marinate in the refrigerator for at least 30 minutes or up to overnight. Grill tenderloin or roast until an internal temperature of 170° F. is reached. *Preparation time = 5 minutes. Marinating time = 30 minutes. Grilling time = 15 minutes.*

Nutrition Facts
Serving size = 4 oz. • Servings per recipe = 4 • Calories = 261 • Calories from fat = 72

% Daily Value
Total fat 8 gm. = 13% • Saturated fat 2 gm. = 8% • Cholesterol 79 mg. = 26% • Sodium 372 mg. = 12% • Total carbohydrate 20 gm. = 7% • Dietary fiber = 0 • Protein 25 gm. = 43% • Calcium 23 mg. = 3%

Exchange Values: 4 lean meat, 1/2 fruit

HONEY-AND-MAPLE BAKED HAM

2 lb. ready-to-eat ham
1 1/2 c. white wine
2 Tbsp. French's® Dijon mustard
2 Tbsp. honey
2 Tbsp. maple syrup
1/2 c. chicken broth
1 tsp. cornstarch

Preheat oven to 400° F. Trim rind from ham and place ham in a baking dish. Pour wine over ham. Cover and bake for 15 minutes. Meanwhile, combine remaining ingredients in a small saucepan. Heat over medium flame, using a whisk to stir mixture smooth. Remove ham from oven and pour honey-and-mustard sauce over it. Return ham to the oven and bake 10 minutes longer. Slice and serve with boiled new potatoes. *Preparation time = 25 minutes*

Nutrition Facts

Serving size = 4 oz. • Servings per recipe = 8 • Calories = 255 • Calories from fat = 90

% Daily Value

Total fat 10 gm. = 15% • Saturated fat 3 gm. = 15% • Cholesterol 46 mg. = 15% • Sodium 634 mg. = 21% (To reduce sodium, select low-sodium ham and chicken broth.) • Total carbohydrate 10 gm. = 3% • Dietary fiber = 0 • Protein 24 gm. = 42% • Calcium 22 mg. = 3%

Exchange Values: 4 lean meat, 1/2 fruit

HOT CRAB SANDWICH MELTS

8 oz. imitation crab meat, snipped into
   bite-sized pieces
3 oz. Philadelphia® Free cream cheese, softened
4 drops hot pepper sauce
1 Tbsp. chopped onion
3 Tbsp. mayonnaise
2 Tbsp. lemon juice
1/2 tsp. Worcestershire sauce
4 English muffins, split
8 slices tomato
2 oz. Kraft® Healthy Favorites cheddar cheese,
   shredded

Preheat oven to 325° F. Combine first seven ingredients. Spread
crab mixture on top of English muffin halves. Top each with one
slice of tomato and shredded cheese. Place on a baking sheet and
bake for 20 minutes. *Preparation time = 30 minutes.*

Nutrition Facts
Serving size = 2 muffin halves • Servings per recipe = 4 • Calories = 299 •
Calories from fat = 17

% Daily Value
Total fat 8 gm. = 13% • Saturated fat 2 gm. = 12% • Cholesterol 19 mg. =
6% • Sodium 885 mg. = 30% (To reduce sodium, choose reduced-sodium
cheese.) • Total carbohydrate 39g. = 13% • Dietary fiber = 0 • Protein 17 gm. =
30% • Calcium 296 mg. = 37% (High in calcium)

Exchange Values: 2 lean meat, 2 bread/starch, 1 vegetable

LEMONY STEAMED FISH

4 4-oz. halibut, scrod, or cod fillets, fresh or frozen
1 small onion, finely chopped
1/4 c. chopped parsley
1 tsp. dillweed
1 tsp. paprika
1/4 tsp. salt
1/8 tsp. pepper
1 Tbsp. ReaLemon® lemon juice

Preheat oven to 400° F. Center each fillet on a 12-inch square of aluminum foil. Sprinkle with onion, parsley, dillweed, paprika, salt, pepper, and lemon juice. Fold foil over each fillet to make a packet, pleating the seams to securely seal. Place on a baking sheet and bake for 30 minutes.

Preparation time = 10 minutes. Baking time = 30 minutes.

Nutrition Facts
Serving size = 4 oz. • Servings per recipe = 4 • Calories = 99 •
Calories from fat = 14

% Daily Value
Total fat 1 gm. = 1% • Saturated fat = 0 • Cholesterol = 0 • Sodium 199 mg.
= 7% • Total carbohydrate 2 gm. = 1% • Dietary fiber 0.5 gm. = 2% • Protein
20 gm. = 34% • Calcium 27 mg. = 3%

Exchange Values: 2 lean meat

MANDARIN CHICKEN

1 11-oz. can Giesha Girl® mandarin oranges
1/4 c. teriyaki sauce
2 whole chicken breasts, skinned and boned
1 Tbsp. vegetable oil
1/4 tsp. garlic powder
1 medium onion, chopped
10 oz. frozen snap peas
1/4 lb. fresh mushrooms, sliced

Drain oranges, reserving 2 Tbsp. of liquid. Blend reserved orange syrup with teriyaki sauce in a glass cup and set aside. Cut chicken into 1-inch pieces. Heat oil in a large skillet over high heat. Add chicken and garlic and stir-fry for 3 minutes. Remove chicken from the pan. Add onion, peas, and mushrooms to the pan and stir-fry for 3 minutes until or onions are tender. Add chicken and teriyaki-sauce mixture; cook and stir to heat chicken and vegetables through. Gently stir in drained mandarin oranges just before serving over hot white rice. *Preparation time = 20 minutes.*

Nutrition Facts
Serving size = 4 oz. • Servings per recipe = 4 • Calories = 245 •
Calories from fat = 63

% Daily Value
Total fat 7 gm. = 11% • Saturated fat 1 gm. = 6% • Cholesterol 73 mg. = 24% • Sodium 719 mg. = 24% • Total carbohydrate 28 gm. = 9% • Dietary fiber 3 gm. = 12% • Protein 20 gm. = 58% • Calcium 78 mg. = 10%

Exchange Values: 1 fruit, 3 lean meat, 1 vegetable

ONE-DISH ORIENTAL CHICKEN AND RICE

1 6-oz. package Uncle Ben's® long grain and
  wild rice mix
1 Tbsp. vegetable oil
2 medium carrots, peeled and sliced thin
6 oz. frozen snow peas, thawed
4 green onions, cut fine
4 skinless, boneless chicken breast halves
1/2 tsp. garlic powder
1 tsp. ground ginger
3 Tbsp. water
1 Tbsp. cornstarch
1 c. orange juice
2 tsp. finely grated orange peel
1 Tbsp. soy sauce

Preheat oven to 400° F. Empty rice from mix into a 2 1/2 quart
casserole dish. Add seasoning packet and 4 cups of water and stir to
mix. Next, layer sliced carrots, thawed peas, sliced onions, and
boneless chicken breasts. In a small glass cup, combine remaining
ingredients. Pour over chicken and cover. Bake for 45 minutes.
Preparation time = 15 minutes. Baking time = 45 minutes.

Microwave Method: Bake at 70% power for 20 minutes, turning
twice during cooking. *Microwave cooking time = 20 minutes.*

Nutrition Facts
Serving size = 4 oz. meat + 1 cup rice and vegetables • Servings per recipe = 4 •
Calories = 339 • Calories from fat = 63

% Daily Value
Total fat 7 gm. = 11% • Saturated fat 1 gm. = 6% • Cholesterol 73 mg. =
24% • Sodium 333 mg. = 11% • Total carbohydrate 35 gm. = 12% • Dietary
fiber 4 gm. = 16% • Protein 32 gm. = 56% • Calcium 93 mg. = 12%

Exchange Values: 3 lean meat, 1 vegetable, 2 bread/starch

ORANGE CHICKEN

2 chicken breasts, skinned and halved
3/4 c. Uncle Ben's® brown rice
1 c. orange juice
1 c. chicken broth
8 oz. fresh mushrooms, sliced thin
1 large onion, chopped fine
2 Tbsp. fresh parsley, chopped fine
1/4 tsp. allspice
1/4 c. white wine

Optional garnish:
Grated orange rind
Fresh chopped parsley

Preheat oven to 350° F. Place chicken breasts on a baking pan and bake for 30 minutes. Microwave Method: Chicken can also be cooked in a covered glass baking dish at 70% power for 8 to 12 minutes, turning twice during cooking. While chicken is cooking, mix remaining ingredients in a medium saucepan. Simmer over medium heat for 20 minutes until thick, whisking to be sure there are no lumps. The rice and vegetable mixture should be of a stewed consistency, not lumpy. On a serving platter, layer chicken with rice mixture on top. Garnish with orange rind and parsley.
Preparation time = 15 minutes. Microwave cooking time = 12 minutes. Conventional baking time = 30 minutes.

Nutrition Facts
Serving size = 4 oz. chicken + 1 cup vegetables • Servings per recipe = 4 •
Calories = 291 • Calories from fat = 36

% Daily Value
Total fat 4 gm. = 6% • Saturated fat 1 gm. = 5% • Cholesterol 73 mg. = 24% •
Sodium 145 mg. = 5% • Total carbohydrate 29 gm. = 10% • Dietary fiber
2 gm. = 8% • Protein 31 gm. = 54% • Calcium 124 mg. = 15%

Exchange Values: 1 bread/starch, 1 fruit, 3 lean meat

ORIENTAL CHICKEN WITH STIR-FRY VEGETABLES

1/2 c. chicken broth
1/4 c. La Cloy® soy sauce
1 Tbsp. pineapple juice
1 Tbsp. dry sherry
1/2 tsp. ground ginger
2 boneless, skinless chicken breasts, cut in half
1/2 tsp. garlic powder
1/2 c. chopped red or green pepper
1/2 c. sliced celery
1 c. thinly sliced mushrooms
6 oz. La Choy® frozen snow peas, thawed
2 c. bean sprouts

Combine chicken broth, soy sauce, pineapple juice, sherry and ginger. Coat a large skillet with Pam®and heat over high heat. Brown chicken and garlic and remove. Stir-fry peppers, celery, mushrooms, and snow peas for 2 minutes. Add soy mixture and chicken and continue cooking for 2 minutes. Add sprouts just before serving and heat through. *Preparation time = 20 minutes.*

Nutrition Facts
Serving size = 4 oz. chicken + 1 cup vegetables • Servings per recipe = 4 •
Calories = 150 • Calories from fat = 36

% Daily Value
Total fat 4 gm. = 5% • Saturated fat 1 gm. = 4% • Cholesterol 73 mg. =
24% • Sodium 1074 mg. = 36% (To reduce sodium, use reduced-sodium soy
sauce and chicken broth.) • Total carbohydrate 11 gm. = 4% • Dietary fiber
2 gm. = 8% • Protein 20 gm. = 54% • Calcium 56 mg. = 7%

Exchange Values: 1 vegetable, 2 lean meat

Picadillo Rolls

1 1/2 lb. lean ground beef
3 medium tomatoes, chopped
2 medium onions, finely chopped
1 tsp. garlic powder
3 Tbsp. chopped fresh or canned jalapeño peppers
1 Tbsp. sugar
1/2 tsp. cinnamon
1/4 tsp. cloves
1 Tbsp. cider vinegar
2 oz. Kraft® Healthy Favorites cheddar cheese, shredded
8 French rolls, warmed

In a large skillet, brown ground beef and drain well. Return drained meat to the skillet and add tomatoes, onions, garlic, peppers, sugar, cinnamon, cloves, and vinegar. Cover and simmer on low heat for 15 minutes. Remove from heat and stir in cheese. To serve, spoon mixture into warm French rolls. *Preparation time = 25 minutes.*

Nutrition Facts
Serving size = 1 roll • Servings per recipe = 8 • Calories = 299 • Calories from fat = 117

% Daily Value
Total fat 13 gm. = 20% • Saturated fat 5 gm. = 24% • Cholesterol 67 mg. = 23% • Sodium 294 mg. = 10% • Total carbohydrate 23 gm. = 8% • Dietary fiber 0.5 gm. = 3% • Protein 24 gm. = 41% • Calcium 113 mg. = 14%

Exchange Values: 3 1/2 lean meat, 1 vegetable, 1 bread/starch

POLYNESIAN SHRIMP

1/4 c. sugar
3 Tbsp. cornstarch
1/2 tsp. ground ginger
1/4 c. white vinegar
2 Tbsp. La Choy® soy sauce
13-oz. can Dole® pineapple chunks in juice
1 lb. frozen uncooked shrimp, thawed
3 green onions, sliced thin
1 small green pepper, cut into strips
1 medium tomato, chopped

Mix sugar, cornstarch, and ginger in a microwave-safe 2-quart casserole dish. Blend in vinegar and soy sauce and then add all remaining ingredients except tomato. Cover and microwave on high power for 10 minutes or until shrimp turn pink, stopping to stir every 4 minutes. Gently stir in tomato and let casserole stand, covered, for 5 minutes before serving over steamed rice. *Preparation time = 25 minutes.*

Nutrition Facts

Serving size = 4 oz. shrimp + 3/4 cup fruit and vegetable • Servings per recipe = 4 • Calories = 283 • Calories from fat = 18

% Daily Value

Total fat 2 gm. = 3% • Saturated fat < 1 gm. = 2% • Cholesterol 174 mg. = 58% • Sodium 690 mg. = 23% • Total carbohydrate 41 gm. = 14% • Dietary fiber 1 gm. = 4% • Protein 25 gm. = 43% • Calcium 84 mg. = 10%

Exchange Values: 3 lean meat, 2 vegetable, 1 fruit

PORK STEAK POCKET

4 4 - oz. boneless pork steaks
1/4 c. chopped onion
1/4 c. chopped celery
1 tsp. margarine
1 slice wheat bread, cut into 1/2-inch cubes
1 Tbsp. raisins
1 c. Tree Top® apple juice

Pound pork steaks until thin. Meanwhile, sauté onion and celery in margarine for 3 minutes. Stir in bread cubes and raisins. Place 1/4 of the bread mixture on each pork steak, fold it in half and secure the edges with wooden picks. Pour apple juice in a large skillet, add the stuffed pork steaks. Cover and braise over low heat for 30 minutes. *Preparation time = 10 minutes. Cooking time = 30 minutes.*

Nutrition Facts
Serving size = 4 oz. • Servings per recipe = 4 • Calories = 202 • Calories from fat = 45

% Daily Value
Total fat 5 gm. = 8% • Saturated fat 2 gm. = 7% • Cholesterol 79 mg. = 26% • Sodium 120 mg. = 4% • Total carbohydrate 13 gm. = 4% • Dietary fiber 1 gm. = 4% • Protein 25 gm. = 44% • Calcium 23 mg. = 3%

Exchange Values: 3 lean meat, 1/2 bread/starch

Salmon Florentine

1 10-oz. pkg. Bird's Eye® frozen spinach, thawed
and well drained
1 17-oz. can red salmon
1 Tbsp. margarine
1/4 c. flour
1/2 tsp. dry mustard
Skim milk
1/4 tsp. salt
3 Tbsp. Parmesan cheese

Preheat oven to 425° F. Place thawed spinach in an 8-inch baking dish sprayed with Pam®. Drain liquid from salmon, saving the liquid in a glass measuring. Use a fork to flake salmon into small pieces and sprinkle it over spinach. Melt margarine in a medium saucepan. Add flour and dry mustard and blend. Add enough milk to the salmon liquid to measure 1 1/2 cups. Stir the liquid and salt into the flour mixture and bring to a boil, stirring constantly. Add 3 Tbsp. Parmesan cheese, stirring to blend; then pour sauce over the salmon. Bake uncovered for 25 minutes. As an alternative, salmon may be cooked in the microwave at 70% power for 15 minutes, turning dish twice during cooking. *Preparation time = 10 minutes. Conventional baking time = 25 minutes. Microwave cooking time = 15 minutes.*

Nutrition Facts
Serving size = 8 oz. • Servings per recipe = 4 • Calories = 301 •
Calories from fat = 117

% Daily Value
Total fat 13 gm. = 20% • Saturated fat 4 gm. = 20% • Cholesterol 11 mg. = 4% • Sodium 1064 mg. = 35% (To reduce sodium, omit salt.) • Total carbohydrate 18 gm. = 6% • Dietary fiber = 0 • Protein 33 gm. = 56% • Calcium 519 mg. = 65% (High in calcium)

Exchange Values: 4 lean meat, 1/2 skim milk, 2 vegetable

SATURDAY NIGHT SEAFOOD SCRAMBLE

3 Tbsp. La Choy® teriyaki sauce
2 Tbsp. water
2 Tbsp. orange juice
1/4 tsp. garlic powder
1 lb. orange roughy or other firm whitefish, cut into
    4 portions
1 onion, chopped fine
1 zucchini, sliced thin
1 green pepper, chopped
1 large carrot, sliced thin

In a 7-by-11-inch baking dish, combine first four ingredients, using a spatula to evenly coat bottom of pan with mixture. Next, layer fish, onion, zucchini, pepper, and carrot. Cover and microwave on high power for 10 minutes, turning twice during cooking. *Preparation time = 10 minutes. Microwave cooking time = 10 minutes.*

Nutrition Facts
Serving size = 8 oz. • Servings per recipe = 4 • Calories = 154 •
Calories from fat = 8

% Daily Value
Total fat 4 gm. = 6% • Saturated fat = 0 • Cholesterol 15 mg. = 5% • Sodium 618 mg. = 21% • Total carbohydrate 17 gm. = 5% • Dietary fiber 2 gm. = 8% • Protein 20 gm. = 35% • Calcium 112 mg. = 14%

Exchange Values: 2 vegetable, 2 lean meat

SAVORY BAKED FISH

1/2 c. chopped celery
1 lb. sole fillets or other firm whitefish
1/4 tsp. salt
1/4 tsp. rosemary
1/4 tsp. pepper
1/4 tsp. paprika
1 c. Del Monte® chopped tomatoes, well drained
1/2 c. chopped green onions
1/4 c. dry white wine

Preheat oven to 350° F. Sprinkle celery in a shallow baking pan. Arrange fish over celery, slightly overlapping. Sprinkle with salt, rosemary, pepper and paprika. Top with tomatoes and onion and add wine. Bake for 25 minutes until fish flakes. *Preparation time = 10 minutes. Conventional baking time = 25 minutes.*

Microwave Method: Follow directions above, but instead of baking, cover and microwave on high power for 10 minutes or until fish flakes easily with a fork, turning dish twice during cooking. *Preparation time = 10 minutes. Microwave cooking time = 10 minutes.*

Nutrition Facts
Serving size = 6 oz. • Servings per recipe = 4 • Calories = 116 • Calories from fat = 6

% Daily Value
Total fat 3 gm. = 5% • Saturated fat = 0 • Cholesterol 15 mg. = 5% • Sodium 339 mg. = 11% • Total carbohydrate 6 gm. = 2% • Dietary fiber 1 gm. = 4% • Protein 18 gm. = 31% • Calcium 98 mg. = 12%

Exchange Values: 2 lean meat

SAVORY STUFFED PEPPERS

1 lb. lean ground beef
1/4 c. chopped onion
12-oz. can Del Monte® whole-kernel corn, drained
8-oz. can tomato sauce
1 c. cooked rice
1/4 c. A-1® steak sauce
1/4 tsp. ground black pepper
8 large green peppers

Preheat oven to 375° F. In a skillet, over medium heat, brown meat and cook onion until done; drain well. Return meat to the skillet and stir in corn, tomato sauce, rice, steak sauce, and pepper; set aside. Cut tops off peppers and remove seeds. Spoon meat mixture into the peppers, arrange in a 9-inch square baking pan and bake for 25 minutes. *Preparation time = 10 minutes. Baking time = 25 minutes.*

Nutrition Facts
Serving size = 1 pepper • Servings per recipe = 8 • Calories = 253 • Calories from fat = 13

% Daily Value
Total fat 8 gm. = 12% • Saturated fat 3 gm. = 14% • Cholesterol 42 mg. = 14% • Sodium 297 mg. = 10% • Total carbohydrate 33 gm. = 11% • Dietary fiber 5 gm. = 20% • Protein 17 gm. = 29% • Calcium 33 mg. = 4%

Exchange Values: 2 lean meat, 1 vegetable, 1 1/2 bread/starch

SEAFOOD BROIL

4 Tbsp. reduced-fat 1000 Island salad dressing
4 toasted English muffins, cut in half
1/2 lb. imitation crab, sliced fine
8 slices fresh tomato, about 2 medium tomatoes
4 oz. Kraft® Healthy Favorites mozzarella cheese,
    cut into 8 slices

On a baking sheet, place English muffin halves and spread with salad dressing. Place one tomato slice on each muffin half. Sprinkle with crab and top with cheese. Broil on "low", 4-inches from heating element until cheese melts, about 6 minutes.

Preparation time = 10 minutes. Cooking time = 6 minutes.

Nutrition Facts
Serving size = 2 muffin halves • Servings per recipe = 4 • Calories = 310 • Calories from fat = 72

% Daily Value
Total fat 8 gm. = 13% • Saturated fat 3 gm. = 16% • Cholesterol 28 mg. = 9% • Sodium 1099 mg. = 37% (To reduce sodium, select reduced-sodium cheese.) • Total carbohydrate 38 gm. = 13% • Dietary fiber = 0 • Protein 20 gm. = 35% • Calcium 316 mg. = 40%

Exchange Values: 2 bread/starch, 3 lean meat

SHRIMP CREOLE

1 Tbsp. margarine
1 medium onion, chopped
1 green pepper, chopped
1/2 c. chopped celery
8-oz. can tomato sauce
1 lb. peeled, deveined shrimp
1 Tbsp. Kikkoman® soy sauce
1 tsp. sugar

Melt margarine in a heavy skillet. Add onion, green pepper, and celery. Cook until vegetables are tender, but not browned, stirring occasionally. Mix in remaining ingredients, cover and simmer for 15 minutes. Serve hot over cooked rice or noodles. *Preparation time = 25 minutes.*

Nutrition Facts

Serving size = 1 cup • Servings per recipe = 4 • Calories = 209 • Calories from fat = 36

% Daily Value

Total fat 4 gm. = 6% • Saturated fat < 1 gm. = 3% • Cholesterol 174 mg. = 58% • Sodium 827 mg. = 28% (To reduce sodium, select reduced-sodium soy sauce.) • Total carbohydrate 14 gm. = 4% • Dietary fiber 4 gm. = 16% • Protein 26 gm. = 45% • Calcium 102 mg. = 13%

Exchange Values: 3 lean meat, 2 vegetable

SIRLOIN STRIPS SAUTÉ

1 tsp. instant beef bouillon
1 1/2 c. boiling water
1 Tbsp. vegetable oil
1 lb. boneless sirloin, cut into thin strips
4 oz. fresh mushrooms, thinly sliced
3 green onions, sliced fine
10 oz. frozen Bird's Eye® chopped broccoli, thawed
1 Tbsp. cornstarch
2 Tbsp. water

Dissolve bouillon in boiling water and set aside. Heat large skillet over medium heat and add oil. Stir in sirloin and brown on all sides. Add mushrooms and green onions and sauté for 2 minutes. Add broccoli and bouillon mixture. Simmer for 5 minutes, stirring occasionally. Dissolve cornstarch in cold water and stir into skillet mixture. Simmer stirring occasionally for three minutes or until slightly thick. Serve over rice or noodles. *Preparation time = 20 minutes.*

Nutrition Facts
Serving size = 8 oz. • Servings per recipe = 4 • Calories = 224 •
Calories from fat = 72

% Daily Value
Total fat 8 gm. = 12% • Saturated fat 2 gm. = 9% • Cholesterol 59 mg. =
20% • Sodium 287 mg. = 10% • Total carbohydrate 10 gm. = 3% • Dietary
fiber 0.7 gm. = 3% • Protein 28 gm. = 48% • Calcium 46 mg. = 6%

Exchange Values: 2 vegetable, 3 lean meat

SUGAR-CRUSTED HAM

1 lb. Wilson's® 99% Lean Ham, cut into 4 slices
1/4 c. brown sugar
2 Tbsp. horseradish
2 Tbsp. lemon juice

Score ham slices diagonally with a sharp knife, and place on a broiling pan or baking sheet. Combine brown sugar, horseradish, and lemon juice in a glass measuring cup. Microwave on 70% power for 2 minutes. Pour sauce over ham. Broil ham slices on "low" 6 inches from heating element for 10 minutes.

Preparation time = 10 minutes. Broiling Time = 10 minutes.

Nutrition Facts

Serving size = 4 oz. • Servings per recipe = 4 • Calories = 216 • Calories from fat = 11

% Daily Value

Total fat 6 gm. = 10% • Saturated fat 2 gm. = 10% • Cholesterol 60 mg. = 20% • Sodium 1368 mg. = 46% (To reduce sodium, select reduced-sodium ham.) • Total carbohydrate 15 gm. = 5% • Dietary fiber = 0 • Protein 24 gm. = 41% • Calcium 21 mg. = 3%

Exchange Values: 3 lean meat, 1 fruit

SUMMER GRILL

1 lb. raw shrimp or raw, cubed chicken
4 c. assorted fresh vegetables,
   cut into 1-inch chunks
1/2 c. La Choy® sweet and sour or teriyaki sauce

Thread shrimp or chicken with raw vegetable chunks onto 4 skewers. Grill for 6 minutes on each side, 6-inches from heating element. Brush with sauce twice during cooking.
Preparation time = 10 minutes. Grilling time = 6 minutes.

Nutrition Facts
Serving size = 2 cups • Servings per recipe = 4 • Calories = 294 •
Calories from fat = 15

% Daily Value
Total fat 2 gm. = 4% • Saturated fat < 1 gm. = 2% • Cholesterol 38 mg. =
13% • Sodium 889 mg. = 30% (To reduce sodium, replace 1/4 cup sauce
with 1/4 cup beer.) • Total carbohydrate 38 gm. = 13% • Dietary fiber 9 gm. =
36% • Protein 32 gm. = 56% • Calcium 126 mg. = 16%

Exchange Values: 4 lean meat, 2 vegetable, 1/2 fruit

SWEET 'N SALSA GRILLED CHOPS

4 4-oz. boneless pork chops, cut 1/2-inch thick
1/2 c. Chi Chi's® medium salsa
2 Tbsp. water
2 Tbsp. orange marmalade

Place chops in a plastic bag. In a glass measuring cup, combine salsa, water, and marmalade, blending well. Pour mixture over pork, turning to coat. Marinate for at least 30 minutes or up to overnight. When ready to grill, remove chops, reserving marinade. Place chops on grill 6 inches above medium-hot coals. Grill 5-7 minutes per side, basting with reserved marinade twice during cooking. *Preparation time = 5 minutes. Marinating time = 30 minutes. Grilling time = 15 minutes.*

Nutrition Facts
Serving size = 4 oz. • Servings per recipe = 4 • Calories = 231 •
Calories from fat = 90

% Daily Value
Total fat 10 gm. = 15% • Saturated fat 4 gm. = 19% • Cholesterol 79 mg. = 26% • Sodium 347 mg. = 12% • Total carbohydrate 8 gm. = 3% • Dietary fiber = 0 • Protein 24 gm. = 42% • Calcium 7 mg. = 1%

Exchange Values: 3 lean meat

SWEET 'N SALSA GRILLED CHICKEN

Substitute 4 skinless, boneless chicken breast halves for the pork chops in the preceding recipe. *Preparation time 5 = minutes. Marinating time = 30 minutes. Grilling time = 12 minutes.*

Nutrition Facts
Serving size = 4 oz. • Servings per recipe = 4 • Calories = 177 •
Calories from fat = 9

% Daily Value
Total fat 4 gm. = 6% • Saturated fat 1 gm. = 7% • Cholesterol 63 mg. = 21% • Sodium 347 mg. = 12% • Total carbohydrate 8 gm. = 3% • Dietary fiber = 0 • Protein 24 gm. = 42% • Calcium 7 mg. = 1%

Exchange Values: 3 lean meat

SWEET-AND-SOUR SAUCE FOR CHICKEN

1 c. Simply Fruit® apricot preserves
1 Tbsp. vinegar
1 Tbsp. lemon juice
2 tsp. soy sauce

Combine all ingredients in a 2-cup glass measuring cup. Microwave on high for 5 minutes, stirring once. Pour over boneless chicken breasts from the grill. *Preparation time = 10 minutes.*

Nutrition Facts
Serving size = 2 Tbsp. • Servings per recipe = 8 • Calories = 46 • Calories from fat = 3

% Daily Value
Total fat = 0 • Saturated fat = 0 • Cholesterol = 0 • Sodium 93 mg. = 3% • Total carbohydrate 13 gm. = 4% • Dietary fiber 0.3 gm. = 1% • Protein = 0 • Calcium 4 mg. = 1%

Exchange Values: 1 fruit

TACO PITA POCKETS

1 lb. lean ground pork
2/3 c. Chi Chi's® medium salsa
2 green onions, sliced
1 small zucchini, cut into julienne strips
1 red or green pepper, cut into julienne strips
4 large pita breads, halved

Accompaniments:
Shredded lettuce
Reduced-fat shredded cheese

Brown ground pork in a skillet and drain well. Stir in salsa, onions, zucchini, and pepper. Heat through. To serve, line each pita half with shredded lettuce, ladle meat-and-vegetable mixture into pocket and garnish with cheese. *Preparation time = 15 minutes.*

Nutrition Facts
Serving size = 1/2 pita + 1/2 cup filling • Servings per recipe = 8 •
Calories = 218 • Calories from fat = 63

% Daily Value
Total fat 7 gm. = 12% • Saturated fat 2 gm. = 12% • Cholesterol 40 mg. = 13% • Sodium 288 mg. = 13% • Total carbohydrate 23 gm. = 7% • Dietary fiber 3 gm. = 12% • Protein 16 gm. = 27% • Calcium 21 mg. = 2%

Exchange Values: 2 lean meat, 1 bread/starch, 1 vegetable

TERIYAKI MARINADE FOR CHICKEN, PORK OR BEEF

1/2 c. A-1® steak sauce
1/4 c. soy sauce
2 Tbsp. vegetable oil

Combine all ingredients in a plastic or glass container, stirring to mix. Use as a marinade with chicken, pork, or beef.
Preparation time = 10 minutes.

Nutrition Facts
Serving size = 2 Tbsp. • Servings per recipe = 8 • Calories = 36 • Calories from fat = 2

% Daily Value
Total fat 4 gm. = 6% • Saturated fat = 0 • Cholesterol = 0 • Sodium 474 mg. = 16% • Total carbohydrate = 0 • Dietary fiber = 0 • Protein 1 gm. = 2% • Calcium 2 mg. = < 1%

Exchange Values: 1 fat

Teriyaki Sirloin on the Grill

1 lb. lean sirloin, cut into 1-inch cubes
8 green onions, cut into 1-inch pieces
1/3 c. Kikkoman® teriyaki sauce
1/4 tsp. garlic powder
1 fresh tomato, cut into 4 wedges

Thread beef cubes and green onions on metal skewers. Combine teriyaki sauce and garlic in a small bowl. Grill beef and onions over medium heat for 6 to 9 minutes for medium doneness, brushing with sauce twice during grilling. Add tomatoes to the skewers the during last several minutes of cooking. Brush with sauce just before serving.

Preparation time = 10 minutes. Grilling time = 10 minutes.

Nutrition Facts
Serving size = 6 oz. • Servings per recipe = 4 • Calories = 191 •
Calories from fat = 40

% Daily Value
Total fat 4 gm. = 7% • Saturated fat 2 gm. = 7% • Cholesterol 59 mg. = 20% •
Sodium 926 mg. = 31% (To reduce sodium, select reduced-sodium teriyaki
sauce.) • Total carbohydrate 10 gm. = 3% • Dietary fiber 1 gm. = 4% •
Protein 27 gm. = 47% • Calcium 24 mg. = 3%

Exchange Values: 4 lean meat

TERIYAKI-ORANGE CHICKEN

1/3 c. Kikkoman® teriyaki sauce
1/4 c. orange juice
1 Tbsp. vegetable oil
Dash cayenne
1 Tbsp. sesame seeds
2 boneless, skinless chicken breasts, cut in half

Combine teriyaki sauce, orange juice, oil, cayenne, and sesame seeds in a small bowl. Broil chicken breasts on "low," 4-inches from heating element for about 12 minutes. Brush with sauce twice during cooking. *Preparation time = 20 minutes.*

Nutrition Facts
Serving size = 4 oz. • Servings per recipe = 4 • Calories = 219 •
Calories from fat = 72

% Daily Value
Total fat 8 gm. = 13% • Saturated fat = 0 • Cholesterol 73 mg. = 24% •
Sodium 931 mg. = 31% (To reduce sodium, select reduced-sodium teriyaki sauce.) • Total carbohydrate 6 gm. = 2% • Dietary fiber 0.5 gm. = 2% •
Protein 29 gm. = 50% • Calcium 25 mg. = 3%

Exchange Values: 4 lean meat

TUNA PATTIES

2 7-oz. cans Chicken of the Sea® water-packed tuna
3/4 c. whole-wheat bread crumbs
1 Tbsp. dried onion
1 Tbsp. chopped dried parsley
2 egg whites
1/4 tsp. dried mustard
1/4 tsp. paprika
1 tsp. vegetable oil

Drain tuna well, then combine with all ingredients, except oil, in a small bowl. Shape mixture into four patties. Brown patties in a nonstick skillet brushed with oil, about 4 minutes on each side. *Preparation time = 15 minutes.*

Nutrition Facts
Serving size = 6 oz. • Servings per recipe = 4 • Calories = 182 • Calories from fat = 27

% Daily Value
Total fat 3 gm. = 4% • Saturated fat < 1 gm. = 2% • Cholesterol 29 mg. = 10% • Sodium 447 mg. = 15% • Total carbohydrate 11 gm. = 4% • Dietary fiber 1 gm. = 4% • Protein 27 gm. = 47% • Calcium 30 mg. = 4%

Exchange Values: 3 lean meat, 1/2 bread

TUNA SPECIAL

2 7-oz. cans Chicken of the Sea® water-packed tuna
2 slices bread, crumbled
1 green pepper, diced
1/4 c. diced pimiento
1 medium onion, chopped fine
1 Tbsp. chopped parsley
1/2 tsp. garlic powder
1/3 c. chicken broth
2 tsp. lemon juice

Preheat oven to 400° F. Spread drained tuna in a shallow 1-quart baking dish. Cover with bread crumbs. Combine green pepper, pimiento, onion, parsley, and garlic powder; sprinkle over the tuna. Combine chicken broth with lemon juice and pour over the top. Bake for 20 minutes.
Preparation time = 10 minutes. Baking time = 20 minutes.

Nutrition Facts
Serving size = 6 oz. • Servings per recipe = 4 • Calories = 182 • Calories from fat = 18

% Daily Value
Total fat 2 gm. = 2% • Saturated fat < 1 gm. = 2% • Cholesterol 29 mg. = 10% • Sodium 409 mg. = 14% • Total carbohydrate 13 gm. = 4% • Dietary fiber 2 gm. = 8% • Protein 28 gm. = 48% • Calcium 40 mg. = 5%

Exchange Values: 3 lean meat, 1/2 bread/starch

VEGETABLE MEATLOAF

1 lb. lean ground beef
1/2 pkg. Knorr® vegetable soup mix
1/4 c. bread crumbs
1/3 c. skim milk

Preheat oven to 400° F. In a medium bowl, combine all ingredients, mixing well. Pat mixture into a draining meatloaf pan. (A draining meatloaf pan is an aluminum pan with holes in the bottom, set into another loaf-size pan. This allows all the meat fat to drip away from the meatloaf into the second pan.) Bake for 40 minutes. *Preparation time = 10 minutes. Baking time = 40 minutes.*

Nutrition Facts below

FRENCH ONION MEATLOAF

.

Substitute 1/2 package Lipton® french onion soup and recipe mix for the vegetable soup mix in the recipe above.
Preparation time = 10 minutes. Baking time = 40 minutes.

Nutrition Facts for both vegetable and french onion meatloaf
Serving size = 4 oz. • Servings per recipe = 4 • Calories = 203 • Calories from fat = 45

% Daily Value
Total fat 5 gm. = 32% • Saturated fat 2 gm. = 8% • Cholesterol 71 mg. = 24% • Sodium 445 mg. = 15% • Total carbohydrate 9 gm. = 3% • Dietary fiber 0.3 gm. = 1% • Protein 29 gm. = 50% • Calcium 52 mg. = 6%

Exchange Values: 4 lean meat

WESTERN STYLE BARBEQUE SAUCE FOR GRILLED MEATS

1 c. Light Western® dressing
2 Tbsp. Worcestershire sauce
1 Tbsp. honey
1 Tbsp. lemon juice
1/8 tsp. black pepper

Combine all ingredients in a glass or plastic container that has a lid. Use as a sauce for any grilled meat. *Preparation time = 10 minutes.*

Nutrition Facts
Serving size = 2 Tbsp. • Servings per recipe = 8 • Calories = 50 • Calories from fat = 3

% Daily Value
Total fat 2 gm. = 3% • Saturated fat = 0 • Cholesterol 2 mg. = 1% • Sodium 536 mg. = 8% • Total carbohydrate 9 gm. = 3% • Dietary fiber = 0 • Protein = 0 • Calcium 4 mg. = 5%

Exchange Values: 1 fruit

WHITE-FISH WITH WINE SAUCE

1 13-oz. can Campbell's® Healthy Request
cream of mushroom soup
1 1/2 tsp. Worcestershire sauce
1 Tbsp. lemon juice
1/4 tsp. prepared mustard
1/8 tsp. white pepper
4 drops Tabasco® sauce
2 Tbsp. skim milk
1/4 tsp. garlic powder
1 tsp. dried parsley
2 Tbsp. white wine
1 lb. whitefish fillets

Preheat oven to 400° F. Combine first all ingredients except fish, in a medium mixing bowl. Place fillets in a baking dish and pour the mushroom-wine sauce over fillets. Bake for 35 minutes or until fish flakes easily with a fork.

Preparation time = 10 minutes. Baking time = 35 minutes.

Nutrition Facts

Serving size = 6 oz. • Servings per recipe = 4 • Calories = 141 •
Calories from fat = 7

% Daily Value

Total fat 7 gm. = 11% • Saturated fat 1 gm. = 5% • Cholesterol = 0 • Sodium 590 mg. = 17% • Total carbohydrate 4 gm. = 1% • Dietary fiber = 0 • Protein 18 gm. = 31% • Calcium 95 mg. = 12%

Exchange Values: 3 lean meat

VEGETABLES

ASPARAGUS AND ALMONDS

1 lb. bunch fresh asparagus
2 tsp. margarine
1 Tbsp. lemon juice
2 Tbsp. Blue Diamond® slivered almonds, toasted
1/8 tsp. salt
1/8 tsp. pepper

Wash asparagus and cut into 1-inch diagonal slices. Heat margarine in a medium skillet over medium heat. Add asparagus and sauté for 4 minutes until tender-crisp. Toss asparagus with lemon juice, almonds, salt, and pepper. Serve with a meat-and-potatoes meal. *Preparation Time = 10 minutes.*

Nutrition Facts below

ZUCCHINI AND ALMONDS

Substitute 4 medium-sized zucchini, sliced thin, for asparagus in the above recipe. *Preparation time = 10 minutes.*

Nutrition Facts for both asparagus and zucchini and almonds
Serving size = 1 cup • Servings per recipe = 4 • Calories = 82 •
Calories from fat = 6

% Daily Value
Total fat 6 gm. = 9% • Saturated fat 1 gm. = 5% • Cholesterol = 0 • Sodium 103 mg. = 3% • Total carbohydrate 7 gm. = 2% • Dietary fiber 4.5 gm. = 18% • Protein 6 gm. = 11% • Calcium 64 mg. = 8%

Exchange Values: 1 vegetable, 1 fat

ASPARAGUS DELICIOUS

1 Tbsp. margarine
1 Tbsp. flour
1/8 tsp salt
1/4 tsp. dill seed
1/8 tsp. white pepper
1 c. skim milk
1 oz. Kraft® Healthy Favorites
   cheddar cheese, shredded
2 lb. fresh asparagus

Place margarine in a small mixing bowl and microwave for 15 seconds. Stir in flour, salt, dill seed, and pepper until smooth. Using a wisk, slowly add skim milk, mixing smooth. Microwave on 70 power for 3 minutes, stopping twice during cooking to wisk. Mixture will become thick. Stir in shredded cheese and cook 45 seconds more on high power. Remove from microwave oven, cover and set aside. Meanwhile, clean and cut asparagus. Place in a casserole serving dish, and cover with 1 Tbsp. water. Cover and microwave on high for 5 minutes. Remove from oven, drain off liquid, and top with cheese sauce. Serve at once. *Preparation time = 15 minutes.*

Nutrition Facts
Serving size = 1 cup • Servings per recipe = 8 • Calories = 59 • Calories from fat = 18

% Daily Value
Total fat 2 gm. = 3% • Saturated fat 1 gm. = 3% • Cholesterol 3 mg. = 1% • Sodium 76 mg. = 3% • Total carbohydrate 8 gm. = 3% • Dietary fiber = 4.5 gm. = 18% • Protein 6 gm. = 10 • Calcium 93 mg. = 12%

Exchange Values: 1 vegetable, 1/2 fat

BAKED CORN WITH SOUR CREAM AND JACK CHEESE

2 eggs or 1/2 c. liquid egg substitute
1 c. Land 'O Lakes® nonfat sour cream
16 oz. frozen whole kernel corn
1/2 c. bread crumbs
1 4-oz. can chopped green chilies
1/4 tsp. salt
1/4 tsp. pepper
2 oz. Kraft® Healthy Favorites
   Monterey Jack cheese, shredded

Preheat oven to 350° F. Spray a 10-inch quiche dish or 2-quart casserole dish with Pam®. Beat eggs and sour cream in a large bowl. Stir in corn, bread crumbs, chilies, salt, pepper, and shredded cheese. Pour into a prepared dish. Bake for 40 minutes, or until firm. *Preparation time = 10 minutes. Baking time = 40 minutes.*

Microwave Method: Once casserole is assembled, microwave on 70% power for 20 minutes, turning twice during cooking. May cut into wedges to serve. *Preparation time = 10 minutes. Microwave cooking time = 20 minutes.*

Nutrition Facts
Serving size = 3/4 cup • Servings per recipe = 8 • Calories = 132 • Calories from fat = 7

% Daily Value
Total fat 2 gm. = 4% • Saturated fat 1 gm. = 5% • Cholesterol 6 mg. = 2% with egg substitute • Cholesterol 59 mg. = 20% with real egg • Sodium 243 mg. = 8% • Total carbohydrate 21 gm. = 7% • Dietary fiber 0.3 gm. = 1% • Protein 9 gm. = 16% • Calcium 171 mg. = 22% (High in calcium)

Exchange Values: 1 vegetable, 1 bread/starch, 1/2 fat

BROCCOLI WITH WALNUTS

1/4 c. water
1 medium bunch broccoli, cut into florets
1/8 tsp. salt
2 Tbsp. chopped walnuts
1 Tbsp. I Can't Believe It's Not Butter® margarine

Measure 1/4 cup water in a large saucepan. Heat to boiling, then add broccoli and salt. Cover and reduce heat to low. Steam for 5 minutes. Drain and place in a serving bowl. In the same pan, cook walnuts in margarine over medium heat for 2 minutes or until golden brown. Pour over broccoli, toss, and serve. *Preparation time = 15 minutes.*

Nutrition Facts
Serving size = 1 cup • Servings per recipe = 4 • Calories = 88 •
Calories from fat = 54

% Daily Value
Total fat 6 gm. = 9% • Saturated fat 1 gm. = 4% • Cholesterol = 0 • Sodium 130 mg. = 4% • Total carbohydrate 8 gm. = 3% • Dietary fiber 4 gm. = 16% • Protein 7 gm. = 12% • Calcium 62 mg. = 8%

Exchange Values: 1 fat, 1 vegetable

CABBAGE-AND-POTATO PIE

4 slices bacon, cut into small pieces
2 Tbsp. I Can't Believe It's Not Butter® margarine
4 large potatoes, peeled and shredded
1/2 head cabbage, shredded
1/2 tsp. salt
1/4 tsp. pepper

Cook bacon in a large nonstick skillet over medium heat until crisp (about 5 minutes). Drain well and place cooked bacon on a paper towel. In the same large skillet, melt margarine. Add potatoes, cabbage, salt, and pepper to the skillet and mix well. Cover and cook over low heat for 10 minutes. Then remove cover and cook for 10 more minutes on medium-low heat. The bottom of the mixture will become crisp. Just before serving, sprinkle crisp bacon pieces over the top of the mixture. Transfer pie to a large round serving plate. Cut and serve. *Preparation time = 25 minutes.*

Nutrition Facts

Serving size = 1/8 pie • Servings per recipe = 8 wedges •
Calories = 103 • Calories from fat = 5

% Daily Value

Total fat 3 gm. = 5% • Saturated fat 1 gm. = 4% • Cholesterol 3 mg. = 1% •
Sodium 228 mg. = 8% • Total carbohydrate 17 gm. = 6% • Dietary fiber 3 gm. =
12% • Protein 3 gm. = 5% • Calcium 34 mg. = 4%

Exchange Values: 1 bread/starch, 1 fat

CALIFORNIA CARROTS

1 lb. carrots, peeled and cut into 1/4-inch thick slices
(about 2 1/2 cups)
1/4 c. water
Grated rind of 1/2 orange
1 orange, peeled, seeded, and cut into
bite-sized pieces
1 Tbsp. I Can't Believe It's Not Butter® margarine
1 Tbsp. chopped green onion

Place peeled carrots and water in a casserole dish. Cover and
microwave on high power for 7 minutes, stopping once during
cooking to stir. Meanwhile, melt margarine in a small skillet. Add
grated rind, orange pieces, and green onion. Cook for just 3 minutes. Drain carrots well, return to the casserole dish, pour oranges
over the top, toss and serve. *Preparation time = 20 minutes.*

Nutrition Facts

Serving size = 1 cup • Servings per recipe = 4 • Calories = 77 •
Calories from fat = 18

% Daily Value

Total fat 2 gm. = 3% • Saturated fat < 1 gm. = 1% • Cholesterol = 0 • Sodium
72 mg. = 2% • Total carbohydrate 15 gm. = 5% • Dietary fiber 4 gm. = 16% •
Protein 2 gm. = 3% • Calcium 43 mg. = 5%

Exchange Values: 2 vegetable, 1/2 fat

California Casserole

16 oz. frozen Bird's Eye®
  California-blend vegetables
1 13 oz. can Campbell's® Healthy Request
  cream of mushroom soup
1/4 c. Cheese Whiz®
1/4 c. skim milk

Place frozen vegetables in a microwave-safe casserole dish. Cover and microwave on high power for 6 minutes. Remove from oven and hold. Meanwhile, in a small mixing bowl, wisk together soup, cheese, and milk until mixture is smooth. Microwave on high power for 2 minutes. Pour over cooked vegetables and serve. *Preparation time = 15 minutes.*

Nutrition Facts
Serving size = 1 cup • Servings per recipe = 8 • Calories = 83 •
Calories from fat = 27

% Daily Value
Total fat 3 gm. = 5% • Saturated fat 1 gm. = 6% • Cholesterol 5 mg. = 2% •
Sodium 351 mg. = 12% • Total carbohydrate 10 gm. = 3% • Dietary fiber 2 gm.=
8% • Protein 3 gm. = 6% • Calcium 59 mg. = 8%

Exchange Values: 2 vegetable, 1/2 fat

CARROT CASSEROLE

2 slices bacon, diced fine
2 lb. fresh carrots
1/2 tsp. dry mustard
1/2 c. chopped green onion
1 13-oz. can Campbell's® Healthy Request
tomato soup

Cook diced bacon in a small skillet over medium-high heat until crisp. Drain bacon well on a paper towel. Meanwhile, peel carrots and slice into coins. Combine carrots, cooked bacon, mustard, green onion, and soup in a casserole dish. Microwave on high power for 14 to 16 minutes, until carrots are tender-crisp. Serve. *Preparation time = 20 minutes.*

Nutrition Facts below

GREEN BEAN CASSEROLE

Substitute 2 lb. fresh or frozen green beans for carrots in the recipe above. *Preparation time = 20 minutes.*

Nutrition Facts for both carrot and green bean casserole
Serving size = 1 cup • Servings per recipe = 8 • Calories = 82 •
Calories from fat = 4

% Daily Value
Total fat 2 gm. = 3% • Saturated fat < 1 gm. = 2% • Cholesterol 2 mg. = 1% •
Sodium 245 mg. = 8% • Total carbohydrate 16 gm. = 6% • Dietary fiber 4 gm.
= 16% • Protein 3 gm. = 4% • Calcium 36 mg. = 5%

Exchange Values: 2 vegetable, 1/2 fat

CARROT SAUTÉ

1/4 tsp. garlic powder
1 Tbsp. margarine
1 Tbsp. La Choy® soy sauce
1 1/2 tsp. water
1/2 tsp. sugar
1 lb. sliced fresh carrots
1/2 c. finely diced onion
1/2 c. sliced celery

In a large skillet, cook garlic in margarine for 1 minute over medium heat. Stir in soy sauce, water, and sugar. Bring mixture to a boil. Add carrots, onion, and celery. Reduce heat to medium-low and sauté until tender-crisp, about 8 minutes. Serve.
Preparation time = 15 minutes.

Nutrition Facts
Serving size = 1 cup • Servings per recipe = 4 • Calories = 78 •
Calories from fat = 4

% Daily Value
Total fat 2 gm. = 3% • Saturated fat < 1 gm. = 1% • Cholesterol = 0 • Sodium 348 mg. = 12% • Total carbohydrate 15 gm. = 5% • Dietary fiber 4 gm. = 16% • Protein 2 gm. = 4% • Calcium 46 mg. = 6%

Exchange Values: 2 vegetable, 1/2 fat

CARROTS ELEGANTE

1 lb. fresh carrots, thinly sliced
1/4 c. golden raisins
1 Tbsp. I Can't Believe It's Not Butter® margarine
3 Tbsp. honey
1 Tbsp. lemon juice
1/4 tsp. ground ginger
1/4 c. slivered almonds

Place carrots in a microwave-safe casserole dish. Sprinkle with 2 Tbsp. water. Cover and microwave on high power for 6 to 8 minutes, stopping once during cooking to stir. When carrots are tender-crisp, remove from microwave oven, drain well, cover again, and set aside. Meanwhile, in a small mixing bowl, combine raisins, margarine, honey, lemon juice, ginger, and almonds. Microwave raisin mixture on 70 power for 4 minutes. Pour over cooked carrots and serve. *Preparation time = 20 minutes.*

Nutrition Facts
Serving size 3/4 cup • Servings per recipe = 8 • Calories = 112 • Calories from fat = 36

% Daily Value
Total fat 4 gm. = 7% • Saturated fat < 1 gm. = 2% • Cholesterol = 0 • Sodium 35 mg. = 1% • Total carbohydrate 18 gm. = 6% • Dietary fiber 2 gm. = 8% • Protein 2 gm. = 4% • Calcium 38 mg. = 4%

Exchange Values: 1 vegetable, 1 fat, 1/2 fruit

CHEESY ITALIAN
POTATOES

6 medium potatoes
Pam® nonstick cooking spray
1/4 c. Kraft® Parmesan cheese
1/8 tsp. garlic powder
1/8 tsp. onion powder
1/2 tsp. Italian seasoning

Cut each potato lengthwise into 8 wedges. Spray potato surfaces with Pam®. Combine cheese and seasonings in a small plastic bag. Add potato wedges to the bag and shake to coat. Arrange potato slices in layers in a microwave-safe baking dish. Cover and microwave on high power for 15 minutes, rotating dish twice during cooking. Serve with red meats. *Preparation time = 5 minutes. Microwave cooking time = 15 minutes.*

Nutrition Facts
Serving size = 3/4 cup • Servings per recipe = 8 • Calories = 120 •
Calories from fat = 6

% Daily Value
Total fat 3 gm. = 4% • Saturated fat 2 gm. = 6% • Cholesterol 8 mg. = 3% •
Sodium 113 mg. = 4% • Total carbohydrate 21 gm. = 7% • Dietary fiber 2 gm. =
8% • Protein 5 gm. = 8% • Calcium 108 mg. = 14%

Exchange Values: 1 bread/starch, 1 fat

CITRUS-GLAZED BRUSSELS SPROUTS

16 oz. frozen Bird's Eye® brussels sprouts
2 Tbsp. chopped pecans
1 Tbsp. margarine
1/4 tsp. salt
3 Tbsp. lemon juice
2 Tbsp. orange juice
3 Tbsp. chopped fresh parsley
1 Tbsp. finely sliced green onions

Place Brussels sprouts in a microwave-safe baking dish and sprinkle with 1/4 cup water. Cover and microwave on high power for 8 minutes. Meanwhile, heat margarine in a large skillet over high heat. Add pecans and cook over low heat for 1 minute. Add cooked sprouts, salt, lemon juice, orange juice, chopped parsley, and onions. Toss and cook over medium heat for 2 minutes. Serve. *Preparation time = 15 minutes.*

Nutrition Facts
Serving size = 3/4 cup • Servings per recipe = 8 • Calories = 57 • Calories from fat = 36

% Daily Value
Total fat 4 gm. = 6% • Saturated fat < 1 gm. = 2% • Cholesterol = 0 • Sodium 96 mg. = 3% • Total carbohydrate 6 gm. = 2% • Dietary fiber 2 gm. = 8% • Protein 3 gm. = 4% • Calcium 19 mg. = 3%

Exchange Values: 1 vegetable, 1/2 fat

CONFETTI CORN

4 medium tomatoes
1 Tbsp. margarine
1/3 c. chopped green onion
1/3 c. chopped red pepper
10 oz. Bird's Eye® frozen whole-kernel corn
2 Tbsp. vinegar
2 Tbsp. chopped fresh cilantro (optional)
1/4 tsp. garlic salt

Cut 1/4 inch off top of tomatoes and hollow out, reserving pulp. Chop tomato pulp into bite-sized chunks and set aside. In a medium skillet, melt margarine and sauté green onion and bell pepper. Add corn, vinegar, tomato pulp, optional cilantro, and garlic salt. Blend well. Heat for 5 minutes or until flavors are blended. Spoon corn mixture into tomato shells and serve.
Preparation time = 20 minutes.

Nutrition Facts
Serving size = 1 cup • Servings per recipe = 4 • Calories = 106 • Calories from fat = 5

% Daily Value
Total fat 2 gm. = 3% • Saturated fat < 1 gm. = 2% • Cholesterol = 0 • Sodium 181 mg. = 6% • Total carbohydrate 23 gm. = 7% • Dietary fiber 2 gm. = 8% • Protein 3 gm. = 6% • Calcium 13 mg. = 2%

Exchange Values: 1 bread/starch, 1 vegetable

CORN AND TOMATO CASSEROLE

16-oz. frozen Bird's Eye® whole-kernel corn
14-oz. can Del Monte® chopped tomatoes,
   drained well
1 tsp. Italian seasoning
1/2 c. bread crumbs
1/4 c. grated Parmesan cheese
1 Tbsp. margarine, melted

Preheat oven to 400° F. Combine corn and tomatoes in a 3-quart casserole dish. Stir in Italian seasonings. In a small mixing bowl, combine bread crumbs, cheese, and margarine until well-blended. Sprinkle over corn and tomatoes. Bake for 20 minutes. Serve. *Preparation time = 10 minutes. Baking time = 20 minutes.*

Nutrition Facts
Serving size = 3/4 cup • Servings per recipe = 8 • Calories = 121 • Calories from fat = 27

% Daily Value
Total fat 3 gm. = 5% • Saturated fat 2 gm. = 7% • Cholesterol 7 mg. = 2% • Sodium 265 mg. = 9% • Total carbohydrate 19 gm. = 6% • Dietary fiber 2 gm. = 8% • Protein 6 gm. = 10% • Calcium 130 mg. = 26% (High in calcium)

Exchange Values: 1 vegetable, 1 bread/starch, 1/2 fat

CREAMY BROCCOLI BAKE

1 large bunch of fresh broccoli
10-oz. can Campbell's® Healthy Request
  cream of mushroom soup
1/4 c. skim milk
2 oz. Kraft Healthy Favorites®
  cheddar cheese, shredded
1/2 c. Light Bisquick® baking mix
2 Tbsp. margarine, melted

Preheat oven to 400° F. Clean broccoli and chop into small pieces. Place in a 3-quart microwave-safe baking dish, sprinkle with 2 Tbsp. water, and cover. Microwave on high power for 6 to 8 minutes until tender crisp. Meanwhile, wisk together soup and skim milk in a small bowl. Drain broccoli well and pour soup mixture over the top. Sprinkle with shredded cheese. Mix melted margarine with Light Bisquick® and sprinkle over the cheese. Bake for 15 minutes or until top of casserole is browned. *Preparation time = 25 minutes.*

Nutrition Facts
Serving size = 3/4 cup • Servings per recipe = 8 • Calories = 129 • Calories from fat = 7

% Daily Value
Total fat 5 gm. = 7% • Saturated fat 2 gm. = 7% • Cholesterol 4 mg. = 2% • Sodium 239 mg. = 8% • Total carbohydrate 20 gm. = 7% • Dietary fiber 3 gm. = 10% • Protein 7 gm. = 12% • Calcium 121 mg. = 15%

Exchange Values: 2 vegetable, 1/2 bread/starch, 1/2 skim milk

FRESH CORN ON THE GRILL

2 tsp. grated lemon rind
1 Tbsp. La Choy® soy sauce
2 Tbsp. vegetable oil
1/4 tsp. garlic powder
1/4 tsp. black pepper
8 ears of corn, husks removed

Combine lemon rind, soy sauce, oil, garlic and pepper. Pour over corn in a shallow baking dish or pan. Cover and refrigerate for at least 30 minutes or as long as overnight. Wrap each ear of corn in foil, twisting foil ends to seal. Cook directly over medium-hot coals on grill for 30 minutes, turning several times.

Preparation time = 10 minutes. Marinating time = 30 minutes. Grilling time = 30 minutes.

Nutrition Facts

Serving size = 1 ear • Servings per recipe = 8 • Calories = 92 • Calories from fat = 5

% Daily Value

Total fat 4 gm. = 6% • Saturated fat < 1 gm. = 2% • Cholesterol = 0 • Sodium 129 mg. = 5% • Total carbohydrate = 0 • Dietary fiber 2 gm. = 8% • Protein 2 gm. = 5% • Calcium 3 mg. = 1%

Exchange Values: 1 bread/starch, 1/2 fat

Glazed Acorn Squash

4 small acorn squash
1/4 c. Brer Rabbit® molasses
1/4 tsp. salt
1 Tbsp. finely grated orange rind
1 Tbsp. melted margarine

Preheat oven to 375° F. Wash squash and halve lengthwise; remove seeds and stringy portion. Place squash, cut side down, in a shallow baking pan sprayed with Pam®. Bake at 375° for 30 minutes or microwave on high power for 15 minutes. Remove squash from oven; turn right side up. Combine remaining ingredients in a small mixing bowl and divide it among the halves. Return the squash to the oven and bake for 30 minutes longer or microwave on high power for 10 more minutes, or until squash is tender. Cooking time varies with thickness of squash.

Preparation time = 10 minutes. Conventional baking time = 60 minutes. Microwave cooking time = 25 minutes.

Nutrition Facts
Serving size = 1/2 squash • Servings per recipe = 8 • Calories = 95 • Calories from fat = 5

% Daily Value
Total fat 1 gm. = 2% • Saturated fat < 1 gm. = 1% • Cholesterol = 0 • Sodium 91 mg. = 3% • Total carbohydrate 23 gm. = 8% • Dietary fiber 1 gm. = 4% • Protein 2 gm. = 2% • Calcium 70 mg. = 9%

Exchange Values: 1 vegetable, 1 bread/starch

GREEN BEANS RISI

1 Tbsp. margarine, melted
16 oz. frozen Bird's Eye® French-style green beans
2 c. cooked rice
3 green onions, chopped fine
2 tsp. lemon juice
1/4 tsp. pepper
1/4 c. chopped pimientos

Melt margarine in a large skillet over medium heat. Add thawed beans, cooked rice, scallions, lemon juice and pepper. Cook, stirring until heated through. Spoon into a serving dish and garnish with pimiento. *Preparation time = 15 minutes.*

Nutrition Facts
Serving size = 3/4 cup • Servings per recipe = 8 • Calories = 128 • Calories from fat = 7

% Daily Value
Total fat 1 gm. = 2% • Saturated fat < 1 gm. = 1% • Cholesterol = 0 • Sodium 21 mg. = 1% • Total carbohydrate = 0 • Dietary fiber 2 gm. = 8% • Protein 5 gm. = 8% • Calcium 30 mg. = 4%

Exchange Values: 2 vegetable, 1 bread/starch

JANE'S AFRICAN VEGETABLE MIX

My friend, Jane Seibrecht, won approval with this dish prepared for a traditional African dinner.

16 oz. frozen whole-kernel corn
16 oz. frozen okra
14-oz. can Del Monte® chopped tomatoes, well drained
1 Tbsp. sugar
1 tsp. salt
1/2 tsp. pepper

Combine all ingredients in a 3-quart casserole dish. Stir to mix well. Microwave on high power for 10 to 12 minutes, until vegetables are cooked through. *Preparation time = 15 minutes.*

Nutrition Facts
Serving size = 3/4 cup • Servings per recipe = 8 • Calories = 83 • Calories from fat = 4

% Daily Value
Total fat < 1 gm. = 1% • Saturated fat = 0 • Cholesterol = 0 • Sodium 352 mg. = 12% • Total carbohydrate 20 gm. = 7% • Dietary fiber 2 gm. = 8% • Protein 4 gm. = 6% • Calcium 71 mg. = 9%

Exchange Values: 2 vegetable, 1/2 bread/starch

LOW-FAT HASH BROWNS

14 oz.-pkg. Betty Crocker® hash brown potatoes
4 c. very hot tap water
1/4 tsp. salt
Pam® cooking spray

Cover potatoes with water in a 2 1/2-quart bowl. Stir in salt and let stand uncovered for 10 minutes. Drain well. Spray a 10-inch skillet generously with Pam®. Over medium heat, spread potatoes firmly and evenly in the skillet. Cook uncovered, without turning or stirring for 10 minutes. Spray the top of the mixture generously with Pam®. Turn the mixture with a spatula and cook until the bottom is brown, (about 3 more minutes). Cut into four wedges and serve. *Preparation time = 25 minutes.*

Nutrition Facts
Serving size = 1 wedge • Servings per recipe = 4 • Calories = 165 • Calories from fat = 9

% Daily Value
Total fat 1 gm. = 2% • Saturated fat = 0 • Cholesterol = 0 • Sodium 160 mg. = 5% • Total carbohydrate 36 gm. = 12% • Dietary fiber = 0 • Protein 3 gm. = 5% • Calcium = 0

Exchange Values: 2 bread/starch

NEW ORLEANS GREEN BEANS

1 c. chopped onion
1 Tbsp. vegetable oil
14 oz.-can Del Monte® chopped tomatoes, drained
16 oz. frozen green beans
1/2 tsp. basil
1/2 tsp. tarragon
1/4 tsp. salt
1/4 tsp. pepper

In a medium saucepan, sauté onion in oil until tender. Add all remaining ingredients and cook on medium-low heat until beans are tender. *Preparation time = 20 minutes.*

Nutrition Facts
Serving size = 3/4 cup • Servings per recipe = 8 • Calories = 45 • Calories from fat = 18

% Daily Value
Total fat 2 gm. = 3% • Saturated fat = 0 • Cholesterol = 0 • Sodium 82 mg. = 3% • Total carbohydrate 10 gm. = 3% • Dietary fiber 1.3 gm. = 5% • Protein 1 gm. = 2% • Calcium 30 mg. = 4%

Exchange Values: 2 vegetable

ONION ROASTED POTATOES

1 envelope Lipton® onion soup mix
4 large potatoes, cut into large chunks
2 Tbsp. vegetable oil

Preheat oven to 450 °F. In a large plastic bag, add all ingredients. Close the bag and shake to cover potatoes with soup mix and oil. Empty potatoes into a shallow baking pan. Bake for 40 minutes, until potatoes are tender.

Nutrition Facts
Serving size = 1/2 cup • Servings per recipe = 8 • Calories = 95 •
Calories from fat = 13

% Daily Value
Total fat 2 gm. = 3% • Saturated fat < 1 gm. = 1% • Cholesterol 3 mg. = 1% •
Sodium 339 mg. = 12% • Total carbohydrate 15 gm. = 5% • Dietary fiber
1 gm. = 4% • Protein 2 gm. = 3% • Calcium 9 mg. = 1%

Exchange Values: 1 bread/starch

OVEN-BAKED
THYME CARROTS

This dish goes great with baked fish.

1 16-oz. pkg. Bird's Eye® frozen
   whole baby carrots
2 tsp. dried thyme
1/2 c. water
1/4 tsp. salt
1 Tbsp. margarine
1 Tbsp. lemon juice
1/4 tsp. black pepper

Preheat oven to 400° F. Combine carrots, thyme, water, and salt
in a 13-by-9 inch baking pan. Cover tightly with aluminum foil.
Bake for 30 minutes. Drain, toss with margarine, lemon juice, and
pepper, and serve.
Preparation time = 10 minutes. Baking Time = 30 minutes

Nutrition Facts
Serving size = 1/2 cup • Servings per recipe = 8 • Calories = 35 •
Calories from fat = 2

% Daily Value
Total fat 1 gm. = 2% • Saturated fat = 0 • Cholesterol = 0 • Sodium 104 mg. =
4% • Total carbohydrate 6 gm. = 2% • Dietary fiber 2 gm. = 8% • Protein
1 gm. = 1% • Calcium 15 mg. = 2%

Exchange Values: 1 vegetable

POTATOES WITH WHITE WINE

16 new potatoes
1/2 tsp. salt
1/4 tsp. pepper
1/2 c. dry white wine
2 Tbsp. I Can't Believe It's Not Butter® margarine

Scrub potatoes, cut into 1/4-inch slices, and place in a large saucepan with cold water to cover. Bring to a boil and simmer for 15 minutes being careful not to overcook. Meanwhile, combine salt, pepper, wine, and margarine in a glass measuring cup. Microwave on 50% power for 2 minutes. Drain potatoes, transfer to a serving bowl, pour wine mixture over them, and serve. *Preparation time = 10 minutes. Cooking time = 20 minutes.*

Nutrition Facts
Serving size = 3/4 cup • Servings per recipe = 8 • Calories = 124 • Calories from fat = 3

% Daily Value
Total fat < 1 gm. = 1% • Saturated fat = 0 • Cholesterol = 0 • Sodium 148 mg. = 5% • Total carbohydrate 27 gm. = 9% • Dietary fiber 1 gm. = 4% • Protein 2 gm. = 4% • Calcium 8 mg. = 1%

Exchange Values: 1 1/2 bread/starch

SAVORY GRILLED POTATOES

1/3 c. Kraft® Free (mayonnaise-type) salad dressing
1/2 tsp. garlic powder
1/2 tsp. paprika
1/4 tsp. salt
1/4 tsp. pepper
4 large baking potatoes, cut into 1/4-inch slices
1 c. chopped onion

Mix salad dressing and seasonings in a large bowl until well blended. Stir in potatoes and onions to coat. Divide potato mixture evenly among 8 12-inch squares of foil. Seal each to form a packet. Place foil packets on the grill over medium heat for 25 minutes, until potatoes are tender. *Preparation time = 10 minutes. Grilling time = 25 minutes.*

Nutrition Facts
Serving size = 1/2 cup • Servings per recipe = 8 • Calories = 75 • Calories from fat = 9

% Daily Value
Total fat 1 gm. = 2% • Saturated fat = 0 • Cholesterol = 0 • Sodium 140 mg. = 5% • Total carbohydrate 17 gm. = 6% • Dietary fiber 2 gm. = 8% • Protein 2 gm. = 3% • Calcium 11 mg. = 2%

Exchange Values: 1 bread/starch

Spinach Soufflé

16 oz. frozen chopped spinach
3 Tbsp. flour
3 eggs, beaten, or 3/4 c. liquid egg substitute
1 c. 1% fat cottage cheese
2 oz. Kraft® Healthy Favorites cheddar cheese,
shredded

Preheat oven to 400° F. Thaw spinach and drain thoroughly. In a large mixing bowl, mix spinach with flour to coat. Add eggs, salt, cheese, add cottage cheese and stir well. Place mixture in a 3-quart baking dish sprayed with Pam®. Bake for 45 minutes or cook in the microwave.

Microwave Method: Cook on high power for 22 minutes. *Preparation time = 15 minutes. Conventional baking time = 45 minutes. Microwave cooking time = 22 minutes.*

Nutrition Facts
Serving size = 3/4 cup • Servings per recipe = 8 • Calories = 92 • Calories from fat = 18

% Daily Value
Total fat 2 gm. = 4% • Saturated fat 1.0 gm. = 6% • Cholesterol 6 mg. = 2% with egg substitute • Cholesterol 86 mg. = 27% with real egg • Sodium 219 mg. = 8% • Total carbohydrate 9 gm. = 3% • Dietary fiber 2 gm. = 8% • Protein 11 gm. = 19% • Calcium 149 mg. = 19%

Exchange Values: 2 vegetable, 1/2 skim milk

SQUASH CASSEROLE

2 10-oz. pkg. frozen squash
1 Tbsp. I Can't Believe It's Not Butter® margarine
1/2 c. chopped onion
4 oz. seasoned croutons for stuffing
2 Tbsp. walnuts
2 Tbsp. chopped parsley

Preheat oven to 375° F. Remove squash from package and place in a shallow microwave-safe baking dish. Cover and microwave 7 minutes on high power. Meanwhile, in a large skillet, melt margarine and sauté onion until tender. Add the croutons, walnuts, and parsley, blending well. When squash is cooked, use a spoon to spread it evenly over the baking dish. Sprinkle crouton mixture over the top. Bake for 15 minutes and serve.

Preparation time = 15 minutes. Baking time = 15 minutes.

Nutrition Facts
Serving size = 6 oz. • Servings per recipe = 4 • Calories = 155 •
Calories from fat = 8

% Daily Value
Total fat 7 gm. = 11% • Saturated fat 1 gm. = 4% • Cholesterol = 0 • Sodium
433 mg. = 14% • Total carbohydrate 21 gm. = 7% • Dietary fiber 3 gm. =
12% • Protein 5 gm. = 8% • Calcium 65 mg. = 8%

Exchange Values: 1 1/2 bread/starch, 1 fat

Sweet and Sour Cabbage

1 11-oz. can Dole® mandarin orange segments
6 c. shredded cabbage
1/2 c. chopped onion
1/4 tsp. garlic powder
1 Tbsp. vegetable oil
1/4 c. white-wine vinegar
1 tsp. caraway seeds
1/4 tsp. salt
1 c. Dole® pineapple chunks

Drain oranges and reserve syrup. In a large skillet, sauté cabbage, onion, and garlic in oil until onion is soft. Stir in reserved syrup, vinegar, caraway seeds, and salt. Cover and simmer for 10 minutes. Stir in pineapple and oranges, continuing to heat for 3 minutes just to warm through. Serve with pork. *Preparation time = 25 minutes.*

Nutrition Facts
Serving size = 1 cup • Servings per recipe = 8 • Calories = 78 •
Calories from fat = 27

% Daily Value
Total fat 3 gm. = 4% • Saturated fat = 0 • Cholesterol = 0 • Sodium 81 mg. = 3% • Total carbohydrate 10.3 gm. = 1% • Protein 2 gm. = 4% • Dietary fiber 4.5 gm. = 18% • Calcium 60 mg. = 8%

Exchange Values: 1 vegetable, 1/2 fruit, 1/2 fat

YAM-BROSIA

17-oz. can vacuum-packed sweet potatoes, sliced
2 bananas, sliced
2 Tbsp. light corn syrup
2 Tbsp. I Can't Believe It's Not Butter® margarine
3 Tbsp. orange juice
1 tsp. Worcestershire sauce
1/4 tsp. salt
1/3 c. flaked coconut

Preheat oven to 375° F. In a 2-quart casserole, alternate layers of sweet potatoes and bananas. Set aside. In a small saucepan, combine all remaining ingredients, except coconut. Heat until margarine is melted. Pour over potato mixture. Cover and bake for 20 minutes. Remove cover, sprinkle with coconut, and bake 10 more minutes. This tastes best as a side dish with ham.

Preparation time = 10 minutes. Baking time = 30 minutes.

Nutrition Facts
Serving size = 3/4 cup • Servings per recipe = 8 • Calories = 180 • Calories from fat = 54

% Daily Value
Total fat 6 gm. = 8% • Saturated fat 4 gm. = 21% • Cholesterol = 0 • Sodium 61 mg. = 8% • Total carbohydrate 30 gm. = 10% • Dietary fiber 3 gm. = 12% • Protein 2 gm. = 4% • Calcium 30 mg. = 3%

Exchange Values: 1 bread/starch, 1 fruit, 1 fat

Zucchini-Carrot Sauté

1 1/2 c. shredded, pared carrots
1/2 c. sliced scallions
1 Tbsp. margarine
3 c. shredded zucchini
1/4 tsp. salt
1 Tbsp. ReaLemon® lemon juice

Sauté carrots and onions in melted margarine in a large skillet over medium heat for 3 minutes. Add zucchini and salt. Cook for 3 minutes more. Sprinkle with lemon juice and serve.
Preparation time = 15 minutes.

Nutrition Facts
Serving size = 3/4 cup • Servings per recipe = 8 • Calories = 35 • Calories from fat = 2

% Daily Value
Total fat 1 gm. = 2% • Saturated fat = 0 • Cholesterol = 0 • Sodium 95 mg. = 2% • Total carbohydrate 7 gm. = 2% • Dietary fiber 1 gm. = 4% • Protein 2 gm. = 3% • Calcium 24 mg. = 3%

Exchange Values: 1 vegetable

DESSERTS

ANGEL FOOD AND PINEAPPLE REFRIGERATED DESSERT

2 3-oz. pkg. cook-and-serve vanilla pudding mix
2 c. skim milk
1 1/2 c. Dole® pineapple juice
1/4 c. raisins
8 oz. reduced-fat whipped topping, thawed
1 8-oz. can crushed pineapple
1 prepared angel food cake
1/2 c. Simply Fruit® raspberry preserves
2 Tbsp. almonds

Cook pudding with milk and pineapple juice according to package directions. Cool. Stir raisins and whipped topping into the pudding. Cut cake into 1-inch chunks. Pour 1 cup of pudding mixture into a 3-quart glass bowl. Top with half of each: cake, preserves, drained pineapple, and pudding. Repeat layers and chill at least 20 minutes. Garnish with almonds.

Preparation time = 20 minutes. Chilling time = 20 minutes.

Nutrition Facts
Serving size = 1/12 wedge from bowl • Servings per recipe = 12 •
Calories = 240 • Calories from fat = 36

% Daily Value
Total fat 4 gm. = 6% • Saturated fat 2 gm. = 6% • Cholesterol = 0 • Sodium 289 mg. = 10% • Total carbohydrate 48 gm. = 16% • Dietary fiber 1 gm. = 4% • Protein 6 gm. = 10% • Calcium 118 mg. = 15%

Exchange Values: 1 fruit, 1 skim milk, 1 bread/starch

ANNIE'S FRUIT DIP

When you want dessert time to last and last, use this!
The recipe is from Annie Cull.

> 3 oz. Philadelphia® Free cream cheese
> 7 oz. marshmallow creme
> 1/4 tsp. lemon extract
> 2 drops red food coloring
> 4 c. prepared fresh fruits for dipping, such as pears, apples, oranges, grapes, and bananas

Place cream cheese and marshmallow creme in a 1 1/2-quart bowl. Microwave on 50% power for 2 minutes. Stir. Repeat cooking and stir smooth. Fold in lemon extract and food coloring and transfer to a serving bowl. Refrigerate until serving time. Prepare assorted fresh fruits for dipping. Soak bananas, apples, and pears in chilled orange juice to prevent browning. Provide toothpicks for fruit dippers. *Preparation time = 15 minutes.*

Nutrition Facts
Serving size = 1/2 cup fruit + 1/8 cup dip • Servings per recipe = 8 • Calories = 154 • Calories from fat = 6

% Daily Value
Total fat 1 gm. = 1% • Saturated fat = 0 • Cholesterol 2 mg. = 6% • Sodium 31 mg. = 1% • Total carbohydrate 39 gm. = 13% • Dietary fiber 2 gm. = 8% • Protein 1 gm. = 2% • Calcium 39 mg. = 5%

Exchange Values: 2 1/2 fruit

APPLE PIE
FOR MORGAN

Adapted from a recipe loved by Morgan Nederhizer.

4 c. sliced tart apples, pared
1 1/4 tsp. cinnamon
1/4 tsp. nutmeg
3/4 c. skim milk
2 eggs or 1/2 c. liquid egg substitute
1/2 c. sugar
1/2 c. Light Bisquick® baking mix

Streusel Topping:

1/2 c. Light Bisquick® baking mix
2 Tbsp. chopped nuts
1/4 c. brown sugar
1 Tbsp. margarine

Preheat oven to 375° F. Mix apples and spices together in a 10-inch pie pan sprayed with Pam®. Beat milk, eggs, sugar and 1/2 c. baking mix until smooth. Pour over apples. Mix ingredients for streusel in a small bowl until crumbly. Sprinkle on top of pie. Bake for 1 hour, until a knife inserted in the center comes out clean. *Preparation time = 20 minutes. Baking time = 60 minutes.*

Nutrition Facts
Serving size = 1/12 pie • Servings per recipe = 12 • Calories = 188 • Calories from fat = 36

% Daily Value
Total fat 3 gm. = 5% • Saturated fat < 1 gm. = 2% • Cholesterol = 0 with egg substitute • Cholesterol 36 mg. = 12% with real egg • Sodium 63 mg. = 2% • Total carbohydrate 42 gm. = 14% • Dietary fiber 2 gm. = 8% • Protein 5 gm. = 9% • Calcium 38 mg.= 5%

Exchange Values: 1 1/2 bread/starch, 1 fruit

Baked Peach Pudding

4 peaches, peeled, pitted, and sliced
4 Tbsp. sugar, divided
2 c. Carnation® evaporated skimmed milk
3 eggs or 3/4 c. liquid egg substitute
1/4 c. flour
1/2 tsp. almond extract
1/2 tsp. vanilla

Sauce:

1/3 c. sugar
2 Tbsp. cornstarch
2/3 c. water
2 Tbsp. orange juice
1 Tbsp. lemon juice

Preheat oven to 375° F. In an 8-inch round baking dish, combine peaches with 2 Tbsp. sugar, mixing well. In a blender, combine 2 Tbsp. sugar, milk, eggs, flour, almond extract and vanilla. Cover and blend for 15 seconds. Pour over fruit. Bake for 40 minutes or until a knife inserted in the center comes out clean. While pie is baking, prepare sauce. Whisk together sugar, cornstarch, water, orange, and lemon juice in a 1-quart bowl until smooth. Microwave on 70% power for 4 minutes, stopping twice to stir. Pour warm sauce over slices of baked peach pudding. *Preparation time = 20 minutes. Baking time = 40 minutes.*

Nutrition Facts

Serving size = 1/8 pie • Servings per recipe = 8 • Calories = 175 • Calories from fat = 9

% Daily Value

Total fat 1 gm. = 2% • Saturated fat = 0 • Cholesterol 2 mg. = 1% with egg substitute • Cholesterol 80 mg. = 27% with real egg • Sodium 108 mg. = 4% • Total carbohydrate 36 gm. = 12% • Dietary fiber 1.5 gm. = 6% • Protein 9 gm. = 15% • Calcium 182 mg.= 23%

Exchange Values: 1 1/2 bread/starch, 1 fruit

BAKED APPLE PUDDING

Substitute 4 apples for the peaches in the previous recipe. Substitute 3 Tbsp. apple juice for the orange and lemon juice in the sauce. *Preparation time = 20 minutes. Baking time = 40 minutes.*

Nutrition Facts
Serving size = 1/8th pie • Servings per recipe = 8 • Calories = 175 • Calories from fat = 9

% Daily Value
Total fat 1 gm. = 2% • Saturated fat = 0 • Cholesterol 2 mg. = 1% • Sodium 108 mg. = 4% • Total carbohydrate 36 gm. = 12% • Dietary fiber 0.5 gm. = 2% • Protein 9 gm. = 15% • Calcium 182 mg. = 23% (High in calcium)

Exchange Values: 1 1/2 bread/starch, 1 fruit

BANANA BUNDT® CAKE WITH PINEAPPLE

1 Pillsbury® Lovin' Lites yellow cake mix
1 c. mashed bananas
1 c. crushed pineapple, drained well

Preheat oven to 350° F. Mix ingredients until smooth. Pour into a Bundt® pan sprayed with Pam®. Bake for 45 minutes or until cake tests done with a toothpick. Remove cake from pan, slice, and top with rainbow sherbet.
Preparation time = 10 minutes. Baking time = 45 minutes.

Nutrition Facts
Serving size = 1/12 cake • Servings per recipe = 12 • Calories = 97 • Calories from fat = 5

% Daily Value
Total fat 1 gm. = 1% • Saturated fat = 0 • Cholesterol = 0 • Sodium 212 mg. = 7% • Total carbohydrate 22 gm. = 7% • Dietary fiber 1 gm. = 4% • Protein 2 gm. = 3% • Calcium 42 mg. = 5%

Exchange Values: 1 bread/starch, 1/2 fruit

BERRY CHOCOLATE PIE

1 regular or deep-dish pie crust, baked empty
   according to package instructions
1/3 c. milk-chocolate chips
1 Tbsp. skim milk
1 tsp. vanilla
1 qt. Kemps® nonfat strawberry frozen yogurt

In a medium microwave-safe bowl, combine chocolate chips and milk. Microwave on 50% power for 1 minute, stopping once to stir. Stir in vanilla. Pour chocolate into baked pie crust and place in the freezer for at least 15 minutes. Soften frozen yogurt and spoon over chocolate layer. Freeze until firm, at least 30 minutes. Garnish with slices of fresh berries. Slice into 12 pieces. *Preparation time = 15 minutes. Chilling time = 45 minutes.*

Nutrition Facts
Serving size = 1/12 pie • Servings per recipe = 12 • Calories = 205 • Calories from fat = 16

% Daily Value
Total fat 9 gm. = 14% • Saturated fat 4 gm. = 18% • Cholesterol 2 mg. = 1% • Sodium 133 mg. = 5% • Total carbohydrate 28 gm. = 9% • Dietary fiber = 0 • Protein 4 gm. = 6% • Calcium 110 mg. = 14%

Exchange Values: 1 bread/starch, 1 1/2 fat, 1 fruit

BLUEBERRY BUTTERMILK CAKE

1 Duncan Hines® DeLights devil's food cake mix
3 eggs or 3/4 c. liquid egg substitute
1 1/3 c. buttermilk
1 c. fresh blueberries
1 Tbsp. finely grated lemon rind

Preheat oven to 350° F. Combine cake mix with buttermilk in a large bowl, mixing until smooth. Pour cake batter into a Bundt pan that has been sprayed with Pam®. Mix berries with lemon rind and then sprinkle on top of the batter. Gently press berries into the cake batter. Bake for 45 to 50 minutes, until a toothpick inserted in the center comes out clean. *Preparation time = 20 minutes. Baking time = 45 minutes.*

Nutrition Facts
Serving size = 1/12 cake • Servings per recipe = 12 • Calories = 104 • Calories from fat = 5

% Daily Value
Total fat 1 gm. = 2% • Saturated fat = 0 • Cholesterol 6 mg. = 2% with egg substitute • Cholesterol 53 mg. = 18% with real egg • Sodium 269 mg. = 9% • Total carbohydrate = 0 • Dietary fiber 0.6 gm. = 3% • Protein 5 gm. = 8% • Calcium 81 mg. = 10%

Exchange Values: 1 bread/starch, 1/2 fruit

Blueberry-Peach Cobbler

1 1/2 c. fresh sliced peaches
1 1/2 c. fresh blueberries
1/3 c. sugar
1 1/2 tsp. cornstarch
1/2 c. Bisquick® Light baking mix
2 Tbsp. chopped nuts
4 Tbsp. brown sugar
1/2 tsp. cinnamon
4 Tbsp. skim milk
2 c. nonfat vanilla ice milk

Preheat oven to 350° F. Prepare fresh fruit and mix with sugar and cornstarch in a large bowl. Transfer to an 8-inch square baking pan. In a medium mixing bowl, combine baking mix, nuts, brown sugar, and cinnamon. Add milk and stir just until moistened. Drop topping in small mounds over fruit. Bake for 20 minutes until topping is light golden brown in color and a toothpick inserted into the topping comes out clean. Serve warm with vanilla ice milk. *Preparation time = 20 minutes. Baking time = 20 minutes.*

Nutrition Facts
Serving size = 2- x 4-inch slices • Servings per recipe = 8 • Calories = 253 • Calories from fat = 45

% Daily Value
Total fat 5 gm. = 8% • Saturated fat 2 gm. = 10% • Cholesterol 9 mg. = 3% • Sodium 77 mg. = 3% • Total carbohydrate 53 gm. = 18% • Dietary fiber 2 gm. = 8% • Protein 6 gm. = 10% • Calcium 111 mg. = 14%

Exchange Values: 1 bread/starch, 2 fruit, 1 fat

BUBBLY BERRIES

1 qt. fresh strawberries, hulled
1/4 c. champagne or sparkling wine
4 Tbsp. sugar
3/4 c. orange juice
3 Tbsp. ReaLemon® lemon juice
1 c. vanilla ice milk

Coarsely chop cleaned berries with champagne and sugar in a medium bowl. Stir in orange and lemon juices. Cover and refrigerate at least 30 minutes or as long as overnight. Ladle into chilled bowls and place ice milk in the center of each serving. *Preparation time = 15 minutes. Chilling time = 30 minutes.*

Nutrition Facts
Serving size = 4 oz. • Servings per recipe = 8 • Calories = 102 •
Calories from fat = 9

% Daily Value
Total fat 1 gm. = 2% • Saturated fat 1 gm. = 4% • Cholesterol 4 mg. = 1% •
Sodium 20 mg. = 1% • Total carbohydrate 2 gm. = 7% • Dietary fiber 2 gm. =
8% • Protein 2 gm. = 4% • Calcium 71 mg. = 9%

Exchange Values: 1 1/2 fruit

CARROT SPICE CAKE

1 Duncan Hines® DeLights Yellow Cake Mix
1 c. water
2 eggs or 1/2 c. liquid egg substitute
1 tsp. cinnamon
1/2 tsp. ground allspice
1 c. shredded fresh carrot
1/2 c. raisins (optional)

Frosting:

3 oz. Philadelphia® Free cream cheese
1 1/2 c. powdered sugar
2 tsp. vanilla
2 Tbsp. milk

Preheat oven to 350° F. In a large mixing bowl, beat cake mix with water, eggs, and spices until smooth. Fold in carrots and optional raisins. Pour cake batter into a 13-by-9 pan sprayed with Pam®. Bake for 35 to 40 minutes, until cake tests done. *For frosting,* soften cream cheese to room temperature, then beat in powdered sugar, vanilla, and milk. Spread over cooled cake. *Preparation time = 15 minutes. Baking time = 40 minutes.*

Nutrition Facts
Serving size = 1/20 of cake • Servings per recipe = 20 • Calories = 105 • Calories from fat = 5

% Daily Value
Total fat 1 gm. = 1% • Saturated fat = 0 • Cholesterol = 0 with egg substitute • Cholesterol 21 mg. = 7% with real egg • Sodium 149 mg. = 5% • Total carbohydrate 24 gm. = 8% • Dietary fiber 0.8 gm. = 3% • Protein 2 gm. = 4% • Calcium 47 mg. = 6%

Exchange Values: 1 1/2 bread/starch

CHOCOLATE
BERRY CHILL

1 prepared graham-cracker crust
2 pints softened strawberry ice milk
1/2 c. Hershey's® chocolate syrup
8 oz. reduced-fat whipped topping, thawed

Spread softened ice milk onto bottom of crust. Spread chocolate syrup evenly over ice milk. Cover with whipped topping. Chill until firm, at least 1 hour. *Preparation time = 10 minutes. Chilling time = 60 minutes.*

Nutrition Facts • Serving size = 1/12 pie • Servings per recipe = 12 • Calories = 263 • Calories from fat = 99

% Daily Value
Total fat 11 gm. = 16% • Saturated fat 6 gm. = 26% • Cholesterol 12 mg. = 4% • Sodium 170 mg. = 6% • Total carbohydrate 38 gm. = 13% • Dietary fiber = 0 • Protein 5 gm. = 8% • Calcium 117 mg. = 9%

Exchange Values: 1 bread/starch, 1 1/2 fruit, 2 fat

CHOCOLATE BUNDT® CAKE

1 Duncan Hines® DeLights chocolate cake mix
1 1/3 c. water
2 eggs
1 Tbsp. grated orange peel
1 Tbsp. instant coffee powder
1/4 c. chocolate chips
1/4 c. chopped nuts

Preheat oven to 350° F. In a large mixing bowl, beat cake mix, water, eggs, orange peel, and instant coffee powder until smooth. Spray a Bundt® pan generously with Pam®. Sprinkle chocolate chips and chopped nuts over the bottom of the pan, spreading them out evenly over the surface. Pour in cake batter and spread evenly. Bake for 40 minutes or until cake tests done. Allow cake to cool before removing from the pan.

Preparation time = 15 minutes. Baking time = 40 minutes.

Nutrition Facts

Serving size = 1/16 wedge of cake • Servings per recipe = 16 •
Calories = 100 • Calories from fat = 27

% Daily Value

Total fat 3 gm. = 5% • Saturated fat = 0 • Cholesterol = 0 with egg substitute • Cholesterol 26 mg. = 9% with real egg • Sodium 204 mg. = 7% • Total carbohydrate 16 gm. = 5% • Dietary fiber 0.3 gm. = 1% • Protein 3 gm. = 5% • Calcium 37 mg. = 5%

Exchange Values: 1 bread/starch, 1/2 fat

CHOCOLATE CRINKLES

1 Duncan Hines® DeLights devil's food cake mix
2 eggs
3 Tbsp. water
1/3 c. margarine
powdered sugar

Preheat oven to 375° F. Combine cake mix, eggs, water, and margarine. Mix with a spoon until well blended. Shape dough into balls the size of walnuts. Roll balls in powdered sugar. Place on a baking sheet sprayed with Pam®. Bake at for 8 to 10 minutes. *Preparation time = 20 minutes. Baking time = 20 minutes.*

Nutrition Facts
Serving size = 1 cookie • Servings per recipe = 36 • Calories = 34 • Calories from fat = 9

% Daily Value
Total fat 1 gm. = 1% • Saturated fat = 0 • Cholesterol = 0 • Sodium 95 mg. = 3% • Total carbohydrate 7 gm. = 2% • Dietary fiber = 0 • Protein 1 gm. = 1% • Calcium 15 mg. = 2%

Exchange Values: 1/2 bread/starch

CINNAMON CRINKLES

Substitute a yellow cake mix for the devil's food cake mix in the previous recipe. Add 2 tsp. cinnamon to the mix.
Preparation time = 20 minutes. Baking time = 20 minutes.

Nutrition Facts
Serving size = 1 cookie • Servings per recipe = 36 • Calories = 34 • Calories from fat = 9

% Daily Value
Total fat 1 gm. = 1% • Saturated fat = 0 • Cholesterol = 0 • Sodium 95 mg. = 3% • Total carbohydrate 7 gm. = 2% • Dietary fiber = 0 • Protein 1 gm. = 1% • Calcium 15 mg. = 2%

Exchange Values: 1/2 bread/starch

CRANBERRY-YOGURT PARFAITS

3/4 c. whole-berry cranberry sauce
2 c. Dannon® plain nonfat yogurt
1/2 c. Kellogg's® low-fat granola

Place about 2 tablespoons cranberry sauce in the bottom of 4 parfait glasses. Layer yogurt, remaining cranberry sauce, and granola on top. Chill until serving. *Preparation time = 15 minutes.*

Nutrition Facts
Serving size = 3/4 cup • Servings per recipe = 4 • Calories = 181 • Calories from fat = 18

% Daily Value
Total fat 2 gm. = 3% • Saturated fat = 0 • Cholesterol 3 mg. = 1% • Sodium 103 mg. = 3% • Total carbohydrate 33 gm. = 11% • Dietary fiber 0.8 gm. = 3% • Protein 8 gm. = 3% • Calcium 232 mg. = 29% (High in calcium)

Exchange Values: 1 fruit, 1 bread/starch, 1/2 skim milk

CREAM-CHEESE PIE WITH CRUNCHY CRUST

1 c. oatmeal
2 Tbsp. chopped nuts
1/4 c. brown sugar
1 Tbsp. melted margarine
6 oz. Philadelphia® Free cream cheese
1/3 c. sugar
1 Tbsp. lemon juice
1 tsp. vanilla
3 eggs or 3/4 c. liquid egg substitute
4 c. sliced fresh strawberries or other
  fresh fruit of choice

Preheat oven to 350° F. Combine oatmeal, nuts, brown sugar, and margarine, mixing well. Firmly press mixture onto bottom and sides of a 9-inch pie plate. Bake for 10 minutes, then cool. In a large mixing bowl, combine cream cheese, sugar, lemon juice and vanilla. Beat on medium speed with an electric mixer until well blended. Add eggs, one at a time, mixing well after each. Pour into prepared crust and bake for 30 minutes. Allow to cool, then chill until serving. At serving time, slice pie and top each serving with 1/2 c. fresh berries. *Preparation time = 20 minutes. Baking time = 40 minutes.*

Nutrition Facts
Serving size = 1/8th pie • Servings per recipe = 8 • Calories = 160 • Calories from fat = 36

% Daily Value
Total fat 4 gm. = 7% • Saturated fat = 0 • Cholesterol 2 mg. with egg substitute = 1% • Cholesterol 80 mg.= 27% with real egg • Sodium 121 mg. = 4% • Total carbohydrate 26 gm. = 9% • Dietary fiber 2 gm. = 8% • Protein 6 gm. = 11% • Calcium 127 mg. = 16%

Exchange Values: 1 bread/starch, 1 fruit, 1/2 fat

CREAMY FROZEN FRUIT POPS

3 c. grape juice
1 14-oz. can Carnation® evaporated
   skimmed milk
12 3-oz. paper cups
12 wooden sticks

Mix juices and milk in a bowl using a wire whisk. Carefully pour 1 oz. of the mixture into each paper cup. Freeze for 20 minutes, then insert a wooden stick into the mixture in each cup. Pour remaining liquid in and around the sticks and return them to the freezer, allowing 5 hours for fruit pops to freeze hard. *Preparation time = 20 minutes. Freezing time = 5 hours.*

Nutrition Facts below

PIÑA COLADA POPS

Substitute 3 cups orange-pineapple juice for grape juice in the previous recipe. Substitute 2 8-ounce cartons Dannon® piña colada yogurt for milk. *Preparation time = 20 minutes. Freezing time = 5 hours.*

Nutrition Facts for both creamy frozen fruit pops and piña colada pops
Serving size = 1 pop • Servings per recipe = 12 • Calories = 65 •
Calories from fat = 3

% Daily Value
Total fat 1 gm. = 1% • Saturated fat = 0 • Cholesterol = 0 • Sodium 40 mg. =
1% • Total carbohydrate 13 gm. = 4% • Dietary fiber = 0 • Protein 3 gm. =
5% • Calcium 101 mg. = 13%

Exchange Values: 1 fruit

DANNON® BROWNIES

1 16-oz. regular brownie mix
   (do not use reduced-fat mix)
1/2 c. Dannon® plain nonfat yogurt
Amount of water as shown on the mix

Preheat oven to 350° F. Spray the bottom of a 13-by-9 inch baking pan with Pam®. Combine brownie mix, yogurt, and water in a large mixing bowl, beating until smooth. Spread batter evenly in pan and bake for 30 minutes or until brownie begins to pull away from the edge of the pan. Cool before cutting.

Preparation time = 10 minutes. Baking time = 30 minutes.

Nutrition Facts

Serving size = 1/24 of recipe • Servings per recipe = 24 • Calories = 100 • Calories from fat = 18

% Daily Value

Total fat 2 gm. = 3% • Saturated fat < 1 gm. = 2% • Cholesterol = 0 • Sodium 90 mg. = 3% • Total carbohydrate 17 gm. = 2% • Dietary fiber = 0 • Protein 1 gm. = 2% • Calcium 22 mg. = 3%

Exchange Values: 1 1/2 bread/starch

DATE-NUT CUSTARD

2 eggs, well beaten or 1/2 c. liquid egg substitute
3 c. skim milk
1 c. Minute® rice, uncooked
3 Tbsp. sugar
1 Tbsp. melted margarine
1/2 c. dates, chopped fine
1/4. chopped nuts
1/8 tsp. nutmeg
1 tsp. vanilla

Combine all ingredients in a large mixing bowl and mix well. Pour into a 1 1/2-quart baking dish sprayed with Pam®. Set the dish in a pan of hot water, about 1-inch deep. Bake for 1 hour or until a knife inserted near the center of the custard comes out clean. *Preparation time = 15 minutes. Baking time = 1 hour.*

Nutrition Facts below

APRICOT CUSTARD

Substitute 1/2 c. diced dried apricots for the dates in the recipe above. *Preparation time = 15 minutes. Baking time = 1 hour.*

Nutrition Facts
Serving size = 1/12 wedge • Servings per recipe = 12 • Calories = 176 • Calories from fat = 9

% Daily Value
Total fat 3 gm. = 5% • Saturated fat 1 gm. = 1% • Cholesterol 2 mg. = 1% • Sodium 136 mg. = 5% • Total carbohydrate 33 gm. = 10% • Dietary fiber 0.3 gm. = 1% • Protein 8 gm. = 14% • Calcium 176 mg. = 22% (High in calcium)

Exchange Values: 1/2 fruit, 1 1/2 bread/starch, 1/2 fat

DOROTHY'S BRUNCH CAKE

A low-fat favorite from nurse Dorothy Tangeman.

> 3/4 c. coarsely crushed Wheaties® cereal
> 1/2 tsp. cinnamon
> 1 pkg. Betty Crocker® 1-Step angel food cake mix

Move oven rack to lowest position. Preheat oven to 350° F. Mix cereal and cinnamon. Prepare cake mix as directed on package, folding cereal mixture into the batter last. Pour into an ungreased Bundt® cake pan. Bake 40 to 45 minutes, or until top of cake is golden brown. Immediately turn pan upside down onto a heat-proof funnel. Let hang for 1 1/2 hours until cool, then remove cake from the pan. Serve with fresh fruit topping. *Preparation time = 15 minutes. Baking time = 45 minutes.*

Nutrition Facts
Serving size = 1/12 cake • Servings per recipe = 12 • Calories = 79 • Calories from fat = 4

% Daily Value
Total fat < 1 gm. = 1% • Saturated fat = 0 • Cholesterol = 0 • Sodium 235 mg. = 8% • Total carbohydrate 18 gm. = 6% • Dietary fiber 0.6 gm. = 2% • Protein 2 gm. = 3% • Calcium 43 mg. = 5%

Exchange Values: 1 bread/starch

FROSTED PISTACHIO LAYER CAKE

1 18-oz. pkg. Duncan Hines® DeLights
  devil's food cake mix
1 1/2 c. water
3 eggs or 3/4 c. liquid egg substitute

Filling:
2 pkg. pistachio instant pudding and pie filling mix
3 c. skim milk

Garnish:
2 Tbsp. slivered almonds

Preheat oven to 350° F. In a large mixing bowl, beat cake mix with water and eggs for 3 minutes. Pour batter into two 8-inch round cake pans sprayed with Pam®. Bake for 25 minutes or until cakes test done. Remove cakes from pans and cool on wire racks. Meanwhile, whisk pudding mix with milk, blending until smooth. When cakes are cooled, frost top of one round cake with pudding, place second cake on top and frost. Slice and serve. Garnish with slivered almonds. Refrigerate leftover cake. *Preparation time = 15 minutes. Baking time = 30 minutes.*

Nutrition Facts
Serving size = 1/12 cake • Servings per recipe = 12 • Calories = 136 • Calories from fat = 7

% Daily Value
Total fat 2 gm. = 3% • Saturated fat < 1 gm. = 2% • Cholesterol 1 mg. = 1% with egg substitute • Cholesterol 53 mg. = 18% with real egg • Sodium 290 mg. = 10% • Total carbohydrate 23 gm. = 8% • Dietary fiber 0.6 gm. = 2% • Protein 6 gm. = 11% • Calcium 132 mg. = 17%

Exchange Values: 1 bread/starch, 1/2 skim milk

FROZEN CITRUS PIE

6 oz. frozen orange juice concentrate
3 oz. Philadelphia® Free cream cheese
2 c. vanilla ice milk, softened
4 oz. reduced-fat frozen whipped topping, thawed
1 prepared graham-cracker crust

Topping:
2 c. canned mandarin oranges, drained

Beat orange juice concentrate and cream cheese in a mixing bowl. Fold in ice milk and whipped topping. Pour into a prepared crust. Freeze at least 1 hour. Remove from the freezer 10 minutes before serving. Top each slice with 1/4 cup drained mandarin oranges. *Preparation time = 20 minutes. Freezer time = 1 hour.*

Nutrition Facts
Serving size = 1/8th pie • Servings per recipe = 8 • Calories = 178 • Calories from fat = 45

% Daily Value
Total fat 5 gm. = 9% • Saturated fat 3 gm. = 15% • Cholesterol 4 mg. = 1% • Sodium 80 mg. = 2% • Total carbohydrate 30 gm. = 9% • Dietary fiber 3 gm. = 12% • Protein 3 gm. = 4% • Calcium 124 mg. = 9%

Exchange Values: 1/2 skim milk, 1 fruit, 1 bread/starch

Fruit-filled Angel Cakes

1 Betty Crocker® 1-Step angel food cake mix
1 tsp. lemon juice
1/4 c. peach schnapps
2 Tbsp. honey
1 1/2 tsp. ground ginger
3 c. fresh peaches, pears, or strawberries, sliced

Garnish:
1 Tbsp. sifted powdered sugar

Preheat oven to 350° F. Insert 12 paper liners into muffin tins. Prepare cake batter as directed on the package. Fill liners two-thirds full. Bake for 12 to 14 minutes or until tops are golden brown. Remove cupcakes from tins and cool on a wire rack. While cupcakes are cooling, combine lemon juice, schnapps, honey, and ginger in a medium bowl. Add fresh fruit and refrigerate for at least 30 minutes. Remove cupcakes from liners, slice in half horizontally. When ready to serve, spoon fresh fruit over the bottom half and replace the top half at an angle. Garnish with sifted powdered sugar.

Nutrition Facts
Serving size = 1 cupcake • Servings per recipe = 12 • Calories = 113 • Calories from fat = 6

% Daily Value
Total fat < 1 gm. = 1% • Saturated fat = 0 • Cholesterol = 0 • Sodium 212 mg. = 7% • Total carbohydrate 27 gm. = 9% • Dietary fiber 1 gm. = 4% • Protein 2 gm. = 4% • Calcium 44 mg. = 5%

Exchange Values: 1 bread/starch, 1/2 fruit

FRUIT-FILLED CRUMB BARS

1 pkg. Pillsbury® Lovin' Lites yellow cake mix
1/2 c. oatmeal
1 tsp. cinnamon
1/4 c. margarine
2 Tbsp. milk
1 egg or 1/4 c. liquid egg substitute
20 oz. apple, blueberry, or cherry pie filling
1/3 c. oatmeal

Preheat oven to 350° F. Combine dry cake mix with 1/2 c. oatmeal, cinnamon, margarine, milk, and egg until crumbly. Reserve 1 cup of this mixture for topping. Press remaining crumbs into the bottom of a 13-by-9 inch baking pan that has been sprayed with Pam®. Bake for 13 minutes. Remove from pan and spread pie filling over the top. Mix 1/3 cup oatmeal with reserved crumbs and sprinkle over pie filling. Return to the oven and bake 22 minutes longer. Cool and slice. *Preparation time = 20 minutes. Baking time = 35 minutes.*

Nutrition Facts
Serving size = 1/24 cake • Servings per recipe = 24 • Calories = 104 •
Calories from fat = 9

% Daily Value
Total fat 1 gm. = 2% • Saturated fat < 1 gm. = 1% • Cholesterol = 0 with egg substitute • Cholesterol = 9 mg. = 3% with real egg • Sodium 156 mg. = 5% • Total carbohydrate 23 gm. = 8% • Dietary fiber 1 gm. = 4% • Protein 2 gm. = 4% • Calcium 38 mg. = 5%

Exchange Values: 1 bread/starch, 1/2 fruit

German-Chocolate Brownies

1 pkg. Pillsbury® Lovin' Lites brownie mix
1/4 c. evaporated skimmed milk
3 Tbsp. brown sugar
1 Tbsp. margarine
1 Tbsp. flour
1/3 c. coconut
1/3 c. chopped pecans
1/2 tsp. vanilla

Prepare brownie mix according to package directions using a 9 x 13 pan; and let cool for 20 minutes. Meanwhile, in a 1-quart microwave-safe bowl, combine evaporated skimmed milk, sugar, margarine, and flour. Microwave on high power for 3 minutes or until mixture is thick, stopping to stir twice during cooking. Spread topping on the brownies. Allow brownies to cool for 15 minutes, then slice and serve. *Preparation time = 20 minutes. Baking time = 30 minutes. Cooling time = 15 minutes.*

Nutrition Facts
Serving size = 2-inch square • Servings per recipe = 16 • Calories = 135 • Calories from fat = 63

% Daily Value
Total fat 7 gm. = 9% • Saturated fat 3 gm. = 11% • Cholesterol 4 mg. = 1% • Sodium 78 mg. = 3% • Total carbohydrate 16 gm. = 6% • Dietary fiber = 0 • Protein 1 gm. = 2% • Calcium 29 mg. = 3%

Exchange Values: 1 bread/starch, 1 fat

GLORIFIED RICE

1 c. instant rice
1 c. orange juice
1 c. miniature marshmallows
9-oz. can Dole® crushed pineapple in juice
8 oz. nonfat sour cream
2 Tbsp. chopped maraschino cherries,
    optional garnish

Place rice and orange juice in a 2-quart microwave-safe bowl. Cover and cook on high power for 3 minutes. Stir in marshmallows, pineapple with juice, and nonfat sour cream and blend well. Transfer to a serving bowl. Garnish top with chopped cherries. Chill for 30 minutes before serving. *Preparation time = 10 minutes. Chilling time = 30 minutes.*

Nutrition Facts
Serving size = 1/2 cup • Servings per recipe = 12 • Calories = 161 •
Calories from fat = 8

% Daily Value
Total fat 2 gm. = 3% • Saturated fat = 0 • Cholesterol = 0 • Sodium 37 mg. =
1% • Total carbohydrate 34 gm. = 12% • Dietary fiber 0.5 gm. = 2% •
Protein 3 gm. = 6% • Calcium 60 mg. = 7%

Exchange Values: 1 1/2 fruit, 1 bread/starch

Holiday Green Cake

1/3 c. chopped pecans
1/3 c. sugar
2 Tbsp. cinnamon
1 Duncan Hines® DeLights white cake mix
3 oz. package instant pistachio pudding
4 large eggs or 1 c. liquid egg substitute
1 c. nonfat sour cream
3/4 c. orange juice
2 Tbsp. vegetable oil
1 tsp. vanilla

Preheat oven to 350° F. Combine pecans, sugar, and cinnamon. Sprinkle a third of the pecan mixture into the bottom and up the sides of a Bundt cake pan sprayed with Pam®. In a mixing bowl, blend remaining ingredients with an electric mixer. Alternate layers of batter and remaining nut mixture. Swirl with a fork. Bake for 35 to 45 minutes or until top of cake is browned and cake tests done. *Preparation time = 10 minutes. Baking time = 45 minutes.*

Nutrition Facts
Serving size = 1/16th wedge • Servings per recipe = 16 • Calories = 152 • Calories from fat = 59

% Daily Value
Total fat 7 gm. = 10% • Saturated fat < 1 gm. = 3% • Cholesterol = 0 with egg substitute • Cholesterol 53 mg. = 18% with real egg • Sodium 208 mg. = 7% • Total carbohydrate 19 gm. = 6% • Dietary fiber 0.8 gm. = 3% • Protein 5 gm. = 8% • Calcium 79 mg. = 10%

Exchange Values: 2 bread/starch

HONEY OF A PUMPKIN PIE

1 1/2 c. Libby's® canned pumpkin
1 egg or 1/4 c. liquid egg substitute
1 1/4 c. skim milk
1 Tbsp. cornstarch
1/3 c. honey
1 1/4 tsp. cinnamon
1/8 tsp. ginger
1/8 tsp. nutmeg
1/8 tsp. cloves
1 prepared graham-cracker crust

Preheat oven to 350° F. Combine all ingredients for pie in a blender and process smooth. Pour into prepared crust and bake for 1 hour. Garnish top of pie with twisted orange slice. *Preparation time = 10 minutes. Baking time = 60 minutes.*

Nutrition Facts
Serving size = 1/8th pie • Servings per recipe = 8 • Calories = 223 • Calories from fat = 11

% Daily Value
Total fat 8 gm. = 12% • Saturated fat 2 gm. = 8% • Cholesterol 1 mg. = 1% with egg substitute • Cholesterol 26 mg. = 9% with real egg • Sodium 209 mg. = 7% • Total carbohydrate 36 gm. = 12% • Dietary fiber = 0 • Protein 4 gm. = 7% • Calcium 70 mg. = 9%

Exchange Values: 2 bread/starch, 1 fat

JELLO® POKE CAKE

1 18-oz. pkg. Duncan Hines® DeLights white cake
  mix, baked and cooled
1 c. boiling water
1 3-oz. pkg. Jello® gelatin, any flavor
  (may use sugar-free gelatin)
1/2 c. cold water
2 c. fresh fruit topping

Prepare cake according to package directions in a 13-by-9 inch pan. When cake is baked and cooled, prick the cake with a large two-pronged fork at 1/2-inch intervals. Dissolve gelatin in boiling water in a small mixing bowl. Add cold water and gently spoon gelatin over cake. Chill for 4 hours. Serve with fresh fruit topping.

Favorite combinations:
- *orange gelatin with fresh peaches*
- *lime gelatin with kiwi and bananas on top*
- *raspberry gelatin with fresh berries*
- *lemon gelatin with tropical fruit mixture*

Preparation time = 10 minutes. Baking time = 25 minutes. Chilling time = 4 hours.

Nutrition Facts
Serving size = 1/24 of cake • Servings per recipe = 24 • Calories = 67 • Calories from fat = 3

% Daily Value
Total fat = 0 • Saturated fat = 0 • Cholesterol = 0 • Sodium 124 mg. = 4% • Total carbohydrate 15 gm. = 5% • Dietary fiber 0.5 gm. = 2% • Protein 2 gm. = 3% • Calcium 22 mg. = 3%

Exchange Values: 1 bread/starch

LEMON BARS

1 c. flour
1/4 c. powdered sugar
3 oz. Philadelphia® Free cream cheese
1 Tbsp. vegetable oil
2 eggs or 1/2 c. liquid egg substitute
1/2 c. sugar
1 1/2 Tbsp. grated lemon peel
2 Tbsp. flour
1/2 tsp. baking powder
1/4 tsp. salt
1/3 c. lemon juice

Preheat oven to 350° F. In a large bowl, stir together flour and powdered sugar. Using a pastry cutter, cut in cream cheese and oil until crumbly. Press mixture into the bottom of an 8-inch square baking pan. Bake for 20 minutes, until light golden in color. In a mixing bowl, beat eggs with sugar and lemon peel until smooth. Whisk in flour, baking powder, salt, and finally lemon juice. Pour into the hot crust and bake for 20 minutes until the top is light golden and set. *Preparation time = 20 minutes. Baking time = 40 minutes.*

Nutrition Facts
Serving size = 1/12 of recipe • Servings per recipe = 12 • Calories = 136 • Calories from fat = 7

% Daily Value
Total fat 2 gm. = 3% • Saturated fat = 0 • Cholesterol = 0 with egg substitute • Cholesterol 35 mg. = 12% with real egg • Sodium 68 mg. = 2% • Total carbohydrate 31 gm. = 10% • Dietary fiber = 0 • Protein 4 gm. = 7% • Calcium 26 mg. ᵁ 3%

Exchange Values: 1 fruit, 1 bread/starch

LEMON LOVER'S CAKE

1 18-oz. pkg. Duncan Hines® DeLights
  yellow cake mix
12 oz. lemonade
2 eggs or 1/2 c. liquid egg substitute

Preheat oven to 350° F. Combine cake mix with lemonade and eggs in a large mixing bowl. Beat for 1 minute on slow speed, scraping the sides of the bowl often. Beat 2 minutes longeron medium speed. Pour cake batter into a prepared Bundt® pan sprayed with Pam®. Bake for 45 minutes. Cool. Serve with nonfat lemon yogurt as a topping. *Preparation time = 10 minutes. Baking time = 45 minutes.*

Nutrition Facts
Serving size = 1/24 cake • Servings per recipe = 24 • Calories = 41 • Calories from fat = 2

% Daily Value
Total fat < 1 gm. = 1% • Saturated fat = 0 • Cholesterol = 0 with egg substitute • Cholesterol 18 mg. = 6% with real egg • Sodium 116 mg. = 4% • Total carbohydrate 8 gm. = 3% • Dietary fiber = 0 • Protein 2 gm. = 3% • Calcium 26 mg. = 3%

Exchange Values: 1/2 bread/starch

LEMON RICE PUDDING

1/2 c. Minute® rice, uncooked
3/4 c. lemonade
3-oz. pkg. instant lemon pudding mix
1 1/2 c. skim milk
2/3 c. nonfat plain yogurt

Combine rice with lemonade in a 1-quart mixing bowl. Cover and microwave on high power for 3 minutes, then cool. Meanwhile, prepare instant pudding with milk in a 2-quart mixing bowl; then fold in yogurt. Fold rice into pudding and spoon into individual serving dishes. Chill until serving, at least 30 minutes. Garnish with twisted lemon slice or crushed lemon-drop candy.
Preparation time = 20 minutes. Chilling time = 30 minutes.

Nutrition Facts

Serving size = 1/2 cup • Servings per recipe = 8 • Calories = 78 •
Calories from fat = 4

% Daily Value

Total fat = 0 • Saturated fat = 0 • Cholesterol 1 mg. = 1% • Sodium 35 mg. =
1% • Total carbohydrate 16 gm. = 5% • Dietary fiber 0.3 gm. = 2% • Protein
2 gm. = 5% • Calcium 83 mg. = 11%

Exchange Values: 1 bread/starch

LEMON-YOGURT FLUFF

1/2 c. Dannon® nonfat vanilla yogurt
2 tsp. frozen lemonade concentrate
1/2 c. reduced-fat frozen whipped topping
2 c. fresh fruit

Combine yogurt, lemonade concentrate, and whipped topping in a
small bowl. Spoon over fresh fruits. *Preparation time = 10 minutes.*

Nutrition Facts

Serving size = 1/2 cup fruit + 1/4 cup topping • Servings per recipe = 4 •
Calories = 61 • Calories from fat = 3

% Daily Value

Total fat 2 gm. = 4% • Saturated fat = 0 • Cholesterol = 0 • Sodium 28 mg. =
1% • Total carbohydrate 9 gm. = 3% • Dietary fiber 2 gm. = 8% • Protein
2 gm. = 3% • Calcium 60 mg. = 8%

Exchange Values: 1 fruit

Low-fat Brownies from a Conventional Mix

21-oz. pkg. Pillsbury® fudge brownie mix
1/2 c. flour
1/4 c. water
1/2 c. low-fat buttermilk
2 eggs or 1/2 c. liquid egg substitute
2 Tbsp. sifted powdered sugar

Mix ingredients in a large mixing bowl for 3 minutes or until smooth. Pour brownie batter into a 13-by-9 inch baking pan sprayed with Pam®. Bake for 28 minutes. Cool. Dust with powdered sugar just before serving. *Preparation time = 10 minutes. Baking time = 28 minutes.*

Nutrition Facts

Serving size = 1/24 of cake • Servings per recipe = 24 • Calories = 103 • Calories from fat = 18

% Daily Value

Total fat 2 gm. = 1% • Saturated fat = 0 • Cholesterol = 0 with egg substitute • Cholesterol = 18 mg. = 6% with real egg • Sodium 181 mg. = 6% • Total carbohydrate 19 gm. = 7% • Dietary fiber = 0 • Protein 3 gm. = 6% • Calcium 43 mg. = 6%

Exchange Values: 1 1/2 bread/starch

NO-GUILT BROWNIES

3 oz. unsweetened baker's chocolate,
  chopped into small pieces
1 c. sugar
3/4 c. flour
3/4 c. Kemp's® low-fat cottage cheese
2 eggs or 1/2 c. liquid egg substitute
1 tsp. vanilla extract
1/4 tsp. salt

Preheat oven to 350° F. Place pieces of chocolate in a microwave-safe bowl. Heat at 60% power for 4 minutes, stopping twice to stir mixture. Meanwhile, in a blender or food processor, puree all remaining ingredients until smooth. Stir in melted chocolate. Pour into an 8-inch square baking pan sprayed with Pam®. Bake for 22 minutes. Cut into squares. Serve with nonfat ice milk. *Preparation time = 15 minutes. Baking time = 22 minutes.*

Nutrition Facts
Serving size = 1/12 of recipe • Servings per recipe = 12 • Calories = 164 • Calories from fat = 8

% Daily Value
Total fat 5 gm. = 7% • Saturated fat 2 gm. = 11% • Cholesterol 1 mg. = 1% with egg substitute • Cholesterol 36 mg. = 12% with real egg • Sodium 114 mg. = 4% • Total carbohydrate 31 gm. = 10% • Dietary fiber 1 gm. = 4% • Protein 5 gm. = 9% • Calcium 19 mg. = 2%

Exchange Values: 2 bread/starch

OAT-BRAN BROWNIES

3 Tbsp. cocoa powder
1 Tbsp. instant coffee
1 Tbsp. water
2 medium bananas, very ripe and mashed smooth
2 c. sugar
3 eggs or 3/4 c. liquid egg substitute
1 tsp. vanilla
1 c. Quaker® oat bran
1/4 tsp. salt
1/4 c. chopped nuts

Preheat oven to 350° F. Combine cocoa, coffee, water, and bananas in a large mixing bowl and beat smooth. Add sugar, eggs, and vanilla, mixing well. Stir in oat bran, salt, and nuts. Pour batter into a 8-inch square baking pan sprayed with Pam®. Bake for 40 to 45 minutes. Cut into 12 servings

Preparation time = 20 minutes. Baking time = 40 minutes.

Nutrition Facts

Serving size = 1/12 inch square • Servings per recipe = 12 • Calories = 193 • Calories from fat = 36

% Daily Value

Total fat 4 gm. = 7% • Saturated fat < 1 gm. = 2% • Cholesterol = 0 • Sodium 86 mg. = 3% • Total carbohydrate 38 gm. = 2% • Dietary fiber 0.3 gm. = 1% • Protein 6 gm. = 9% • Calcium 21 mg. = 2%

Exchange Values: 2 bread/starch, 1/2 fruit

OATMEAL BROWNIES

2/3 c. sugar
1/3 c. water
3 Tbsp. vegetable oil
1 tsp. vanilla extract
1 large egg or 1/4 c. liquid egg substitute
1/2 c. flour
1/3 c. Quaker® oatmeal
1/4 c. cocoa powder
3/4 tsp. baking powder
1/8 tsp. salt

Preheat oven to 350° F. In a medium bowl, combine sugar, water, oil, and vanilla extract, mixing well. Stir in eggs and beat smooth. Mix together the flour, oatmeal, cocoa, baking powder, and salt and fold into the sugar mixture, stirring smooth. Pour batter into an 8-inch square pan sprayed with Pam®. Bake for 23 minutes or until a toothpick inserted in the center comes out clean.
Preparation time = 15 minutes. Baking time = 23 minutes.

Nutrition Facts
Serving size = 2-inch square • Servings per recipe = 16 • Calories = 86 • Calories from fat = 4

% Daily Value
Total fat 3 gm. = 5% • Saturated fat = 0 • Cholesterol = 0 with egg substitute • Cholesterol 13 mg. = 4% with real egg • Sodium 25 mg. = 1% • Total carbohydrate 16 gm. = 5% • Dietary fiber = 0 • Protein 2 gm. = 3% • Calcium 20 mg. = 3%

Exchange Values: 1 bread/starch

OATMEAL-RAISIN COOKIES

3/4 c. white sugar
3/4 c. brown sugar
1/4 c. oil
1 egg or 1/4 c. liquid egg substitute
1 tsp. vanilla
3/4 c. water
1 c. flour
1/2 tsp. baking soda
1 tsp. salt
3 c. Quaker® oatmeal
3/4 c. raisins
3/4 c. chopped dates

Preheat oven to 350° F. Cream sugars, oil, egg, and vanilla in a large mixing bowl. Add water and beat on low speed until well mixed. Stir in flour, baking soda, and salt. Fold in oatmeal, raisins, and dates. Stir until blended. Drop dough by spoonfuls onto a baking sheet sprayed with Pam®. Flatten slightly with a fork. Bake for 12 minutes or until cookies are golden brown. *Preparation time = 20 minutes. Baking time = 24 minutes.*

Nutrition Facts
Serving size = 1 cookie • Servings per recipe = 36 • Calories = 104 • Calories from fat = 5

% Daily Value
Total fat 2 gm. = 3% • Saturated fat = 0 • Cholesterol = 0 with egg substitute • Cholesterol 6 mg. = 2% with real egg • Sodium 83 mg. = 3% • Total carbohydrate 22 gm. = 7% • Dietary fiber = 0 • Protein 2 gm. = 3% • Calcium 31 mg. = 4%

Exchange Values: 1 1/2 bread/starch

ORANGE-BANANA BUNDT® CAKE

18-oz. pkg. Duncan Hines® DeLights yellow cake mix
2 medium bananas ripe and mashed smooth
3 eggs or 3/4 c. liquid egg substitute
2/3 c. water
3-oz. pkg. orange gelatin mix
1/2 c. boiling water
6 ice cubes
1 c. nonfat vanilla yogurt
2 tsp. finely grated orange peel

Preheat oven to 350° F. Spray a Bundt® pan with Pam®. In a large mixing bowl, combine cake mix, bananas, eggs, and water and beat for 3 minutes until smooth. Pour batter into the prepared pan and bake for 45 minutes. Remove cake from pan and cool completely on a rack. While the cake is baking, stir gelatin into boiling water in a small mixing bowl. When gelatin is completely dissolved, add ice cubes. Place gelatin in the refrigerator for 15 minutes or until partially set. When cake is cooled, use the handle of a wooden spoon to poke 16 holes, equally spaced, in the top of the cake. The holes should be 2 1/2-inches deep. Carefully pour gelatin into the holes. If the gelatin is absorbed into the cake, it is not set well enough, and should be chilled longer. Refrigerated cake for 1 hour. Slice and serve with nonfat vanilla yogurt as a topping and garnished with finely grated orange peel. *Preparation time = 20 minutes. Baking time = 45 minutes. Chilling time = 1 hour.*

Nutrition Facts
Serving size = 1/16 of cake • Servings per recipe = 16 • Calories = 107 • Calories from fat = 5

% Daily Value
Total fat 1 gm. = 1% • Saturated fat = 0 • Cholesterol 2 mg. = 1% with egg substitute • Cholesterol 42 mg. = 13% with real egg • Sodium 204 mg. = 7% • Total carbohydrate 22 gm. = 7% • Dietary fiber 0.5 gm. = 2% • Protein 4 gm. = 7% • Calcium 62 mg. = 8%

Exchange Values: 1 bread/starch, 1/2 fruit

MELON ICE

6 c. ripe canteloupe chunks
   (may use honeydew or watermelon chunks)
1/2 c. sugar
3 Tbsp. lemon juice
1/2 c. Carnation® evaporated skimmed milk

In a heavy-duty gallon-size plastic bag, combine melon of choice, sugar, and lemon juice. Seal bag and let stand at room temperature for 5 minutes. Place half of melon chunks in a food processor along with 1/4 cup evaporated milk and, process until mixture is smooth. Repeat process adding the remaining other half of melon and milk. Pour mixture into 4 serving dishes. Chill until time to serve. *Preparation time = 20 minutes.*

Nutrition Facts
Serving size = 3/4 cup • Servings per recipe = 8 • Calories = 91 •
Calories from fat = 13

% Daily Value
Total fat < 1 gm. = 2% • Saturated fat = 0 • Cholesterol = 0 • Sodium 17 mg.
= 1% • Total carbohydrate 21 gm. = 7% • Dietary fiber 1 gm. = 4% • Protein
2 gm. = 3% • Calcium 50 mg. = 7%

Exchange Values: 1 1/2 fruit

ORANGE-RUM CUSTARD

1 1/2 c. skim milk
1/3 c. orange juice
2 tsp. rum extract divided
4-oz. pkg. Jello® Vanilla Cook and Serve pudding
1 tsp. finely grated orange peel
4 amaretti cookies, coarsely chopped
1 orange, peeled and sectioned

In a 2-quart microwave-safe dish, combine milk, orange juice, and 1 teaspoon rum extract. Stir in pudding mix. Cover and cook in microwave at high power for 3 minutes. Cook 2 minutes more until mixture boils, stopping to stir twice. Remove pudding from oven and stir in orange peel. Cover and chill until mixture is thickened, at least 30 minutes. Combine remaining 1 teaspoon of rum extract with cookie crumbs. Spoon pudding into four dessert dishes and garnish tops with flavored crumbs and fresh orange sections. *Preparation time = 15 minutes. Chilling time = 30 minutes.*

Nutrition Facts
Serving size = 1/2 cup • Servings per recipe = 4 • Calories = 118 • Calories from fat = 9

% Daily Value
Total fat 1 gm. = 2% • Saturated fat = 0 • Cholesterol = 0 • Sodium 84 mg. = 3% • Total carbohydrate 22 gm. = 0 • Dietary fiber 1.5 gm. = 6% • Protein 5 gm. = 9% • Calcium 177 mg. = 22% (High in calcium)

Exchange Values: 1/2 skim milk, 1 fruit

PINEAPPLE-RUM UPSIDE-DOWN CAKE

2 Tbsp. margarine
2 tsp. rum extract
1/2 c. brown sugar
15-oz. can Dole® sliced pineapple, drained
Drained pineapple juice + enough water to
    equal 1 1/3 cup liquid
18-oz. pkg. Duncan Hines® DeLights
    yellow cake mix
3 eggs or 3/4 c. liquid egg substitute

Melt margarine in a small mixing bowl. Add rum extract and brown sugar and stir to dissolve. Pack mixture firmly and evenly around the bottom of 7-by-11 inch glass baking dish. Drain pineapple juice into a glass measuring cup and set aside. Arrange pineapple slices evenly over the sugar mixture. Prepare cake mix as directed, substituting pineapple juice and water for 1 1/3 cup of liquid and 3 eggs or 3/4 cup liquid egg substitute. Pour batter into the baking pan. Bake for 35 to 40 minutes, or until cake tests done. While cake is still hot, invert onto a serving plate. Cut into 24 squares. Serve warm with ice milk.

Preparation time = 20 minutes. Baking time = 40 minutes.

Nutrition Facts
Serving size = 1/24 of recipe • Servings per recipe = 24 • Calories = 75 • Calories from fat = 4

% Daily Value
Total fat 1 gm. = 1% • Saturated fat = 0 • Cholesterol = 0 with egg substitute • Cholesterol 27 mg. = 9% with real egg • Sodium 133 mg. = 5% • Total carbohydrate 15 gm. = 5% • Dietary fiber = 0 • Protein 2 gm. = 3% • Calcium 31 mg. = 4%

Exchange Values: 1 bread/starch

PUMPKIN BARS FROM A CAKE MIX

1 Betty Crocker® Super Moist Light
   yellow cake mix
16-oz. can Libby's® solid pack pumpkin
3 eggs or 3/4 c. liquid egg substitute
2 tsp. cinnamon
1/2 tsp. ginger
1/2 tsp. cloves

Glaze:
1/2 c. powdered sugar
1/4 tsp. orange extract
1 Tbsp. skim milk

Preheat oven to 350° F. In a large mixing bowl, beat cake mix with pumpkin, eggs and spices for 3 minutes. Pour batter in a 15-by-8 inch jelly roll sized baking pan that has been sprayed with Pam®. Bake for 23 minutes. When bars are cool and just prior to serving, frost bars with glaze prepared from powdered sugar, orange extract, and skim milk. Glaze only the portion of the bars that will be eaten, as this dessert does not keep well once the glaze has been spread on. Unfrosted bars can easily be frozen for later use. *Preparation time = 10 minutes. Baking time = 23 minutes.*

Nutrition Facts
Serving size = 1/24 of recipe • Servings per recipe = 24 • Calories = 60 • Calories from fat = 3

% Daily Value
Total fat 1 gm. = 1% • Saturated fat = 0 • Cholesterol = 0 with egg substitute • Cholesterol 27 mg. = 9% with real egg • Sodium 121 mg. = 4% • Total carbohydrate 13 gm. = 4% • Dietary fiber 1 gm. = 4% • Protein 2 gm. = 4% • Calcium 31 mg. = 4%

Exchange Values: 1 bread/starch

PUMPKIN CHEESECAKE

Crust:
12 gingersnap cookies, crumbled
2 Tbsp. margarine, melted

Filling
6 oz. Philadelphia® Free cream cheese
14-oz. can sweetened condensed milk
16-oz. can pumpkin
3 eggs or 3/4 c. liquid egg substitute
3 Tbsp. orange juice
1 tsp. pumpkin-pie spice
1/4 tsp. salt

Crush gingersnap cookies and mix with melted margarine. Press firmly on bottom and halfway up side of a 9-inch springform pan. Set aside. In a large mixing bowl, beat cheese until fluffy. Gradually beat in sweetened condensed milk and all remaining ingredients. Pour into cookie crust and bake for 1 hour and 15 minutes or until cake springs back when lightly touched. Cool to room temperature. Chill and serve with fresh orange slices as a garnish. *Preparation time = 10 minutes. Baking time = 1 hour, 15 minutes. Chilling time = 25 minutes.*

Nutrition Facts
Serving size = 1/16 wedge of cheesecake • Servings per recipe = 16 • Calories = 165 • Calories from fat = 45

% Daily Value
Total fat 5 gm. = 7% • Saturated fat 2 gm. = 11% • Cholesterol 12 mg. = 4% with egg substitute • Cholesterol 40 mg. = 13% with real egg • Sodium 162 mg. = 6% • Total carbohydrate 26 gm. = 9% • Dietary fiber = 0 • Protein 6 gm. = 10% • Calcium 146 mg. = 18%

Exchange Values: 1 bread/starch, 1 fruit, 1/2 fat

Pumpkin-Spice
Angel Food Cake

1 pkg. Betty Crocker® 1 Step
   angel food cake mix
1 1/4 c. water
1/2 c. canned pumpkin
1/4 tsp. cinnamon
1/4 tsp. ground ginger
1/2 tsp. nutmeg

Preheat oven to 350° F. Using an electric mixer, beat cake mix, water, pumpkin, and spices. Pour batter into a tube pan and bake for 35 to 40 minutes. Cool cake completely before removing it from the pan. Serve with orange sherbet as a topping.
Preparation time = 10 minutes. Baking time = 40 minutes.

Nutrition Facts
Serving size = 1/12 cake • Servings per recipe = 12 • Calories = 76 • Calories from fat = 4

% Daily Value
Total fat 1 gm. = 1% • Saturated fat = 0 • Cholesterol = 0 • Sodium 213 mg. = 7% • Total carbohydrate 17 gm. = 6% • Dietary fiber 0.3 gm. = 1% • Protein 2 gm. = 3% • Calcium 43 mg. = 5%

Exchange Values: 1 bread/starch

RED, WHITE, AND BLUE CHEESECAKE

1 prepared graham-cracker crust

Filling:
2 15-oz. containers Sargento® ricotta cheese
3/4 c. sugar
1/2 c. evaporated skimmed milk
1/3 c. flour
1 tsp. vanilla
1/4 tsp. salt
3 eggs or 3/4 c. liquid egg substitute
1/2 c. Simply Fruit® raspberry preserves
1/2 c. fresh blueberries

In a large mixing bowl, blend ricotta, sugar, milk, flour, vanilla, and salt. Add eggs one at a time, blending until smooth. Pour half of the batter into the crust. Spoon half of raspberry spread over the batter. Top with remaining batter. Spoon remaining raspberry spread randomly over the batter and swirl with a knife for a marbled effect. Bake at 350° for 1 hour or until center is just set. Turn off oven and cool pie in oven with door propped open for 30 minutes. Chill until serving. Decorate the top of the pie with fresh blueberries at serving time. *Preparation time = 10 minutes. Baking time = 40 minutes. Cooling time = 30 minutes.*

Nutrition Facts
Serving size = 1/12 pie • Servings per recipe = 12 • Calories = 209 •
Calories from fat = 15

% Daily Value
Total fat 6 gm. = 12% • Saturated fat 4 gm. = 19% • Cholesterol 24 mg. = 8% with egg substitute • Cholesterol 77 mg. = 26% with real egg • Sodium 182 mg. = 6% • Total carbohydrate 27 gm. = 21% • Dietary fiber = 0 • Protein 13 gm. = 22% • Calcium 251 mg. = 31% (High in calcium)

Exchange Values: 1 fat, 1 skim milk, 1 bread/starch

STRAWBERRY ANGEL CAKE

1 pkg. Betty Crocker® 1 Step angel food cake mix
1 1/4 c. water

Filling:
1 c. reduced-fat whipped topping
2 Tbsp. sifted cocoa
1 c. thinly sliced fresh strawberries

Preheat oven to 350° F. Using an electric mixer, beat cake mix and water following package directions. Pour batter in a tube pan and bake for 35 to 40 minutes. Cool cake completely before removing it from the pan. Slice off entire top of cake, about 1-inch down. Set aside. To form a tunnel, cut around cake 1-inch from outer edge and 1-inch from inner edge, leaving a base of cake 1-inch thick on the bottom. Gently pull out cake within cuts. Place hollowed cake on a serving plate. In a bowl, mix sifted cocoa and whipped topping; fold in sliced fresh strawberries. Spoon berry mixture into the tunnel, pressing down firmly. Replace top of cake, pressing gently. Chill about 15 minutes before slicing to serve. *Preparation time = 20 minutes. Baking time = 40 minutes. Chilling time = 15 minutes.*

Nutrition Facts
Serving size = 1/12 cake • Servings per recipe = 12 • Calories = 92 • Calories from fat = 5

% Daily Value
Total fat 2 gm. = 2% • Saturated fat 1 gm. = 6% • Cholesterol = 0 • Sodium 216 mg. = 7% • Total carbohydrate 18 gm. = 6% • Dietary fiber 0.6 gm. = 3% • Protein 2 gm. = 3% • Calcium 43 mg. = 5%

Exchange Values: 1 bread/starch

Strawberry Dip

3/4 c. fresh strawberries
1 Tbsp. sugar
1/4 c. plain nonfat yogurt
1/4 c. Kraft® Free (mayonaisse-type) salad dressing

Slice berries into a small bowl and sprinkle with sugar. Let stand for 1 hour, then mash with a fork. Fold in yogurt and salad dressing and serve with apples, pears, bananas, and kiwi dippers. *Preparation time = 10 minutes. Standing time = 1 hour.*

Nutrition Facts
Serving size = 1/4 cup • Servings per recipe = 4 • Calories = 36 •
Calories from fat = 2

% Daily Value
Total fat = 0 • Saturated fat = 0 • Cholesterol = 0 • Sodium 22 mg. = 1% •
Total carbohydrate 7 gm. = 2% • Dietary fiber 0.7 gm. = 3% • Protein 2 gm.
= 3% • Calcium 60 mg. = 8%

Exchange Values: 1/2 fruit

SUMMER FRUIT KUCHEN

2 2/3 c. Light Bisquick® baking mix
2/3 c. skim milk
6 thinly sliced fresh peaches, plums, pears,
   nectarines, or apples
1 tsp. cinnamon
1/8 tsp. nutmeg
1 tsp. almond extract
1/4 c. sugar

Preheat oven to 400° F. In a medium bowl, combine baking mix with milk. Beat for 30 seconds to form a dough. With floured hands, shape dough on a cookie sheet into a 9-inch circle. Mix fresh fruit with spices, almond extract, and sugar. Arrange fruit slices in rows around the dough, overlapping slightly, and pressing gently into the dough. Bake for 50 minutes. This is best served warm. *Preparation time = 10 minutes. Baking time = 50 minutes.*

Nutrition Facts
Serving size = 1/12 wedge • Servings per recipe = 12 • Calories = 215 •
Calories from fat = 11

% Daily Value
Total fat 1 gm. = 1% • Saturated fat = 0 • Cholesterol = 0 • Sodium 8 mg. =
1% • Total carbohydrate 56 gm. = 19% • Dietary fiber 0.6 gm. = 2% •
Protein 7 gm. = 12% • Calcium 19 mg. = 2%

Exchange Values: 1 fruit, 2 bread/starch

THREE BOYS' COOKIES

A cookie that comes in handy, from Mary Finch,
who feeds three boys.

1 c. margarine
1 1/2 c. brown sugar
2 eggs or 1/2 c. egg substitute
1/2 c. buttermilk
3 c. Quaker® Oatmeal
1 3/4 c. flour
1 tsp. baking soda
1 tsp. baking powder
1 tsp. salt
1 tsp. cinnamon
1 tsp. nutmeg
1/2 c. raisins

Preheat oven to 400° F. Cream margarine with brown sugar in a large mixing bowl. Stir in eggs, one at a time. Stir in buttermilk. Add all remaining ingredients, stirring well after each addition. Drop dough by spoonfuls onto a baking sheet sprayed with Pam®. Bake for 8 minutes. *Preparation time = 10 minutes. Baking time = 1 hour.*

Nutrition Facts
Serving size = One 2 1/2 inch cookie • Servings per recipe = 72 cookies • Calories = 65 • Calories from fat = 18

% Daily Value
Total fat 2 gm. = 3% • Saturated fat = 0 • Cholesterol = 0 with egg substitute • Cholesterol 6 mg. = 2% with real egg • Sodium 43 mg. = 1% • Total carbohydrate 11 gm. = 4% • Dietary fiber 0.2 gm. = 1% • Protein 1 gm. = 2% • Calcium 15 mg. = 2%

Exchange Values: 1 bread/starch

TROPICAL MERINGUE

20-oz. can Dole® pineapple chunks,
    packed in juice
1 Tbsp. + 2 tsp. cornstarch
1/4 tsp. almond extract
1 c. finely diced dates
3 egg whites
1 tsp. lemon juice
1/3 c. sugar

Preheat oven to 375° F. Pour pineapple juice into a 9-inch square baking dish. Stir in cornstarch and extract until smooth. Add pineapple chunks. Bake uncovered in a preheated oven for 20 minutes. Stir in dates. Beat egg whites and lemon juice with an electric mixer until soft peaks form. Gradually add sugar, beating until stiff peaks form and sugar is dissolved. Spoon over the pineapple mixture, spreading level. Bake 15 minutes more or until golden brown. Serve warm. *Preparation time = 20 minutes. Baking time = 35 minutes.*

Nutrition Facts
Serving size = 1/12 of recipe • Servings per recipe = 12 •
Calories = 82 • Calories from fat

% Daily Value
Total fat = 0 • Saturated fat = 0 • Cholesterol = 0 • Sodium 3 mg. = 1% •
Total carbohydrate 21 gm. = 7% • Dietary fiber 1 gm. = 4% • Protein 1 gm. =
2% • Calcium 25 mg. = 3%

Exchange Values: 1 1/2 fruit

INDEX

INDEX

INDEX

INDEX

INDEX